The South Asian Diaspora

The South Asian diaspora numbers just under 30 million people worldwide, and it is recognised as the most widely dispersed diaspora. It is, moreover, one which of late has seen phenomenal growth, both due to natural increase and the result of a continued movement of professionals and labourers in the late twentieth century and early twenty-first century from the subcontinent to countries such as the United States, the United Kingdom, Canada, Australia and Singapore.

This book uses the concept of transnational networks as a means to understand the South Asian diaspora. Taking into account diverse aspects of formation and development, the concept breaks down the artificial boundaries that have been dominating the literature between the 'old' and the 'new' era of migration. In this way the continued connectedness of most historic South Asian settlements is shown, and the fluid nature of South Asian identities is explored.

Offering a unique and original insight into the South Asian diaspora, this book will be of interest to academics working in the field of South Asian Studies, Diaspora and Cultural Studies, Anthropology, Transnationalism and Globalisation.

Rajesh Rai is Assistant Professor at the South Asian Studies Programme, National University of Singapore. His research interests are in the fields of diaspora studies and transnational identities, nationalism and the post-colonial history and politics of South Asia. He was assistant editor of *The Encyclopedia of the Indian Diaspora* (2006), and has published several articles on various aspects of the South Asian Diaspora particularly in Southeast Asia. **Peter Reeves**, Emeritus Professor of South Asian History at Curtin University (Perth, Western Australia), was Visiting Professor and Head of the South Asian Studies Programme (SASP) at the National University of Singapore from 1999 to 2006. His research interests include the history of the South Asian diaspora, the history of fisheries in colonial South Asia and the maritime history of the Indian Ocean since 1800. He was executive editor of *The Encyclopedia of the Indian Diaspora* (2006).

Routledge contemporary South Asia series

The South Asian Diaspora

Transnational networks and changing identities

**Edited by Rajesh Rai and
Peter Reeves**

Routledge
Taylor & Francis Group

LONDON AND NEW YORK

Transferred to digital printing 2010

First published 2009
by Routledge
2 Park Square, Milton Park, Abingdon, Oxon OX14 4RN

Simultaneously published in the USA and Canada
by Routledge
270 Madison Ave, New York, NY 10016

Routledge is an imprint of the Taylor & Francis Group, an informa business

© 2009 Selection and editorial matter, Rajesh Rai and Peter Reeves;
individual chapters, the contributors

Typeset in Times by Wearset Ltd, Boldon, Tyne and Wear

British Library Cataloguing in Publication Data
A catalogue record for this book is available from the British Library

Library of Congress Cataloging in Publication Data
The South Asian diaspora : transnational networks and changing identities
/ edited by Rajesh Rai & Peter Reeves.
p. cm. – (Routledge contemporary South Asia series) (Routledge
contemporary south asia series)
Includes bibliographical references and index.
1. South Asians–Foreign countries. 2. South Asians–Ethnic identity. 3.
South Asia–Emigration and immigration. 4. South Asian diaspora. I. Rai,
Rajesh. II. Reeves, Peter, 1935–
DS339.4.S667 2008
305.891'4–dc22   2008007131

ISBN10: 0-415-45691-6 (hbk)
ISBN10: 0-415-59616-5 (pbk)
ISBN10: 0-203-89235-6 (ebk)

ISBN13: 978-0-415-45691-3 (hbk)
ISBN13: 978-0-415-59616-9 (pbk)
ISBN13: 978-0-203-89235-0 (ebk)

Contents

Illustrations

Figures

Maps

Tables

Contributors

Marina Carter, DPhil (Oxon), is Research Fellow at the Centre for South Asian Studies, University of Edinburgh. She is currently employed on a two-year, AHRC-funded project 'Mutiny at the Margins' administered by the School of History and Classics, University of Edinburgh. Her principal research interests include Indian labour migration, Indian Ocean, Mascarene islands, Mauritius, South Asian diaspora. Among Carter's publications are *Voices from Indenture: Experiences of Indian Migrants in the British Empire* (London: Leicester University Press, 1996); *Servants, Sirdars and Settlers: Indians in Mauritius, 1834–1874*, (Delhi: Oxford University Press, 1995); *Lakshmi's Legacy: Testimonies of Indian Women in 19th Century Mauritius*, (Mauritius: EOI, 1994). Co-authored publications include: *Coolitude: An Anthology of the Indian Labour Diaspora*, with K. Torabully (London: Anthem Press, 2002) and *Across the Kalapani: the Bihari Presence in Mauritius* (Mauritius: CRIOS, 2000).

Chan E.S. Choenni studied political science and science of philosophy at the University of Amsterdam in the Netherlands. He received his PhD at the University of Utrecht. He is well known for his work on multicultural societies, integration policy and ethnic minorities. He has published on the position of (East) Indians in Trinidad, Guyana and Suriname, and the history of Indians in the Netherlands, labour-market discrimination in the Netherlands, and citizenship and integration policies. Choenni is senior advisor in the Ministry of Justice, Department of Integration Policy in the Netherlands. His main activities are co-ordination of research and reports to the parliament. He is Vice-President of the Dr Jnan Adhin Institute (JAI), an institute that publishes on Indian history, art and culture.

Theresa W. Devasahayam completed her PhD in Cultural Anthropology from Syracuse University, USA. She has held research positions in the Centre for Asia Pacific Social Transformation Studies (CAPSTRANS), University of Wollongong, Australia and the Asia Research Institute (ARI), National University of Singapore, Singapore. Her research areas include: gender and care, women and work, unskilled female labour migration, and women's fertility and reproductive health and rights. Theresa's professional record also includes acting as Consultant to the United Nations Economic and Social Commission for Asia and the Pacific (UNESCAP), the United Nations Population Fund (UNFPA) and the United Nations Development Fund for Women (UNIFEM).

Murari Kumar Jha completed his MA in early-modern history at the Centre for Historical Studies, Jawaharlal Nehru University, India. He wrote his MPhil *The European Trading Companies and Indian Merchants in Gujarat during the Seventeenth Century* at the same university. He currently studies in the Netherlands where he is learning the language and conducting archival research on early modern Gangetic Bihar and its linkages with the maritime world. He is currently an MPhil student under the ENCOMPASS programme run by the Department of History, Leiden University.

Amarjit Kaur is recognised as a leading scholar of Malaysian and Southeast Asian economic history. She has made important contributions to theoretical debates on globalisation, economic development, labour history, international migration and the gendered division of labour in Asia. She has numerous publications on Indian migration to Southeast Asia, and has enhanced the development of theoretical frameworks to the transnational study of migration. Her current research centres on the governance of migration and related security issues; and border-management strategies of major states in the Asia-Pacific region, in the face of transnational economic and social processes and the expanding global governance regime. She is currently Professor of Economic History at the School of Economics, University of New England, Australia.

Habibul Haque Khondker is Professor and Interim Chair of the Department of Social and Behavioral Sciences at Zayed University, Abu Dhabi, UAE. He has a PhD in sociology from the University of Pittsburgh, USA and a Master's in Sociology from Carleton University, Ottawa, Canada. Before joining Zayed University, he taught at the National University of Singapore for two decades. Khondker has published articles on globalisation, state, civil society, democracy, military in politics, famine, internet and science. His current research interests are politics and globalisation, and gender empowerment in comparative settings. He is the co-editor (with Goran Therborn) of *Asia and Europe in Globalization: Continents, Regions, and Nations* (Leiden: Brill, 2006). He is writing a book titled *Globalization: East/West* with Bryan Turner. He is on the editorial board of *Globalizations* (Routledge) and the *Journal of Classical Sociology* (Sage).

Brij V. Lal is Professor of Pacific and Asian History at the Australian National University. He is the recipient of numerous awards and honours, including the Distinguished Pacific Scholar and Fellowship of the Australian Humanities Academy. Amongst his many publications are *Girmitiyas: The Origins of the Fiji Indians* and *Mr Tulsi's Store: A Fijian Journey*, which was voted one of 'Ten Notable Asia-Pacific Books' by the

Committee of the San Francisco-based Kirimaya Prize in 2002. He was General Editor of *The Encyclopedia of the Indian Diaspora* (Singapore: Editions Didier Millet, October 2006).

Claude Markovits is a Directeur de Recherche (Senior Research Fellow) at the CNRS, Paris. He has authored numerous works on the history of colonial India, with particular emphasis on merchants and businessmen, as well as on the politics of Indian nationalism. His publications include *Indian Business and Nationalist Politics 1931–1939* (Cambridge: Cambridge University Press, 1985); *The Global World of Indian Merchants 1750–1947* (Cambridge: Cambridge University Press, 2000); *A History of Modern India 1480–1950* (London: Anthem Press, 2002); and *The Un-Gandhian Gandhi: the Life and Afterlife of the Mahatma* (Delhi: Permanent Black, 2003).

Vijay Mishra is Professor of English Literature at Murdoch University, Australia. He holds doctorates from the Australian National University and Oxford. His research interests include eighteenth-century English literature; literary history and theory; Australian and postcolonial literature; Indian literature and film; diasporas; and narrative fiction and film. His publications include *Devotional Poetics and the Indian Sublime* (Albany, New York: State University of New York Press, 1998); *Bollywood Cinema: Temples of Desire* (New York and London: Routledge, 2002); and *Literature of the Indian Diaspora: Theorizing the Diasporic Imaginary* (London: Routledge, 2007).

Rajesh Rai, Assistant Professor at the South Asian Studies Programme, National University of Singapore, completed his PhD at the School of Historical Studies at the University of Birmingham. His research interests are in the fields of diaspora studies and transnational identities, nationalism and the postcolonial history and politics of South Asia. Assistant Editor of *The Encyclopedia of the Indian Diaspora* (Singapore: Editions Didier Millet, 2006), he has published several articles on various aspects of the South Asian diaspora particularly in Southeast Asia.

Peter Reeves, Emeritus Professor of South Asian History at Curtin University (Perth, Western Australia), was Visiting Professor and Head of the South Asian Studies Programme (SASP) at the National University of Singapore from June 1999 to December 2006. A Fellow of the Academy of Humanities in Australia, he has also taught at the universities of Sussex, Western Australia and Michigan. His research interests are in the following areas: the political and agrarian history of northern India; the maritime history of the Indian Ocean since 1800; the history of fisheries in colonial and postcolonial South Asia; the history of Singapore's inshore and culture fisheries; and the history of the Indian diaspora. He was Executive Editor of *The Encyclopedia of the Indian Diaspora* (Singapore: Editions Didier Millet, 2006).

Tan Li Jen did her MA in History at the National University of Singapore. Her chapter is part of her unpublished dissertation, *Saints and Martyrs in the*

Diaspora: Sikh Identities in Post-Colonial Singapore and Malaysia – a social-cultural history of the Sikh community. Following the completion of her Master's degree, Li Jen worked as a broadcast journalist with a news radio station before joining a publishing firm.

Acknowledgements

The beginning of this project can be traced to the 'International Workshop on the Feasibility of an Encyclopedia of the Indians Overseas' that was convened in Singapore in December 2001. That workshop led to the publication of *The Encyclopedia of the Indian Diaspora* in 2006. However, the connections that we made at this workshop, were also crucial in the development of this volume.

A number of the participants who had attended that initial workshop went on to present papers at an international conference on 'Asian Diasporas' held at the National University of Singapore (NUS), from 5 to 7 April 2004 under the auspices of the Faculty of Arts and Social Sciences (FASS), NUS. This book comprises many of the papers presented at the 'Asian Diasporas' conference. Without the generous financial support of the FASS, NUS, which enabled the conduct of both the workshop and the conference, this book would not have been possible; we wish, therefore to thank the FASS for its invaluable assistance.

We are greatly indebted to the faculty, staff and graduate students at the South Asian Studies Programme at NUS for their support of the project. We would also like to thank our Research Assistants: Ms Fahmida Farzhana, Ms Gauri Pathak, Ms Meera Gopalkrishna and Ms Sadhana Rai.

Finally we would like to dedicate this book to Noelene and Anu for their constant encouragement.

Rajesh Rai and Peter Reeves

Introduction

Rajesh Rai and Peter Reeves

Diaspora

The definition of the term 'diaspora' is both complex and subject to considerable debate in academic circles. Historically, diaspora has been associated with the dispersal of the Jewish people, who experienced its violence and collective exile. However, there is now recognition that many aspects of this experience are applicable as well to other groups of migrants including those from Africa, South Asia and the like. Gerard Chaliand and Jean-Pierre Rageau in *The Penguin Atlas of Diasporas* list four criteria for the diaspora condition:

> *the collective forced dispersion of a religious and/or ethnic group*[;] ... *collective memory, which transmits both the historical facts that precipitated the dispersion and a cultural heritage*[;] ... *the will to survive as a minority by transmitting a heritage*[;] ... [and] *the time factor.* Only time decides whether a minority that meets all or some of the criteria described above having insured its survival and adaptation, is a diaspora.
>
> (Chaliand and Rageau 1995: xiv–xviii)

The evolution of the term in scholarly literature has adopted a pattern where the element of 'forced dispersion' has been downplayed to accommodate a variety of migrant experiences that nevertheless meet most of the underlying principles of the diaspora condition. The expansiveness of the term is apparent in the formulation we adopted in *The Encyclopedia of the Indian Diaspora*, where 'collective memory', 'the will to survive as a minority' and 'the time factor' are affirmed as key markers in defining diaspora:

> A diaspora exists precisely because it remembers the 'homeland'. Without this memory..., these migrants and settlers would be simply people in a new setting, into which they merge, bringing little or nothing to the new 'home', accepting in various ways and forms the mores and attitudes that already exist in their new country and society ... The people of the diaspora, however, do not merely settle in new countries: they recreate in their socio-economic, political and cultural institutions a version of ... that homeland that they remember.
>
> (Reeves and Rai 2006: 18)

History is replete with examples of South Asian movement beyond the subcontinent that conform to even the more exclusive definitions of diaspora. The export of Indian slaves, the expulsion of convicts from the subcontinent to penal settlements in various parts of the Indian Ocean, and the recruitment of labourers through indenture during the colonial period are cases in point. It is apparent, however, that many other South Asian migrant communities may not have experienced a similar degree of violence at the point of dispersion. Would that be a sufficient condition for the exclusion of these groups from being described as a diaspora?

Certainly the experience of South Asian migrant communities born out of slavery, indenture or convict labour was vastly different from that of a contemporary South Asian migrant IT professional who finds his or her niche in 'Silicon Valley', maybe to settle into 'NRI'-dom, maybe to return to the subcontinent. To incorporate the latter's experience even in the most liberal definitions of the diaspora could render the term ineffectual as a conceptual category. Yet, South Asian migrants, since the early nineteenth century, comprised various groups including traders, imperial auxiliaries, 'free' migrants and long-term migrant professionals, whose position vis-à-vis the diaspora condition is more problematic when compared to the two extremities in the continuum of migration set out above.

While these migrant groups may not fulfil all the criteria of the diaspora condition, they exhibit a number of features, including the collective memory of a 'homeland', a sense of 'exile' and 'loss' and the persistence of 'homeland' political and socio-economic identities that allow their incorporation in more inclusive interpretations. Such an interpretation in turn allows the inclusion of a range of South Asian movements whose historical trajectories, once separate, have now come to be increasingly intertwined as they occupy common geographical spaces or share the growing connectivity, which is manifest in the contemporary 'age of globalisation'.

The South Asian diaspora

The South Asian diaspora numbers just under 30 million people worldwide. Smaller than the African and Chinese diasporas in size, it is nonetheless recognised as the most widely dispersed diaspora. It is one which, of late, has seen phenomenal growth both due to natural increase and the result of a continued movement, in the late twentieth century and early twenty-first century, of professionals and labourers from the subcontinent. Prior to the Second World War, the largest South Asian diasporic communities were based in Southeast Asia, South and East Africa, the Caribbean, Mauritius and Fiji. While they remain significant communities in these parts, the period after the Second World War has seen a rapid escalation in the number of South Asians settled in the West. In the United States alone, between 2000 and 2005, the 'Asian Indian' population grew by 38 per cent (15 times the national average) from 1.7 million to over 2.3 million (Little India 2006). Similar increases have been recorded elsewhere, including the United Kingdom, Canada and Australia. To this contemporary movement we can add some five million transient South Asian workers based in the Middle East alone.

This phenomenal growth, alongside recognition of the global economic, political and social significance of the South Asian diaspora, has sparked a concomitant expansion in academic literature on the subject.[1] These works have provided considerable insights on the experience of the diaspora. Scholarly work on the subject has largely adopted an interdisciplinary approach (drawing primarily from historical, human geographic, sociological and cultural studies) in dealing with questions related to the forces that ushered the movement of people to regions far removed from their homeland. A similar approach, moreover, marks the study of the political, social and economic development of these communities in the 'hostland'; the continued linkages between the diaspora and the 'homeland'; and the emergence of complex diasporan identities constructed from the negotiation of cultural values carried from the homeland, generational differences and the multiethnic milieu of 'hostland' societies.

The picture that has emerged from these scholarly interventions is that of two distinct diasporas: one, the 'old' diaspora, born out of the 'age of colonial-capital'; the other, the 'new' diaspora, formed by people intimately connected to the monumental changes that have taken place in the ongoing 'age of globalisation'. While it may be useful to fragment these demarcations further within the matrix of the South Asian diaspora, these categories have allowed important insights into the contrasting experiences of the nineteenth-century and early twentieth-century movement of South Asians – the 'old' diaspora – created as a 'break' from the 'homeland'; and the movement that has continued from the late twentieth century into the twenty-first century. Given the developments in communications, the more recent migrations have given a degree of 'connectedness' between the diaspora and the 'homeland' which was unthinkable in earlier times. The recently published *Encyclopedia of the Indian Diaspora* (2006) explores that contrast in chapters three and four, where the further point is made that 'the mid-20th century saw the beginning of a change in the pattern of Indian migration. For the first time, people went not to the colonial periphery but to the metropolitan centres at the heart of the Empire-Commonwealth' (Lal *et al.* 2006: 66). Early on, this migration was primarily for labouring and service opportunities in the United Kingdom. Increasingly, however, over the last three decades of the twentieth century, it became a steady flow to the United States, Canada, Australia and New Zealand, all of which were economies looking for highly skilled and professional migrants – the migrants who came in the late twentieth century to constitute the 'NRIs' ('Non-Resident Indians'). These 'NRIs' changed the nature of the diaspora very fundamentally – and brought high levels of skill and entrepreneurial flair to their new 'hostlands'.

Wherever South Asians have migrated, moreover, they have carried with them the social, religious and cultural practice (as they remember or are taught them) of the 'homeland'. These may be manifest in the private domains of households or, when there exists a sufficiently large number of South Asians, be represented in more public spaces. It is not surprising, therefore, that South Asian religious and cultural institutions, restaurants, movies, music and fashion shops are a common sight all over the world. In many cosmopolitan cities, entire neighbourhoods have been transformed into 'Little Indias' where one can easily purchase South Asian produce and enter into a recognisable 'Indian' locale.

The social and cultural dynamics of migrant lives have received considerable attention in the scholarly literature. Engaged in understanding the production and negotiation of diasporan identities within a dialectical context of being between 'here' and 'there', these works have shown the inadequacy of traditional notions of identity tied to the politics of place. As Benzi Zhang notes, 'diaspora is the process of crossing and recrossing multiple borders of language, history, race, time and culture [which] must challenge the absolutism of singular place by relocating their identity in the multiplicity of plural relationships' (Zhang 2004: 69). This argument is important but it does not completely answer all the questions that need to be raised. Does the contrast between 'old' and 'new' in the scholarly literature of the South Asian diaspora conceal alternative narratives of migration and transnational community formation? While the *bête noire* of 'indenture' has punctuated accounts of the 'old' diaspora, emphasising notions of fracture, what of those groups, made up particularly, though not solely, of commercial migrants who maintained significant connections with the 'homeland' even as they traversed the *kala pani* ('dark waters') in search of fortune? Given this bifurcated matrix, how do studies on the subject deal with the growing overlap between the 'old' and the 'new', even as members of the diaspora of colonial capital relocate to the West, or as contemporary migrant professionals from South Asia come to occupy sites held by earlier migrants linked to indenture? These are some of the questions taken up in this volume. What these essays endeavour to provide is a view – over time and in widely separated locales – of these factors at work in the establishment, expansion and sustainability of this world-wide movement of the peoples of South Asia that has become 'the diaspora' and made it such a potent element in many situations around the world.

Transnational networks

The first part of the volume looks at the role of 'transnational' networks in providing space and context for the building of the economic and social features of the diaspora communities. Given their separation from the 'homeland', those whose journeyings and activities build the basis of the new communities need such space – space that is freer and more fluid than that within either the homeland or the social realm of the existing 'native' or 'indigenous' society with which the diasporic community has to cope as it seeks to settle itself in the new land and both conserves and adapts the culture that it carries from the homeland to this new world in which it finds itself. Merchants, specialists with new or particular skills, as well as the poor who have found themselves displaced to this strange and difficult new life, need support, solidarity and reinforcement to sustain themselves in that new life. Even as the community grows and is more firmly lodged in the 'hostland', such networking remains a necessity because new arrivals have to negotiate their entrance and acceptance with the longer-settled members of the diasporic society, as well as learning how to operate alongside the native society.

The term 'transnational', which is defined by the *American Heritage Diction-ary* (2004) as 'reaching beyond or transcending national boundaries', has gained currency in academic discourse as a result of the expansion of international migration over the last few decades, and the growing linkages between non-state actors, particularly people, but as well of ideas and goods, across national boundaries. While diaspora acts as a historical precursor to transnationalism in terms of the study of the international movement of people, the corpus of trans-national literature has tended to focus on the greater 'connectedness' evident in the contemporary experience of migration, in terms, for example, of the information communication technology that now links migrants and the 'home-land'. This connectivity poses questions on the attendant conceptions of 'exile' and 'fracture' in diasporic literature especially in its attempts to encompass migrant experience in the contemporary era. Consequently, there now exists a body of scholarly literature that sees the contemporary migration of profession-als between metropolitan cities as best treated within the context of 'transnation-alism', rather than that of diaspora.

Presumably, then, it might seem ill-suited for this volume to place narratives of transnationalism within the corpus of diasporic literature. The argument for incongruity is to some extent appended by the influence of a 'cosmopolitan' philosophy (Wikipedia 'transnationalism') with attendant notions of 'world citi-zenry' and 'a taste or consideration for cultures besides one's own culture of origin' (Wikipedia 'cosmopolitanism') in narratives of transnationalism that is at odds with the centrality of the 'homeland' in expositions of the latter.

Yet, literature on transnationalism itself contains the problematic of whether the cosmopolitan is simply an 'ideal type' in a world where migrant lives and their 'imaginaries' continue to be informed by a dialectical negotiation between 'here' and 'there', in which the negotiation of 'homeland' socio-cultural, polit-ical and economic identities remain important components. Scholars who have adopted a network approach in their studies of transnational migrant communit-ies, even as they have acceded to the 'voluntary' nature of migration, have often put paid to the cosmopolitan imperative by emphasising the need to account for these homeland socio-economic and political institutions and the need to situate 'individual decision makers within groups, and ... [interpose] groups between macroscopic social and economic conditions and actual migrations' (Light *et al.* 1993: 25–6).

While the study of transnational networks has grown from the changes ushered in the contemporary era, there is acknowledgement that such groups existed long before the late twentieth and early twenty-first centuries (thus lending support for a longer reading of the process of globalisation). With regards to South Asia, there is considerable interest, for example, in the study of the early itinerant commercial groups that ventured out of the subcontinent and who, several times in a lifetime, negotiated the caravan routes of Central Asia or the sailing routes of the Indian Ocean. The same can be said for networks of migrant-recruiters such as the *kangani* and *maistry*, and as well indentured émigrés who, upon attaining freedom, traversed the 'homeland' and 'hostland' serving as initiators of chain-migration streams that aided in the relocation of kinsmen. These groups have received relatively little treatment in the scholarly literature of the South Asian diaspora, in part because of the uncomfortable fit with more exclusive definitions of the diaspora condition, and also because they constantly travelled to and from the 'homeland'. While their journeys impacted on both 'homeland' societies and those in the diaspora – features much akin to contemporary transnational migration – yet the literature on transnationalism – predicated on connections between 'nation-states' – has ignored these groups precisely because 'nation-states' in South Asia only emerged as independent entities from 1947 onwards. We take the view, however, that the inclusion of these transnational networks within the broader framework of diaspora adopted in this volume enables the study of these groups about whom information is limited in scholarly works on the subject.

Some of these questions are addressed in Part I of the volume. The four chapters in this section discuss four very different situations in which it is possible to observe networks – of various kinds – in the diaspora and to pose questions about the value of the transnational in understanding how individuals and groups – ethnic groups, social classes, kin groups, caste groups, occupational groups – utilise networking in achieving goals in the diaspora.

Through his case study of two diasporic merchant networks of Hindu Sindhis from the towns of Shikarpur and Hyderabad in Sind, Claude Markovits discusses the nature of trading relations within firms; within the mercantile life of the cities which form their centre of operations; and, in operational terms, in the far-flung trading regions in which individual members of the firms do business. He examines the popular perception of a correlation between certain ethnic groups and their areas of business success. In doing so, Markovits discounts the utility of the transnational approach and looks instead at the importance of circulation and mercantile knowledge in understanding mercantile networks. He combines the 'culturalist' orientation of diaspora studies with a commercial network studies approach which situates trading networks in their historical, political and economic contexts. He rejects the model of 'Asian' capitalism, based on essentialising cultural traits and an emphasis on kinship and ethnicity, demonstrating instead, through his two examples, how South Asian transnational mercantile networks display their own particular specificities and historical trajectories.

Murari Jha's chapter examines the social world of merchants in pre-modern Gujarat and their Indian Ocean networks. Using both indigenous and European sources, his study elucidates upon the interlinked social worlds of these traders, exploring the relationship between the private and semi-public spheres of the family/community, and the wider commercial world of the market at the port cities in Gujarat. Jha's essay emphasises the collaborative relationship forged amongst different groups of traders; the traditional practices employed to resolve disputes on commercial matters; and how access to cotton textiles from the hinterland enabled these traders to develop an expansive transnational trading network that led to Gujarati diasporic movements to various parts of the Indian Ocean.

Marina Carter examines subaltern networks in the colonial Indian labour diaspora of Mauritius. Although the extant literature on colonial Indian labour migrants tends to emphasise the 'forced' aspect of recruitment and the seemingly static aloofness of indentured labourers from the hostland community, Carter argues for a more nuanced approach. Through the case study of Mauritius, she shows that, notwithstanding their subjection to economic oppression and legislative discrimination, Indian labour migrants tapped into both local inter-community, inter-ethnic associations and transnational intra-community, intra-ethnic networks for their socio-economic and settlement objectives. Using a subaltern methodology and investigating colonial archives for the subjective experiences of the men and women who participated in labour migrations, Carter sifts away conventional colonial and historiographical labels to unearth the complexity of detail surrounding the settlement processes of Indian labour migrants to Mauritius.

Peter Reeves' chapter is concerned with operations in the international 'acquisitions & merger' field which has developed in the globalised world economy of the late twentieth and early twenty-first centuries. He outlines the way in which Indian entrepreneurs – operating outside the diaspora as such but being linked to it by some actors in these situations – acquire substantial European operations in steel and tyre production and merge them with corporations which they have built in other sectors of the globalised economy. These 'case studies' are used to suggest that changes may be taking place in the pattern of Indian entrepreneurial activity in which a 'transnational space', opened up by the globalisation of the world economy and made pertinent by India's economic liberalisation allows entrepreneurs to operate independently of Indian economic policies and, by drawing on international resources, to build successfully an international industrial position. It is an outcome which – while the entrepreneurs see themselves as operating independently – nonetheless is seen as being related to India's international economic strengthening.

Changing identities

Insofar as the community development of the diasporic society succeeds, the identity of that migrant population becomes a major issue. The community itself is confronted by major questions: if it is a caste or community-segmented community, what identity can it preserve? What common features of the group are most important to a sense of community identification? How will the community deal with changes that derive from adaptation to the new society in which the community is now living and of which it has necessarily to be a part? Then there are issues beyond those immediate concerns: How can the sense of identity be passed to succeeding generations? Will those succeeding generations, who may come under increasing pressure to adapt to the hostland's demands, be able to preserve the cultural skills required to sustain their diasporic identities?

These questions were – and are – fundamental issues for migrant communities. If the community successfully deals with them it could survive – but that success in itself could open new problem areas. In some diasporic situations, if the migrant community flourishes, this can be a cause for concern on the part of the 'hosts', who may feel threatened by the emergence of a new social entity in their midst, practising strange rites, set in very different ways of social behaviour; and sometimes seemingly allied with the colonial power itself, under whose banner the new group appeared in the native community's homeland.

Equally, attempts by migrant groups to take on some features of the host society can also alarm the older native society: If they succeed, what will that mean for the host society? How then can the native society preserve its identity, unmarked by compromises with a community or communities whose social and cultural practice bore little or no relation to that which had existed before migration began? Moreover, there are likely also to be political consequences, especially if the colonial power introduces new forms of governance, administration and economic regulation (taxes, revenue collection, trading arrangements) with which immigrants may be more familiar or to which they adapt more quickly because they are better grounded in the language of the new forms or are more experienced in handling similar developments in their homeland.

There is no doubt that the first line of development is, almost universally, the road that is taken by the migrant society. This is because there is great pressure on the migrants to preserve the cultural and social elements which they have brought from the 'homeland', even if these are only available in vestigial forms. Over time, some features may become attenuated. Caste, for instance, might lose much of its meaning, although it might still be embodied in family names and some practices; V.S. Naipaul, in *An Area of Darkness*, talks of the community in Trinidad 'playing' at caste:

> caste in India was not what it had been to me in Trinidad. In Trinidad caste had no meaning in our day-to-day life; the caste we occasionally played at was no more than an acknowledgement of latent qualities; ... In India it implied a brutal division of labour...
>
> (Naipaul 1964: 36)

Nonetheless, sustaining some sense of 'Indian-ness' (or 'South Asian-ness') – remains a prime concern. Naipaul captures that exquisitely in *A House for Mr Biswas*:

> In the arcade of Hanuman House ... there was already the evening assembly of old men ... pulling at clay chelums that glowed red and smelt of ganja and burnt sacking ... They could not speak English and were not interested in the land where they lived; it was place where they had come for short

time and stayed longer than expected. They continually talked of going back to India, but when the opportunity came, many refused, afraid of the unknown, afraid to leave the familiar temporariness.

(Naipaul 1961: 174)

The remaining essays in this volume are dedicated to looking at the critical issue of identity and change in the South Asian diaspora. The four chapters in Part II deal with social and economic issues and circumstances in different regions:

Amarjit Kaur's essay entitled 'Indians in Southeast Asia: migrant labour, knowledge workers and the new India' outlines the formation and development of the Indian diaspora in Burma, Malaysia and Singapore. Her chapter shows how political and domestic affairs in India and the hostland impacted on the social, economic and political position of Indians in these multi-ethnic host societies in the colonial period. Kaur goes on to analyse the changes that have been manifest amongst Indian communities in Singapore and Malaysia especially following India's economic transformation in the 1990s that has led to the formation of new patterns of migration and provided opportunities for new alignments with the former 'homeland'.

In 'Indo-Fijians: roots and routes', Brij Lal uses the medium of autobiography to reflect on the changing identities of three generations of Indo-Fijians. By charting the route taken by the practices and attitudes of the generation of his grandfather, his father and his own, he paints a historical picture of the evolving relationship of the Indo-Fijian diaspora to its Indian roots and Fijian experiences. For the modern generation, irrevocably affected by bitter racial politics, the nurturing of their Indian heritage, constantly re-interpreted, becomes an avenue for the expression of pride and choice in their identity, rather than being a marker of the ritualistic reverence and everyday understanding displayed by their indentured, immigrant forebears.

In 'From Bharat to Sri Ram Desh: the emigration of Indian indentured labourers to Suriname', Chan E.S. Choenni re-creates the indenture experience of Indians to Suriname, particularly in terms of the emigration process. He shows how Indians, under the indenture system in Dutch-controlled Suriname, benefited as subjects of the British empire which afforded them better protection and conditions in their emigration to the Dutch colony of Suriname. The essay argues that these improved conditions, impacting on the early settlement of the indentured Indian diaspora in Suriname, had a long-lasting favourable impact on the material well-being of this diaspora as compared with the indenture-fostered Indian diaspora in other parts of the Caribbean.

In his chapter, Habibul Khondker uses ethnographic descriptions to chart the everyday lives and practices of diasporic Bengali-speaking Bangladeshis in Singapore and the USA. Through richly detailed accounts of his own experiences and interactions with white-collar non-resident Bangladeshis, he pieces together a complex picture of a diasporic identity laced with both a 'longing' for and 'reviling' of the 'homeland' and performed through transient, contingent roles.

Community is reproduced in the 'hostland', and imaginary 'homelands' blend into real 'homelands' for the creation of virtual local cultures and hybrid identities.

The chapters in Part III are concerned with the questions of identity in a cultural context.

Rajesh Rai's chapter studies the development of 'minor' South Asian languages in Singapore. Rai argues that even as state policies vis-à-vis language have been particularly crucial in determining the position of these languages, there is a need to factor the impact of contemporary South Asian migration to the island city and developments in transnational media that have played an important role in increasing the communicative domains for these languages. His chapter goes on to analyse why in some cases South Asians in Singapore have ignored possibilities of having their actual 'mother tongue' included in the education curriculum, instead supporting the study of a diglossic complement.

Through a study of cooking and food sharing amongst South Indian women in Malaysia, Theresa Devasahayam argues that in spite of a changing social context where Indian women have come to be engaged in wage work, these activities have remained important cultural channels through which kinship is forged, defining both in- and out-groups. Her chapter shows that although living in a multi-ethnic state has resulted in a change in the type of foods that are cooked and shared, there remains a marked continuation with traditional concerns of 'purity' and 'pollution' in food preparation.

Tan Li Jen looks at the Singaporean Sikh community, part of the 'old diaspora' that migrated during the colonial era, and its efforts to memorialise Bhai Maharaj Singh – a prominent historical and religious figure. Her chapter shows how the colonial past has come to be negotiated and interpreted in the postcolonial period in a complex process that, over time, has imbued layers of significance to Bhai Maharaj Singh. Tan goes on to show how this iconic figure has been creatively employed in the construction of an illustrious 'historical' narrative for Sikhs, which, in addition to alleviating feelings of insecurity that come from being part of minority community, has been useful in the formation of a unique Singaporean Sikh identity.

In his personal narrative, 'The familiar temporariness', Vijay Mishra meditates on the ruptured identity of the old Indian plantation diaspora through the work of V.S. Naipaul. Deeply sensitive to Naipaul's anguish as a writer of a liminal society, a society built upon the trauma of belonging to a land and confessing ownership to a language which is not one's own, Mishra reads in Naipaul's writing the inherent contradiction of the old plantation diaspora's identity – an anti-coloniality firmly placed within colonial discourse. Defending Naipaul from charges of masochistic racism, Mishra sees in him instead the old Indian diaspora's willingness, opposed temperamentally to the new diaspora's postcolonial multiculturalism, to intervene and assimilate in the grand European narratives of modernity by right of vision, albeit not by right of racial connection.

Conclusion

The two themes of this volume – networks and identity – are, of course, not totally separate, even though in some situations or on some occasions, one or the other can be the more important. The essays in this volume exemplify this. What these essays endeavour to provide is a view over time and in widely separated locales of these factors working in the establishment, expansion and sustainability of this world-wide movement of the peoples of South Asia that has become the diaspora and made it such a potent element in many situations around the world.

Note

1 Some recent works include: Paranjpe (2001); Puwar and Raghuram (2003); Jacobsen and Pratap (2004); Jayaram (2004); Thapan (2005); Brown (2006); Rajan and Sharma (2006); Lal *et al.* (2006).

References

Brown, J.M. (2006) *Global South Asians: Introducing the Modern Diaspora*, Cambridge: Cambridge University Press.

Chaliand, G. and J.P. Rageau (1995) *The Penguin Atlas of Diasporas*, New York: Viking.

Dictionary.com 'transnational' (2004) Original source: *The American Heritage® Dictionary of the English Language, Fourth Edition*, Houghton Mifflin Company. Online. Available at: http://dictionary.reference.com/browse/transnational (accessed 21 November 2006).

Jacobsen, K.A. and K.P. Pratap (eds) (2004) *South Asians in the Diaspora: Histories and Religious Traditions*, Leiden; Boston: Brill.

Jayaram, N. (ed.) (2004) *The Indian Diaspora: Dynamics of Migration*, New Delhi; Thousand Oaks: Sage Publications.

Lal, B.V., P. Reeves and R. Rai (eds) (2006) *The Encyclopedia of the Indian Diaspora*, Singapore: Editions Didier Millet.

Light, I., P. Bhachu and S. Karageorgis (1993) 'Migration Networks and Immigration Entrepreneurship', in I. Light and P. Bhachu (eds) *Immigration and Entrepreneurship: Culture, Capital and Ethnic Networks*, New Brunswick: Transaction Publishers, pp. 25–50.

Little India (2006) 'Asian Indian Population 2005', in *Little India*, November. Original source: American Community Survey 2005. Online. Available at: www.littleindia.com/news/132/ARTICLE/1389/2006–11–12.html (accessed 21 November 2006).

Naipaul, V.S. (1964) *An Area of Darkness*, London: André Deutsch.

—— (1961) *A House for Mr Biswas*, London: André Deutsch.

Paranjpe, M. (ed.) (2001) *In Diaspora: Theories, Histories, Texts*, New Delhi: Indialog Publications.

Puwar, N. and P. Raghuram (eds) (2003) *South Asian Women in the Diaspora*, Oxford: Berg Publishers.

Rajan, G. and S. Sharma (2006) *New Cosmopolitanisms: South Asians in the US*, Stanford: Stanford University Press.

Reeves, P. and R. Rai (2006) 'The Indian Context', in B.V. Lal, P. Reeves and R. Rai (eds) *The Encyclopedia of the Indian Diaspora*, Singapore: Editions Didier Millet, pp. 18–31.

Thapan, M. (ed.) (2005) *Transnational Migration and the Politics of Identity*, Thousand Oaks: Sage Publications.

Wikipedia, The Free Encyclopedia. 'Cosmopolitanism'. Online. Available at: http://en.wikipedia.org/wiki/Cosmopolitanism (accessed 21 November 2006).

Wikipedia, The Free Encyclopedia. 'Transnationalism'. Online. Available at: http://en.wikipedia.org/wiki/Transnational (accessed 21 November 2006).

Zhang, B. (2004) 'Beyond Border Politics: the Problematics of Identity in Asian Diaspora Literature', *Studies in the Humanities*, 31(1): 69–91.

Part I
Transnational networks

1 Ethnicity, locality and circulation in two diasporic merchant networks from South Asia

Claude Markovits

This chapter is situated at the intersection between the field of diaspora studies, with its heavy focus on questions of identity and ethnicity and its 'culturalist' orientation, and the field of commercial network studies which has been more preoccupied with situating trading networks in relation to the development of an international economy in Asia.[1] Although few academic studies have tried to combine the two approaches, at a more popular or semi-academic level, it is a commonly held assumption that a strong correlation exists between the success in business of particular groups and their ethnicity. Western commentators trying to account for the surge in the growth of some of the East Asian and Southeast Asian economies in the 1980s and 1990s have often emphasised the crucial role played by overseas Chinese ethnic networks in that success story. They also gave great importance to the prevalence of a specific value system (which they sometimes characterised as 'Asian', whatever that means, or some-times as 'Confucian', which of course is not the same thing), which they saw as partly opposed to the Western value system, but at the same time favourable to entrepreneurship. Although there were some reservations regarding the hierar-chical and authoritarian nature of this so-called 'Asian' value system, it was on the whole praised as having contributed decisively to the spectacular economic development of some Asian countries.

Western academic authors, such as Jack Goody (1996) and André Gunder Frank (1998), each one in his own different way, but both rejecting the 'Euro-centric' orientation of the dominant strand of economic history as practised in the West, attempted to give some historical depth to the upsurge of Asian capitalism by pointing to its longstanding roots. Interestingly, their notion of Asia was inclusive of India as well as of China and Southeast Asia, while South Asia had figured very little in the dominant narrative of 'Asian' capitalism. That narrative, however flawed and inadequate, had the merit of focusing the atten-tion of a Western public away from its usual obsession with its own story, but it suffered from the advent of the 1997 Asian financial crisis, which led to a sudden reversal in perceptions: the same Asian capitalism which had been praised to the skies was suddenly vilified as 'crony capitalism' (as if there had ever been capitalism anywhere without an element of cronyism). The 'ethnic factor', which had been viewed in a positive light as a resource, became open to

a more critical kind of scrutiny, as the nepotism supposedly bred by the dominance of family-based firms in the so-called Asian model of capitalism was
identified as one of the main sources of cronyism. Whatever the ups and downs
in intellectual fashion in the West, which, it should be noted, have had little
influence on perceptions in Asia, it remains a difficult task to combine the diaspora studies approach with the study of trading networks, and I shall make use
here of recently published personal research to question some of the basic
assumptions behind the whole exercise of 'ethnicising' the study of economic
behaviour.

The study of ethnic business networks

The question of the specific role played by certain 'ethnic' groups in the commercial economy exercised the minds of sociologists much more than those of
economists and economic historians. Having been initiated by Weber, Sombart
and Simmel, whose preoccupation was mostly with the specific economic niche
occupied by Jews in medieval and modern Europe, this problematic was refor-
mulated in a more general way by Blalock and Bonacich in the 1960s and
1970s, culminating in the 'theory of middleman minorities' put forward by the
latter in a well-known 1973 article (Bonacich 1973). That theory, it should be
noted, never made it into mainstream economics or economic history. In the
1980s, Philip Curtin, elaborating on an earlier insight from Abner Cohen (1971),
linked it with the emerging 'diaspora' theme to produce his wide ranging theory
of the trade diaspora, which took in some aspects of the middleman minority
paradigm but gave it more anthropological and historical depth (Curtin 1984).
Curtin endowed his trade diasporas with a role mainly as cultural brokers, which
made them redundant once the age of world capitalism had dawned by the early
nineteenth century, producing a degree of uniformisation in the functioning of
markets. Mainstream economists and economic historians, it should again be
noted, remained unmoved. In the meantime Goitein and his pupils had produced
their massive work on the medieval Jewish trading diaspora operating from
Cairo, on the basis of the Geniza documents (Goitein 1967–93), and, from that
horizon, Avner Greif produced a sophisticated analysis of coalitions of Maghribi
traders (Greif 1992), which attracted some attention from mainstream economists. In spite of that, studies of ethnic business communities have remained to
this day the almost exclusive preserve of area specialists, and a 'generalist'
scholar like K.N. Chaudhuri did not hesitate, in his grand synthesis on the Indian
Ocean, to summarily dismiss the notion of trade diaspora (Chaudhuri 1985:
224–6).

   In the growing, but still overall thin, body of literature devoted to diasporic
trading networks, assumptions about their nature often remain implicit, and are
rarely spelt out openly. It is, however, possible to perceive the existence of two
different schools of thought, one which I call 'primordialist', which lays heavy
stress on pre-existing factors, often labelled 'predispositions', in the emergence
of ethnic business networks, and one which could be called 'constructivist',

which emphasises the processual nature of such phenomena. The 'ethnicist' paradigm is just the most widespread version of the dominant 'primordialist' thesis. Although ethnicity in this conception is a fairly polysemic term, since it can apply as much to ethnic groups *stricto sensu* or to religious ones or (in the South Asian context) to caste groups, a common characteristic is the given and somewhat timeless nature of the specific endowments assigned to such groups. It is pointed out that they are already closely knit, for extra-economic reasons, such as the fact of belonging to a persecuted religious minority, and therefore particularly well suited to operating in the field of long-distance exchanges, characterised by the existence of large gaps in information and the absence of reliable transcultural institutions for building trust. Hence the particular focus in this literature on longstanding diasporic communities, such as the Jews and the Armenians, which have been actively involved in international trade since medieval times.

However, when it comes to contemporary Asia, the leading business network ethnicities, those of various South Asian and East Asian groups, are not linked in the same way with the existence of longstanding diasporas created by the political and religious persecution of minority groups. The Asian networks developed in various contexts at different periods in time, mostly in 'majority' communities (such as Hindus in India or Han in China), and in their case it was a mixture of commercial and political factors which led to the emergence of the diaspora. Professor Hamashita (1988), in particular, has shown how the expansion of Chinese networks in Southeast Asia was linked to the Chinese 'tributary' system. In the case of Indian merchants, who (if they were Hindu, which was most often the case) had to brave a religious taboo (of varying severity) to travel and settle overseas, trade expansion was partly linked to the renewal of links to the Islamic world fostered by the establishment of the Mughal empire (Dale 1994).

The study of Asian merchant diasporic networks must therefore pay special attention to the political dimension, given the often direct link between the growth of merchant diasporas and the expansion of specific political systems, including the European commercial-cum-military enterprises which intruded into the Asian commercial sphere from the sixteenth century onwards,[2] and came to largely dominate it by the second half of the nineteenth century. The bewildering ethnic variety of Asian ethnic networks (at least in the South Asian case, but the East Asian one does not appear to be vastly different) is also to be taken into account, for it belies any attempt at finding an obvious link between precise, often discrete, ethnicities, and success in business. Why, to take an example, should a particular sect or subcaste of Gujarati merchants be more successful than another one in the international market place? An answer inevitably involves a deep research into the minutiae of the historical record of various groups, which generally remains rather obscure to the contemporary observer.

In the South Asian field, one study which has tried to combine an anthropological approach putting special emphasis on the role of caste and a more historical one centred on the development of one particular network is David Rudner's work on the Nattukottai Chettiars (Rudner 1994). This American anthropologist saw in the strength of their caste organisation the major competitive advantage of that subcaste of Tamil bankers who dominated rural credit transactions in large parts of mainland Southeast Asia (Burma, Thailand, Malaya, Cochinchina) for half a century, between 1880 and 1930. Using their Saivaite temples as clearing houses, they wove a thick web of transactions linking their homeland of Chettinad, situated in the South Indian princely state of Puddukottai, and the neighbouring big emporium of Madras with Southeast Asia and Ceylon, some of its ramifications extending all the way to Mauritius and South Africa. While basing his analysis of the role of caste on contemporary ethnological observations made in Chettinad, Rudner also delved deep into the historical record of the Chettiars in Southeast Asia, which is fairly well documented. There remains however a certain mismatch between his ethnography and his history. As regards the crucial question of why caste solidarity proved particularly well suited to sustaining such a network, apart from the regulatory framework provided by the caste *panchayat*, Rudner has no really convincing explanation to offer.

My own study of two networks of Hindu merchants based in Sind (Markovits 2000), a province of British India between 1843 and 1947, which is now part of Pakistan, whose operations extended all over Central Asia for one and across the entire world for the other, led me to a reappraisal of the role of ethnic or caste solidarity in the emergence of diasporic merchant communities. Neither of these two groups, contrary to the Chettiars, was either mono-ethnic or mono-caste, and solidarity, which was often breached in fact by various forms of opportunistic behaviour, was much more based on the local patriotism of town dwellers and an ideology of brotherhood, which placed as much emphasis on fictitious as on real blood ties, than on any sense of belonging to one ethnic group or caste. Besides, the success of such networks was crucially based on their ability to develop specific forms of knowledge rather than on a form of 'moral economy'. I was thus led to stress the importance of the cognitive aspects of mercantile activity, an extremely under-researched area of study.

From a methodological point of view, I became alert to the pitfalls of the dominant morphological and synchronic approach to trading networks, which tends to see them as constituted entities, and favoured a more genetic and diachronic approach, which places emphasis on the way such networks were historically constructed. I shall try in the next section to sketch the main outlines of that approach on the basis of my published work.

A plea for diachrony and cognitivism

The preference shown in the literature for a synchronic rather than a diachronic presentation of so-called 'ethnic' business networks has often little to do with a methodological bias as such, but rather tends to reflect the difficulty involved in reconstructing the historical record of groups which do not constitute their own archives (and, even if they do, show a strong reluctance to share them with outsiders) and are often largely absent from the archival records constituted by the various states in which they operate. I was lucky in being able to locate in the records kept by the British Imperial and Indian governments several series of documents which helped me to reconstruct at least partly the historical trajectory of the groups I was researching. That material was not unproblematic, and it offered many challenges to an historian, a question into which I shall not go, but its greatest advantage was that it included many documents, of a mostly judicial nature, emanating from the two groups under study, which allowed a kind of insider's view of the networks (although not unmediated), rather than simply reflected British views of them (which, one must add, oscillated between indifference and hostility).

The first point I would like to stress is the extremely contingent nature of developments in this field, which tends to make all talk of 'predispositions' somewhat dubious. The two groups of merchants I studied originated from two medium-sized towns in a remote province of British India, which had been one of the last to be annexed by the British (in 1843). Prior to the eighteenth century, neither of these two towns appear to have played a significant role in international trade; nor was their geographical situation particularly advantageous in itself. These were two inland towns, one, Shikarpur, situated in Upper Sind, along a caravan route linking Northern India to Afghanistan and Central Asia which took its full importance only after the Kandahar-based Durrani clan had established its hegemony over most of the region by the mid-eighteenth century under its first ruler Ahmad Shah (Gommans 1995).

In an earlier period, it was another town, Multan, situated in the Punjab not very far from the Sind border, which had been the main Indian depot of the caravan trade between Northern India and Central Asia through Afghanistan, a trade which had its origins in the establishment of commercial links accompanying the Ghaznavid and Ghurid penetration of Northern India from the eleventh century onwards and had flourished anew from the sixteenth century onwards with the Mughal conquest of Northern India.[3] The shift from Multan to Shikarpur, which occurred gradually in the second half of the eighteenth century, and which remains clouded in some amount of mystery, was largely due to political factors: the decline of Multan following a short-lived Maratha invasion of the town and the emergence of Kandahar as the true seat of power in the so-called Durrani 'Empire', which gave sudden importance to Shikarpur as the best-placed mart on the route between Kandahar and Northern India. The situational 'advantage' of the town was thus mostly a function of political developments, and had not the Kandahar-based Durranis risen to prominence in Afghanistan, the town would have remained an insignificant mart of only local importance. But within a few decades it became the financial capital of a vast, although loosely held, empire, its bankers, mostly originating from Multan, holding the strings of the Durrani purse, and extending their financial operations across the whole of Central Asia (Gankovsky 1981). The story of the Hyderabad merchants displays even more randomness: based in a town of Lower Sind situated at some distance from the sea, they were bankers to the Baluchi tribal rulers of Sind, who had made the town their capital in the mid-eighteenth century, and financed craft production for the use of the court and the army. Following the British annexation of Sind in 1843, they lost their two major businesses (as well as their share of the Malwa opium trade), while Hyderabad was quickly overtaken by Karachi as a commercial and financial centre. However, within thirty years, using a newly established connection with Bombay (Sind was made part of the Bombay Presidency in 1847), they had managed to establish themselves as silk and curio traders in a vast area stretching from Egypt to the Straits of Malacca, the beginning of a process of worldwide expansion which led them at a later stage to literally reach the four corners of the earth.

If the emergence of these two networks was largely contingent, owing much to sudden geopolitical shifts, of which merchants were at first the victims but which they managed to transform at a later stage into opportunities, their subsequent history confirms the importance of political factors and their primacy over any 'predispositions'. For the merchants of these two towns in their original setting both combined trade with finance, in the manner of traditional Indian *banias*, who are rarely specialised in one field, but tend to spread their investments between different branches. Differences in political contexts, however, led one group, the Shikarpuris, to increasingly specialise in rural money lending, where they could carve for themselves a safe niche in Central Asia, even after the region had largely fallen under Russian domination and the caravan trade between Northern India and Central Asia, their traditional mainstay, had been reduced to insignificance, and thus partly eschew trade, while on the contrary the other group, the Hyderabadis or Sindworkies, increasingly specialised in certain kinds of trading operations and became much less involved in finance, even if it was largely their financial skills that kept them in good stead in their new career as international traders.

If one looks for comparative advantage to explain the (relative) success of these particular groups in the international market place, it is not in the direction of ethnicity that one will find satisfactory answers. For, in a segmented society like that of Sind (and of India), all corporate groups, whether they be castes, religious sects or simply clusters of town dwellers, were closely knit and practised certain forms of solidarity. None was ostensibly better than any other at pooling resources and at ensuring transgenerational transmission of assets, which was facilitated by the *Mitaksara* system of family and inheritance law, prevalent in most of British India (except in Bengal).

The significant differences have to be found elsewhere, and one of my hunches is that an inquiry into knowledge practices could be most enlightening. I must admit that I was not able to carry it very far, but it seems to me that cognitive processes in merchant communities deserve to attract more attention from scholars than they have till now. The importance of information to the running of commercial businesses is well known, but there is not much appreciation of the role of knowledge in fostering success in trading ventures, apart from the specific case of accounting, which is a fairly well-researched area. Trading skills, as distinct from accounting skills, embody certain forms of knowledge:

they are not, contrary to what is often assumed, a static body of recipes which are simply transmitted from one generation to another without any incremental aspect.

Merchant knowledge is not purely routine, but can often be innovative to a certain extent, at least inasmuch as it can adapt itself to changes in political and market conditions. To give an example: the acquisition of linguistic skills was an important requisite for success in the international market place, prior to the emergence of English as the global lingua franca of business, which is a relatively recent phenomenon. It can be argued that all merchant communities did not show themselves equally adept at it. One group which performed particularly well in this respect was that of the Hyderabad Sindworkies, originally a monolingual Sindhi-speaking community which, after it embarked upon its international trade ventures, quickly transformed itself into a polyglot group, acquiring basic proficiency not only in English but in various other languages, depending on the area of their operations. A telling example is provided by a Sindhi merchant testifying before an Australian parliamentary commission that, during a few years passed in Massawah, in present-day Eritrea, he had acquired a good knowledge of the three main languages of the place, Arabic, Amharic and Italian (Markovits 2000: 138). What is interesting in this case is that, contrary to Jewish and Armenian merchants, who already received a multilingual education from childhood, these Sindhi merchants had to start from scratch and become multilingual in a very short time.

At a deeper level, one is struck by the capacity of such merchant groups to process information into a body of knowledge, of a largely pragmatic kind, concerning markets, which gave them often an advantage over competitors and was actively sought out by others. Thus, in Southeast Asia, it was remarked that Japanese companies valued highly the knowledge about markets accumulated by their Sindhi agents (Brown 1994), and that it was their possession of such knowledge which made the Sindhi (Hyderabadi) merchants indispensable intermediaries for some Japanese firms.

Another aspect which deserves more attention than it has received in the literature is the question of opportunistic behaviour. Its occurrence, when it appears frequent, puts in question the most widely held assumptions about the role of ethnicity and kinship in fostering trust in business networks operating across vast distances. In my material, I found many instances of such behaviour, ranging from petty theft to large-scale defrauding of partners. I also observed that often the arbitration mechanisms internal to the communities did not function properly, which led to lengthy and costly court cases. In making my way through the latter, I became aware of the fact that written contracts appeared to be the rule, at least among Hyderabadis, from the early 1900s onwards, which belies another widely held view that in such 'ethnic' networks there is a preference for oral over written contracts. All this led me to a reflection on the nature of trust within diasporic merchant communities. I concluded that there was a constant tension between two concepts of trust, one which laid heavy stress on affective links, in particular the obligations created by the ties of brotherhood (often fictitious, but this was a very powerful fiction), and one which I call 'empirical rational', which laid emphasis on reputation, a reputation which was not based simply on bazaar gossip, but could draw on an accumulated record of transactions, which was often accessible in a written form in a kind of archive of the network.

Basically, I was led to view merchant networks not as given entities based on a shared ethnicity, or even a shared town identity, but as historical constructs being constantly re-created in the flow of transactions which connected the various actors, whether they be purely commercial or monetary transactions, or legal and affective ones, transactions over which a constantly evolving political and economic environment exercised of course decisive influence. Differential ability by merchant groups to construct over time a specific body of knowledge appeared to be one decisive discriminating factor in accounting for success or failure in the international market place. To understand the varied flow of transactions which animated such networks, one has to take a close look at the pattern of circulation which regulated them. That is why I was led to stress circulation rather than migration as a central theme for the study of diasporic merchant networks. In the following section, I examine this point in some detail.

The pattern of circulation in diasporic merchant networks

To analyse the functioning of the two networks under study, I put forward a model based on the circulation between on the one hand what I called the network centre and on the other hand the actual places of business, which in the two cases under review were very clearly separated. This separation could be explained in many ways, but the most decisive factor was the early concentration of capital in the hands of a few families, added, in the case of Shikarpur, to the presence of a large displaced mercantile work force devoid of capital. Although, in the dispersion, some acquired resources and transformed themselves into capitalists, endowment of capital resources remained unequal throughout the history of the two networks. Residing in the network centre and not having to adopt a peripatetic way of life was one sign of superior social status, which probably reflected in part a traditional religious stricture on travel across the seas or the high passes leading to Central Asia.

The network centres, the two medium-sized Sind towns of Shikarpur and Hyderabad (with a population in the range of 50,000–100,000), had thus residential and command functions, but very little of the actual physical activity of production or distribution took place there. They were primarily the places of residence of the principals of the firms, mostly small-scale ones, which dominated the two networks. These principals had agents in the various places of business, who did the actual day-to-day trading or financing, using in part capital provided by their principals, and in part capital borrowed on the spot either from other Sindhis, or from financial institutions, mostly banks. Insofar as the difference between organising merchants and their agents was clearly present, these networks had strong similarities to the Armenian network based in New Julfa which operated across an enormous area (Aslanian 2006). However, they lacked the political organisation and religious homogeneity of the Armenian merchant diaspora. Their actual functioning was characterised by the combination of a high degree of centralisation with a certain amount of initiative left to local agents.

The kind of financial operations which took place in the network centres were the more complex ones: the keeping of yearly or half-yearly accounts of the firms, through the centralisation of the accounts sent from the various branches, the taking of deposits, the business of remittances and, above all, operations of compensation done in informal clearing houses where *hundis* (bills of exchange) drawn on various places were dealt with. Increasingly, some of these complex operations were shifted to Bombay, which was better placed in terms of connections to the world markets.

While goods circulated in the networks, particularly in the Hyderabadi network (which traded mostly in silk and curios), this circulation took place mostly between the various sites at the periphery (i.e. from Kobe or Yokohama in Japan, where silk goods were bought, to various Mediterranean ports where they were sold mostly to ship passengers), and the network centres were not directly involved in it. Circulation within the network between the centre and the periphery was therefore primarily a circulation of credit, in the form of paper, mostly *hundis* and other kinds of bills, although some specie also came from the branches to the headquarters of the firms (for instance until the 1890s, Shikarpuris in Russian Central Asia remitted part of their profits to their home town in the form of golden *tillas*, a Bukharan currency which was valued for its high gold content). Second to the circulation of credit came that of information. Through the means of letters and, increasingly, telegrams, there came from the places of business to the network centres, a constant flow of information on prices and commodities, which allowed the principals to decide on their policies with some measure of confidence (although delays in corresponding with Central Asia remained a problem for Shikarpuri financiers till the end of their operations in the region around 1917, in the wake of the Russian Revolution). From the network centres there originated a reverse flow of information which was both financial and 'social' as the faraway operators remained deeply enmeshed, in their farthest exile, with the current developments in their own small burgher societies.

These networks were also animated by a constant circulation of men (while circulation of women practically did not occur, as brides and spouses remained located in the network centres, even during the long periods of expatriation of their male consorts). As I was able to document, thanks to detailed archival sources, the two towns, in spite of their limited population, were the exclusive recruiting ground for the circulating personnel, agents and salaried employees, who were sent from there to the various places of business. The ability of the principals to continue over a long period (of one to two centuries) to recruit their personnel exclusively from their home towns struck me as one of the most enduring and original traits of these two networks, one which to a certain extent defied economic logic and reflected the capacity of localised sociological realities to shape the modus operandi of men working across distances of thousands of miles.

In my search for a rationale to the obstinacy of the principals in recruiting exclusively from their home towns, while it would have made more sense economically to recruit at least part of their personnel either elsewhere in India (in Bombay for instance, where there was a large pool of skilled commercial manpower) or locally in the places of business, I had my closest encounter with the twin ghosts of ethnicity and kinship. For a simple explanation to the preference shown for townsmen would have been provided by emphasising a common ethnicity and the power of kinship and affinity, with all its potential for trust-building. But I was determined to resist the attraction of simple commonsensical explanations, and besides two facts appeared to throw some doubt on their validity: the first one was the complexity of ethnicity (including caste and religious affiliation) in the specific context of the two towns of Sind under study, and the second one was the frequency of opportunistic behaviour, as already mentioned. While sharing a common ethnicity, generally manifested through webs of kinship and marriage, can contribute to the building of trust, there is also a reverse side to the coin. Actually, although this might sound paradoxical, a relative or an affine is much better placed to swindle you than a perfect stranger, because he knows much more about you, and may also have a much stronger incentive to do so, for various possible reasons (family quarrels, jealousy, etc.). So I did not completely accept the argument about 'trust', although it was often advanced by the merchants themselves when, faced with immigration restrictions in various countries, they had to justify to the authorities their preference for men recruited in their own towns. I tended therefore to go for a more convoluted sociological explanation, focusing on the role of patrons exercised by the principals through their awarding of jobs, a way of maintaining and enhancing status in a mercantile society where social hierarchies were relatively discreet (or at least appear so to the historian who has no insider's knowledge of these vanished communities).

The theme of circulation seems to me to offer a good vantage point from which to survey the rise of diasporic merchant networks in Asia, for it takes in the same breath the strong local roots of such networks and their ability to encompass very extended spaces. It is basically through circulatory mechanisms that, within these networks, the local and the global were articulated in a fashion which tends to relativise the dominant contemporary discourse on globalisation and its radically new character.

The two networks I studied represented instances of a much earlier phase of 'globalisation', that Chris Bayly, in a recent article, has proposed to call 'archaic globalisation' (Bayly 2002), a term which I do not find satisfactory, but which I shall adopt for lack of a better alternative. Actually, what made this early globalisation possible was the skill of the Indian merchants from Sind at settling payments across vast distances through fiduciary instruments, such as *hundis* which, although rustic – the well-known Victorian explorer Sir Richard Burton, who spent some time in Sind, called the *hundi* the 'rude instrument with which the Shikarpuri Rothschild works' (Burton 1877: II 252–3) – proved well suited to the purpose of facilitating long-distance transactions without recourse to the long delays and dangers involved in the transport of specie across the high passes separating India from Central Asia. At a later stage, modern technology, in the form of the steamship and the telegraph, both widely used by the Hyderabadi merchants, undoubtedly propelled a further stage in the process, but did not really revolutionise the functioning of these networks.

Prior to the partition of India, the two networks I studied did not clearly belong to the category of diasporas, since, apart from the fact that the principals remained resident in the network centres and travelled only for inspection tours of their branches, most of those who worked in dispersed locations themselves came back to the network centre after a stint abroad of two or three years, a process which could be often repeated during a lifetime. Only a minority of the network participants settled abroad durably, generally former agents or employees who separated from their principals at some point in time and set up business on their own. Some even married local women and converted to another religion.

It is therefore doubtful if the kind of circulation which took place in these networks can be seen as an early form of 'transnationalism'. Since the pre-1947 non-European world was not yet mostly divided between nation-states, but still largely under the control of various colonial empires, including in indirect ways (for instance through settlements such as those which existed in a certain number of Chinese port-cities), the notion of transnationalism would have to be seriously reworked to be retrospectively applicable to a different pattern of world relations. What is, however, striking in the two networks I have studied is that their operations were not limited to territories in the British Empire, but extended to regions under other imperial sovereignties, whether French (Indochina, Algeria, Morocco), Dutch (the East Indies), Spanish (Canary Islands and Spanish Morocco), Portuguese (Portuguese East Africa), American (the Philippines) or Russian (Central Asia). Yet is should be noted that, with the exception of France before 1904 and Russia before 1907, the other imperial powers involved were British allies, and that the protection of the British Crown generally ensured the Indian merchants (who were, since 1858, Crown subjects) fair treatment, at least prior to the First World War, which generalised the use of the passport and resulted in a less favourable travel regime for merchants. All in all, it would seem to me that it is difficult to think of the pre-1947 world of the Sindhi merchants in terms of a transnational space. In historical terms, transnationalism was largely the product of the universal triumph of nationalism, which occurred only through post-Second World War decolonisation. Prior to that moment, transnationalism has to be seen largely as a dimension of empire, as argued in a recent book (Grant *et al.* 2007).

After 1947, as Sind became part of Pakistan and its Hindu population left it en masse, relocating in India, and more particularly in Bombay, there occurred a significant shift. Bombay, in spite of being the residence of many Sindhi merchants, did not play the role of the network centre in the manner of pre-1947 Hyderabad and Shikarpur. The networks became de-centred or rather polycentred. While the physical operations of production and distribution continued to take place in many locations dispersed across the world, the complex financial operations which had been taking place exclusively in the network centres became spatially spread out. Some took place in Bombay, but most were relocated either to one of the great Asian emporia where many Sindhi firms established their new headquarters (mostly Singapore and Hong Kong), or to the great financial centres of the planet (London, New York), not to mention the fiscal havens where the ultimate controlling firms were often located (Cayman Islands, Bermuda).

Thus South Asian networks blossomed into worldwide diasporas. Most Sindhis settled abroad durably, even if they often tended to shift location regularly, in relation to changing opportunities in the world market place and changing political conditions. They became a kind of classical diaspora, romanticising their lost homeland. But such an evolution was not foreordained; it was the direct result of massive political upheaval, a reminder that contingency, in the form of unpredictable political developments, can play a larger role in shaping the course of the history of merchant networks than the laws of the international market place.

The case study offered here does not easily fit within a general model of the Asian diaspora. It cannot even be held up as a paradigm of the South Asian merchant diaspora. I see it mainly as a plea for combining the dominant 'culturalist' approach to diasporic phenomena with continued attention to economic and political factors. A more balanced view of Asian diasporas could be reached, which would avoid the exaggerated glorification and subsequent debunking of a so-called model of 'Asian' capitalism which was seen in the 1990s. While modern Asian diasporic trading networks display some similarities with European and Middle Eastern networks of an earlier period, their specificities can be best understood through a careful study of their diverse historical trajectories rather than through the device of constructing a model of 'Asian' capitalism based on an essentialisation of randomly selected 'ethnic' and 'cultural' traits of Asian entrepreneurs.

Notes

1 For a recent treatment of that theme, see Sugiyama and Grove (2001).
2 Christine Dobbin (1996) called 'conjoint communities' the Asian entrepreneurial minorities, such as the Peranakan Chinese or the Parsis, which developed special links to the Europeans, groups which had been called 'compradores' in an earlier, Marxist-inspired, literature.
3 For an overall view of commercial exchange between India and Central Asia, see Levi (2002).

References

Aslanian, S. (2006) 'From the Indian Ocean to the Mediterranean: Circulation and the Global Trade Networks of Armenian Merchants from New Julfa, Isfahan, 1606–1747', PhD thesis, New York, Columbia University.

Bayly, C.A. (2002) ' "Archaic" and "Modern" Globalization in the Eurasian and African Arena, *c.*1750–1850', in A.G. Hopkins (ed.) *Globalization in World History*, London: Pimlico, pp. 47–73.

Bonacich, E. (1973) 'A Theory of Middleman Minorities', *American Sociological Review*, 38(4): 583–94.

Brown, R. (1994) *Capital and Entrepreneurship in Southeast Asia*, London: Routledge.

Burton, R. (1877) *Sind Revisited*, 2 vols, London: Richard Bentley and Sons.

Chaudhuri, K.N. (1985) *Trade and Civilisation in the Indian Ocean: An Economic History from the Rise of Islam to 1750*, Cambridge: Cambridge University Press.

Cohen, A. (1971) 'Cultural Strategies in the Organization of Trading Diasporas', in C. Meillassoux (ed.) *The Development of Indigenous Trade and Markets in West Africa*, London: Routledge, pp. 266–78.

Curtin, P.D. (1984) *Cross-Cultural Trade in World History*, Cambridge: Cambridge University Press.

Dale, S.F. (1994) *Indian Merchants and Eurasian Trade 1600–1750*, Cambridge: Cambridge University Press.

Dobbin, C. (1996) *Asian Entrepreneurial Minorities: Conjoint Communities in the Making of the World-Economy, 1570–1940*, London: Curzon Press.

Frank, A. Gunder (1998) *ReOrient: the Global Economy in the Asian Age*, Berkeley, Los Angeles: University of California Press.

Gankovsky, Y. (1981) 'The Durrani Empire', in USSR Academy of Sciences, *Afghanistan Past and Present*, Moscow: Progress Publishers, pp. 76–98.

Goitein, S.D. (1967–93) *A Mediterranean Society: The Jewish Communities of the Arab World as Portrayed in the Documents of the Cairo Geniza*, 6 vols, Berkeley, Los Angeles: University of California Press.

Gommans, J.J.L. (1995) *The Rise of the Indo-Afghan Empire, c.1710–1780*, Leiden, New York, Cologne: E.J. Brill.

Goody, J. (1996) *The East in the West*, Cambridge: Cambridge University Press.

Greif, Avner (1992) 'Contract Enforceability and Economic Institutions in Early Trade: the Maghribi Traders' Coalition', *American Economic Review*, 83(3): 525–48.

Hamashita, T. (1988) 'The Tribute Trade System and Modern Asia', *The Toyo Bunko*, 46(1): 7–24.

Grant, K., P. Levine and F. Trentmann (eds) (2007) *Beyond Sovereignty: Britain, Empire and Transnationalism, c.1880–1950*, Basingstoke, New York: Palgrave.

Levi, Scott C. (2002) *The Indian Diaspora in Central Asia and its Trade 1550–1900*, Leiden; Boston; Cologne: E.J. Brill.

Markovits, C. (2000) *The Global World of Indian Merchants 1750–1947: Traders of Sind from Bukhara to Panama*, Cambridge: Cambridge University Press.

Rudner, D.W. (1994) *Caste and Capitalism in Colonial India: the Nattukottai Chettiars*, Berkeley, Los Angeles: University of California Press.

Sugiyama, S. and L. Grove (eds) (2001) *Commercial Networks in Modern Asia*, Richmond: Curzon Press.

2 The social world of Gujarati merchants and their Indian Ocean networks in the seventeenth century[1]

Murari Kumar Jha

Introduction

This chapter will approach the social history of pre-modern Gujarat by engaging with themes related to merchants and their social world: their communities and their religious practices; the interactions between Indians and Europeans (Valle 1892: 73–4); the cross-cultural exchanges that existed amongst the various communities; and their 'transnational' connections with maritime societies of the Indian Ocean littoral.

By the seventeenth century, the transoceanic movement of people, goods, and ideas made Gujarati port society truly cosmopolitan. Gujarati merchants[2] had developed a network of agents stationed at the great port cities across the Indian Ocean. These networks extended to the Philippines in the east, East Africa in the west, and via maritime and the inland caravan route to Russia in the north.[3] During the seventeenth century Gujarati cotton textiles constituted an important commodity of trade and Gujarati merchants traded in this commodity by establishing commercial networks in the Indian Ocean. Their easy reach to the commodity produced at home put them on an advantageous footing and this enabled them to access distant markets overseas through their transoceanic networks, which led to diasporic movements of Gujarati merchants in the Indian Ocean.

The social world of Gujarati merchants

The social world of merchants in seventeenth-century Gujarat was multi-faceted comprising various communities some of whom had a tradition of involvement in trade and commerce that spanned several generations. Among the Hindus, Banias were prominent, taking to trade and commerce as their calling (Carre 1990: 138).[4] They functioned as brokers and *sarrafs*, issuing promissory notes or bills of exchange, popularly known as *hundis*, to transfer funds from one place to another throughout the Indian Ocean networks of trade (Haynes 1987: 342). Jain merchants also functioned in similar capacities in the commercial world of Gujarat (Khan 1928: 116–17).[5]

Among the Muslims, the Khojas and Bohras played an important role in commercial circles, and some were great ship-owning merchants.[6] Alongside these merchants were representatives from the major trading communities of western Asia who served as an important link between the port cities of western India and west Asia. The Arabs, Turks (especially in Diu), Persians and Egyptians were the other major constituents of the Muslim mercantile society operating from Gujarat, and many had their own houses and commercial establishments (Pearson 1976: 25). Alongside these, there were Parsi and Armenian traders (Torri 1990). Many of these 'foreign' settlers in Gujarat had gradually become part of Gujarati mercantile society, having little or no connection with their places of origin.

Pre-modern Gujarati merchants lived within several distinct, yet interlinked, worlds. The extended joint family was the primary unit, followed by communities linked by caste and faith. The joint family as well as the community were both private and semi-public domains, marked off from outside intrusion, but not free from internal dissent and rivalry (Varadarajan 1976: 227).[7] Related to these was the dynamic world of the market. It was in this world that merchants operated as men of commerce and trade as they came into contact with the outside world.

In cities like Cambay and Surat rivalries were rife. Merchant magnates such as Virji Vora in the seventeenth century and later Ahmed Challaby amongst others competed for commercial gain (Misra 1984: 45–6). Amidst the competition, there also existed co-operation that extended beyond the boundaries of caste and faith. While Hindus and the Jains specialised as *sarrafs*, in brokerage and trade in merchandise such as textiles, spices and so forth, Muslims dealt predominantly in the shipping trade. For successful commercial voyages overseas, there existed a clear interdependence of these groups with Muslim merchants often employing Hindu brokers who generally organised their trade. For the procurement of trading goods in Gujarat, Muslim merchants generally hired the services of Bania and Jain brokers. Accounting and book-keeping of the Muslim merchants were also usually taken care of by the Bania merchants.

In addition there existed institutions such as the *Nagarseth* and *Mahajan* that regulated trade and negotiated with political authorities when required (Mehta 1991: 22). These institutions intervened in the social matters of the community as well. For the Bohras and the Khojas this role was played by the head of their religious community, or the *da'i*. In matters related to community, an absolute autonomy prevailed, and issues were handled by the caste *panchayats* or by the head of the community (Misra 1984: 45).

European sources make clear that Banias were involved in a wide range of mercantile activities, ranging from brokerage – particularly for European and other overseas merchants – to owning shops and dealing in retail trade. François Pyrard de Laval, who visited the East Indies in the early seventeenth century, in his description of the merchants of Cambay noted:

> The principal nation and race there are the *Banianes,* who are in such numbers that one speaks only of the Banians of Cambaye: they are to be found in every port and market in India, along with the Guzerates, who are

Mahometans of Surat and other [neighbouring] lands. The Banians, on the other hand, observe the same manner of life as the Bramenis, albeit they wear not the cord.... No people in the world know so much about pearls and precious stones; and even at Goa the goldsmiths, lapidaries, and other workmen occupied with the finer crafts are all Banians and Bramenis of Cambaye, and have their own streets and shops.

(Pyrard 1888: 249–50)

François Pyrard de Laval's descriptions, like most other contemporaneous European sources and travel accounts, tended to refer to Banias as synonymous with all Hindu and Jain merchants. This was primarily because, in spite of religious differences, there existed numerous similarities between these groups. They belonged to the third rank in the four-fold division of Hindu society, the *vaisya* varna, which was divided into 41 strictly endogamous *jatis* or castes, some sections of which included both Hindus and Jains and were called *meshris* among the Hindus and *shravaks* among the Jains (Alpers 1976: 26; Pearson 1976: 26).

The difficulty of distinguishing Hindus from Jains in most European sources was also because both these communities placed considerable emphasis on living an austere life and tended to practise strict vegetarianism. This was an object of fascination for Western travellers given that meat was an important component of their own diet. Yet descriptions at this time were often unable to account for differences in the extent of reverence given to animal life amongst Banias. Thus accounts of the Banias provided by the European travellers generally matched the lifestyle followed by the Jains. They were deemed to be extremely superstitious, as they refrained from travelling in their carts in the rainy season because of the fear of killing small insects which might come under the wheels or under the feet of the animals (Srivastava 2001: 591–2). Barbosa wrote, 'When these *Baneanes* meet with a swarm of ants on the road they shrink back and seek for some way to pass without crushing them' (Barbosa 1918: 112).

Many European writers attributed the success of the Banias in business and commerce to the training that they received in the family. Describing the role of the family in the apprenticeship of a young merchant, J.B. Tavernier wrote:

They [Gujarati Merchants] accustom their children at an early age to shun slothfulness, and instead of letting them go into the streets to lose their time at play, as we generally allow ours, teach them arithmetic, which they learn perfectly, using for it neither pen nor counters, but the memory alone, so that in a moment they will do a sum, however difficult it may be. They are always with their fathers, who instruct them in trade, and do nothing without explaining it to them at the same time.

(Tavernier 1977: 144)

Such specialisation, over successive generations within a family of a particular occupation, contributed to the enhancement of their skills in business and commerce. Ovington noted that the practice of endogamy ensured that specialised skills and trade 'secrets' were maintained within the caste which he labelled as 'Sect' (Ovington 1929: 165).

Further, François Pyrard records that Banias were always prepared to learn workmanship from the Portuguese, also in turn imparting skills to the Portuguese:

> I have never seen men of wit so fine and polished as are these Indians: they have nothing barbarous or savage about them, as we are apt to suppose. They are unwilling indeed to adopt the manners and customs of the Portuguese; yet do they readily learn their manufactures and workmanship, being all very curious and desirous of learning. In fact the Portuguese take and learn more from them than they from the Portuguese...
>
> (Pyrard 1888: 248–9)

Not all descriptions of the Banias, were as positive as those voiced by Pyrard. Careri believed that the Banias were 'much greater Cheats than the *Armenians* and *Jews*' (Thevenot 1949: 256). The Dutch traveller John Huygen van Linschoten, who visited Gujarat towards the end of the sixteenth century, while acclaiming the business skills of the Bania, also held similar views on their deceitful nature. He wrote:

> Gusarates and Banianes are of the country of Cambaia: ... They are most subtill and expert in casting of accounts, and writing, so that they do not only surpasse and goe beyond all Jewes [*original Dutch*; all other Indians] and other nations thereabouts, but also the Portingales: and in this respect they have no [*original Dutch*; much advantage], for [that] they are very perfect in the trade of merchandise, and very ready to deceive men.
>
> (Linschoten 1885: 60 and 252–3)

The training and specialisation in the traditional calling of the merchant family was not a new development in the seventeenth century. The merchants of Gujarat, both Hindu and Muslim, had been specialising in the organisation of overseas trade for many centuries. Even at the time of Tome Pires' travel to the East Indies in the early sixteenth century, Gujarati merchants had a formidable reputation for their commercial acumen. Pires noted:

> These [people] are [like] Italians in their knowledge of and dealings in merchandise ... they are men who understand merchandise; they are so properly steeped in the sound and harmony of it, that the Gujaratees say that any offence connected with merchandise is pardonable. There are Gujaratees settled everywhere. They work some for some and others for others. They are diligent, quick men in trade. They do their accounts with fingers like ours and with our very writings.
>
> (Pires 1944: 41)

While it is true that the Bania merchants organised and operated their trading activities with the help of their caste fellows or kinsmen, at the same time, they also interacted with the Arab and other Muslim merchants for sale and purchase of commodities.[8] It has been remarked by Cabral that 'These [Arab merchants] spoke their languages, knew their customs and commodities, and through centuries of friendly intercourse had built up commercial relations which in general, were satisfactory' (Cabral 1937: xxvi). During his travels to India in the beginning of the sixteenth century, Cabral found that the Gujarati merchants had their headquarters at Cambay and were active in various networks of trade. Hindu and Muslim merchants from Gujarat had established themselves as important figures in both the Western and Eastern ports in the Indian Ocean at a time when trade with Malacca was flourishing (Cabral 1937: 81). Their trade in this vast region was sustained with the help of agents or 'factors' with whose cooperation they had established factories in different parts of coastal Asia.

The Dutch merchant Francisco Pelsaert noted that the Hindu brokers generally organised Muslim merchants' trade and did brokering for them. He made the observation, however, that Hindu brokers did not deal in the sale and purchase of any living being:

> all the business of the lords' palaces and of the Moslem merchants is done by Hindus – book-keeping, buying, and selling. They are particularly clever brokers, and are consequently generally employed as such throughout all these countries, except for the sale of horses, oxen, camels, elephants, or any living creatures, which they will not handle as the Moslems do.
>
> (Pelsaert 1925: 78)

Some European writers also provide evidence on the relationship between Bania traders and Mughal authorities at the time. The Italian traveller Pietro Della Valle observed that 'the King doeth not persecute his subjects with false accusations, nor deprive them of anything when he sees them live splendidly and with the appearance of riches...' (Valle 1892: 42). Ovington, however, provided views to the contrary, pointing out that the Banias tended to hide their property from the gaze of Mughal officials, transacting money in the darkness of night, or in the obscurity of the morning, because they feared they would be robbed by them (Ovington 1929: 187). While one cannot discount that some Mughal officials might have engaged in such activities, this should not be mistaken as a systematic effort to target at Gujarati Hindu merchants. After all, Mughal officials had various other means of ascertaining the economic standing of a merchant. The sale and purchase of merchandise, for example, could not have been done secretly, and the Mughal customs officials duly collected customs duty on the value of merchandise carried by a merchant (Singh 1970–1: 84–5). It is nevertheless true that the Bania merchants were generally not ostentatious, living frugally in their day to day life even if they had amassed substantial wealth, with the exception of special occasions such as marriages, which were celebrated in a stately manner (Valle 1892: 30–2).[9]

The social world of the Muslim merchants was complex. The heterogeneity of the Muslim merchant community was made up by the trade settlers originating from various countries, as well as by those who were itinerant traders, coming from places like Egypt, Syria, Persia and Afghanistan (Pearson 1976: 25). Among Muslim merchants, the foreign settlers tended to outperform the local Muslim communities in commercial matters with the possible exception of Bohras and Khojas who excelled in trade and commerce. There existed a number of minority communities within the Muslim community, and at times there was discord – and sometimes even open hostility against them from the dominant Sunni Muslims (Misra 1985: 37–8).

John Fryer made a remark that Muslim merchants had a general apathy towards educating their children and a lack of training in accounting and business transactions. He believed that this explained why most Muslim merchants hired Banias for the purposes of accounting and transactions. Fryer noted:

> The *Moors*, who are by Nature slothful, will not take pains being proud, scorn to be taught and jealous of the Baseness of Mankind, dare not trust their Children under tuition, for fear of Sodomy, whereby few of their Great Men or Merchants can read, but keep a Scrivan of the *Gentues*; on which account it is the *Banyans* make all Bargains, and transact all Money-business...
>
> (Fryer 1985: 112)

The Muslims imparted education to their children through *madrassas*, and it is possible that accounting and book-keeping were not included within the curriculum at these religious seminaries.

The Muslim population of Gujarat mainly constituted the foreign immigrant settlers and local converts. The influx of the Muslim adventurers gained momentum from the thirteenth century when Sultanate rule was established in Gujarat. Muslims came in various capacities as military-men, traders and slaves through land and sea routes from West and Central Asia. However, the early pioneers of the Shia trading class, the Bohras, are believed to have come from Yemen as early as the eleventh century. It has been pointed out that in 1067 Abdullah, a missionary *da'i*, was sent from Yemen to Gujarat to gain converts (Majmudar 1965: 39). Through various miracles he was said to have won over many cultivators and artisans.

During the Gujarat Sultanate (circa fifteenth century) the minor Muslim communities or new converts were considered to be heretical and faced persecution by the rulers. Consequently, the Shias did not display their religious books and kept them hidden (Khan 1928: 110; Fryer 1985: 92). In view of the hostility from the Sunnis, the Ismaili Bohra community did not read *namaz* or prayer in the mosque till the end of Sultanate rule in Gujarat. Persecution of these groups declined with the advent of Mughal rule, and with the exception of the reign of Aurangzeb, the Shia Bohras[10] and other minor Muslim communities felt secure enough to openly practise their religious rites (Misra 1985: 25, 34–5). The

prevalence of the Hindu law of inheritance among the Islamic converts, especially Khojas and Bohras, prevented an extensive division of the property on
death and thus provided a pool of capital for further investment in trade and
commerce (Pearson 1976: 27).

In spite of occasional persecution and hostility, commercial towns were
inhabited by people of different religious persuasions. The demographic profile
of Surat comprised different sects of Muslims along with Hindus and Parsis as
has been noted by Thevenot:

> These three sorts of Inhabitants are either Moors, Heathens, or Parsis; by the
> word *Moors* are understood all the Mahometans, Moguls, Persians, Arabi-
> ans or Turks that are in *Indies*, though they be not uniform in their Religion,
> the one being Sunnis and the other Chiais [Shias].
>
> (Thevenot 1949: 22)

In spite of such plurality in the religious fabric of Gujarati society, people of
differing faiths not only co-existed but also interacted closely whenever trade
and commerce necessitated such intercourse (Ray 1983: 109).[11] Della Valle
remarked that in Surat, the Hindu population was far greater than the Muslim
and 'they live all mixt together, and peaceably, because the *Gran Moghel* ...
makes no difference in his Dominions between the one and the other...' (Valle
1892: 30). In the early seventeenth century, François Pyrard also noted that, in
Cambay, 'This country has its own king, who is a vassal of the Grand Mogor,
and a Mahometan by religion, though most of his people are Gentiles. But
every man lives according to his own religion, by reason whereof one sees here
men of all laws and sects' (Pyrard 1888: 249). The *Ardhakathanaka*, a
seventeenth-century autobiography of the Jain merchant Banarsi Das contra-
dicted Ovington's observation that 'Moors often treated gentiles with inhuman-
ity'. Banarsi Das' writing on the period from Humayun to Shahjahan does not
refer to any incident of religious persecution. Erring nobles were often recalled
by the Emperor and sometimes harshly punished (Saran 1973: 185; Das 1957:
31). The treatment of non-Muslims was particularly benevolent during the
reign of Akbar, when the Jain monk Shvetamberacharya Heeravijaya Suri was
felicitated. His successor Jahangir allowed Heeranand Mukim to take out
religious processions, and during his reign hundreds of Jain temples were
consecrated.

The Muslim Ismaili community, the Khojas, represented an unusual degree
of proximity with Hindu ritualistic beliefs and practices. Some *pirs* adopted
Hindu names to attract adherents and converts. Parallels were drawn between
personalities of Islamic and Hindu faiths and many religious and mythological
symbols were shared. Adam was introduced as Lord Vishnu and the Prophet of
Islam as Lord Mahesh. Islam Shah, who was an imam in the fifteenth century,
was represented as an incarnation of Lord Brahma or the creator of universe in
the Hindu canonical tradition. The Pandavas of the Mahabharat were equated
with the first five Imams. The most revered canonical work of the Khojas, the

Dasavatar, dealt with the incarnations of Vishnu. While nine chapters of this work deals with nine different incarnations of Lord Vishnu, the tenth deals with Ali as the tenth *avatara* (Lokhandwalla 1967: 158–9). The inspiration derived by the Khojas from Hindu canonical traditions presents an excellent testimony of Hindu–Muslim syncretistic tradition in Gujarat at the time.

Relations between religious communities in Gujarat, however, deteriorated during the time of Aurangzeb. When Aurangzeb was appointed governor of Gujarat on 27 April 1645, the Bohra and Khoja communities were persecuted precisely because they followed a set of ritual practices that deviated from the *sharia* or Islamic law. Their faith was proscribed in the name of correction of 'forbidden practices'. The most glaring instance is the death sentence given to the 32nd *da'i* Syedna Qutb Khan-u'd-din bin Da'ud Burhan-u'd-din bin Qutb-shahi. Although death sentences in the Mughal empire required confirmation from the Emperor, in this case Aurangzeb did not refer the matter to Shahjahan (Misra 1985: 34). The persecution of Bohras did not stop at the elimination of their *da'i*, and a number of regulations were framed concerning the social behaviour of the community. Sunni Imams were appointed at their mosques and those who did not attend such religious prayers were sternly punished. As the community was hapless to escape such regulations they began to practise two sets of religious ceremonies, one in public and another in private (Misra 1985: 34).

Commercial activities of Gujarati merchants

Gujarati merchants played a crucial role in trade both within the subcontinent and overseas. Goerges Roques informs that Muslim merchants primarily traded in manufactures. Ahmadabad merchants who manufactured silk cloth in great abundance exported these to Agra, Golconda, Bengal and other parts of India. In exchange they received 'turbans, sashes, and extremely fine and light cloth for *cabayes*, which they sell in retail to other merchants' (Ray 1983: 110). The cargo of returning ships also carried tutenag, a metal used for making household utensils, calin an alloy of lead and tin, sapanwood for dyeing, eaglewood and sandal for manufacturing perfumes and all sorts of drugs.

Banias were most forthcoming in the conduct of their trade and were quick to approach ships that arrived at the port. Manucci remarked about the Banias:

> Whenever a loaded vessel arrives, the Hindu traders go aboard, and ask if the captain wishes to sell the whole cargo of the ship. If so, they pay for it in money, or furnish goods for the return cargo, whichever is preferred. This is all done without delays, and merchants can thus acquire whatever merchandise they are in search of, and for which they have left home.
>
> (Manucci 1981: 60)

John Fryer remarked that Surat belonged to two sorts of vermin; the first was fleas and the second, Banias:

The other Vermin are the *Banyans* themselves, that hang like Horseleeches, till they have suck'd both Sanguinem & Succum (I mean Mony) from you: As soon as you have set your Foot on Shore, they crowd in their Service, interposing between you and all Civil Respect, as if you had no other Business but to be gull'd; so that unless you have some to make your way through them, they will interrupt your going, and never leave till they have drawn out something for their Advantage.

(Fryer 1985: 82)

These traders whom Fryer calls 'horseleech' and 'vermin' were either big merchants, or their agents, some of whom had the wherewithal to buy all of the cargoes on board a ship. With licences they had obtained from Mughal authorities to open up marts at the ports, these traders had considerable experience in dealing with foreign merchandise and were instrumental in the conduct of business at Gujarati ports. Perhaps Fryer was astonished to see the expertise of these merchants whom he considered 'worse brokers than Jews'. Of course most of these merchants were Banias who dealt in substantial volumes of trade but nevertheless looked quite modest in their appearance at the port. As Fryer observed:

These generally are the Poorer sort, and set on by the Richer to Trade with the Seamen for the meanest things they bring and notwithstanding they take them at their own rates, get well enough in exchange of Goods with them.... For they well understand the constant turning of cash amounts both to the Credit and Profit of him that is so occupied which these *Banyans* are sensible of, otherwise they would not be so industrious to enslave themselves.

(Fryer 1985: 82)

Brokers played a crucial role in the sale and purchase of sorts of goods in the markets of Gujarat. They acted as intermediaries between the primary producers and merchants who wanted to procure merchandise for the overseas as well as internal markets (Qaisar 1974–5: 223). Georges Roques speaks of the customary rule in India which made it imperative for all merchants, indigenous or Europeans to have a broker for the sale and purchase of commercial goods. There were public as well as private brokers in the market. The post of public broker was given by the governmental authority and could be inherited by the son from his father (Ray 1983: 96–8). In order to get services of a public broker one had to have a private broker. While private brokers took 2 per cent of the value of goods as his fee for the services in helping the European merchants procure cotton textiles, the service of the public broker was 'free' though he took 1 per cent as customary from the buyer and charged 2 per cent from the merchant who wanted to sell his goods. The agreements and contracts made before the public broker were legally binding.

Dispute resolution: oath-taking and ordeals

Disputes were not unknown when merchants dealt in commercial matters. These disputes could involve transactions of commercial goods, as well as payments of money and dealings in credit. Important figures in the merchant society, as well as the institution of *Mahajan*, played an important role in resolving differences between parties. In addition oath-taking and ordeals were also crucial in establishing the truth and dispensing justice. This was true as well for many other merchant societies in the pre-modern world. For example, oath-taking was a common way of resolving differences among the Jewish merchants, as has been demonstrated by Mose Gil by using *Geniza* documents of the eleventh century. Though the Jewish court played a role in the mediation of trade relations according to Jewish law, in exceptionally difficult cases, one or the other party was made to swear. Swearing was considered incontrovertible proof that the person swearing was telling the truth (Gil 2003: 314).

Swearing or oath-taking was equally effective in resolving disputes among the Bania and Muslim merchants of Gujarat. The person who was swearing could do so by taking a flower off an image of Lord Shiva or by placing his hand upon the foot of some deity. Both the parties would have to agree on the mode of oath to be taken. Pelsaert wrote about oath-taking at the shrine of Prince Khusrau:

> he was accepted as a true *pir*, or saint; and they carried matter so far that they were foolish enough never to take an oath except by 'the head of the Sultan,' which was regarded as more binding than if they had sworn by God Himself.
>
> (Pelsaert 1925: 71)

There were different modes of swearing and some of them were considered to be more effective than the others. However, undergoing an ordeal or some painful and daunting observance was considered an even more effective way of establishing the truth. This could take several forms. They ranged from lifting a hot iron ring, taking a ring of three copper coins out of a vessel filled with heated oil, putting on a pair of iron fetters and then walking past the *pir*'s tomb, and creeping through a narrow hole made of stone. This stone was known as the window of truth and falsehood. In Cochin, the accused had to swim across the lagoon which was full of crocodiles and if the person came out safely he was declared innocent (Thevenot 1949: 326).

Among the Hindus, cows and Brahmans were considered very sacred, and it was a great sin to harm them in any way. Roques noted that 'They [Banias] never commit perjury if they take the oath on the back of this animal [cow], fearing that their soul would not be granted entry there' (Ray 1983: 85). The devisers of the oath of course kept this fact in mind. To quote from *Ras Mala*:

> If it be wished to impose on a Hindoo a very binding cold oath, he is compelled to place his hand on the neck of a Brahmin; or if one still more

stringent is called for, the swearer is required to touch with a knife the neck of a cow, the meaning being, that if he breaks the oath he incurs the sin of Brahmin, or cow-murder.

(Forbes 1973: 575)

For small matters, lesser oaths were usually sufficient to end a dispute. However, for disputes of a grave nature, the most powerful oath was administered. If the oath taker was a Brahmin he swore by his sacred thread, in the case of a Rajput, a sword was used, in the case of a Bania, he would swear by the *Suruswutee*, which referred to their account book (Forbes 1973: 575). Ovington noted that Banias 'will be apt rather to venture the loss of Cause, than the taking an Oath' because it brings them great social indignity. He further wrote that 'As we lay our Hands in swearing upon the Holy Bible, so he [Bania] puts his hand upon the venerable Cow...' (Ovington 1929: 138). When a Muslim took an oath it was in the name of Roza or Ramadan or in the name of the Muslim saint or *pir* who dwelt therein. Thus, oaths and ordeals played an important role in adjudicating disputes arising in the commercial world as well as in other social matters.

Gujarati merchants and their Indian Ocean networks

The commercial activities of Gujarati merchants depended much on overseas trade and 'international' contacts during the pre-modern period. The oceanic networks in the Indian Ocean were old and well established, and for centuries Gujarati merchants operated on these networks. The Gujarati proverbial saying from pre-modern times, *Je Java jaye pariya pariya khaye* ('those who visit Java for commercial purposes could be rich and prosperous for generation after generation'), remains prevalent even today in Gujarat.[12] The mobility across the ocean, criss-crossing political boundaries, was an important factor behind Gujarati merchants' trading and commercial eminence. The mobility of Gujarati merchants was not confined to the Indian Ocean, and in the seventeenth century some of were believed to have had travelled as far as to Europe as well (Curtin 1984: 203; Meilink-Roelofsz 1962: 248).[13]

Tome Pires wrote that, 'Cambay chiefly stretches out two arms, with her right arm she reaches out towards Aden and with the other towards Malacca, as the most important place to sail to...' (Pires 1967: 42). This depiction of the overseas trade from Cambay by Pires clearly demonstrates the convergence of two extremely important networks of the Indian Ocean in Gujarat. However, when the Portuguese took over Malacca in 1511, Gujarati merchants had to disperse to other ports in the Archipelago. Even as the Portuguese, and Tamil Hindu merchants collaborated after Malacca fell to the Portuguese, (Meilink-Roelofsz 1962: 169), this impacted negatively on Tamil Hindu merchants' relations with Muslim traders in the Malay world, thus hampering the former's trade to a certain extent (Sandhu 1969: 28). Consequently, even as Gujarati merchants withdrew from Malacca, they were able to shift their trade to other locations that concentrated around the Bay of Bengal, and other parts of Southeast Asia, especially Aceh (Pearson 2003: 164).

After the Vijayanagar empire fell in 1565 and Islam penetrated southern India, Muslim merchants from the south along with Gujarati Muslim merchants became more active in the Southeast Asian trade. The vigorous Muslim commercial activities in Southeast Asia led the process of the gradual spread of Islam in the region (Arasaratnam 1970: 6) in which Gujarati Muslims merchants played an important role (Meilink-Roelofsz 1962: 63). In addition sharing the same religion facilitated trading relationships and occasionally allowed for favourable commercial arrangements. For example, during the first decade of the seventeenth century the *Shahbandar* of Bantam, who was originally from Meliapur on the Coromandel Coast of India, had shown great favours to the Gujarati Muslim merchants trading in pepper in exchange for Gujarati textiles. The *Shahbandar* preferred Gujarati merchants over the Dutch traders even if the latter were willing to pay better prices (Meilink-Roelofsz 1962: 240).

However, in the course of the seventeenth century, the overseas trade of Gujarati merchants was marked by an important shift to the western Indian Ocean.[14] It is probable that the growing commercial and naval dominance of the Dutch in the Indonesian Archipelago discouraged Gujarati merchants to frequent the commercial cities of Southeast Asia. As a result of the Dutch 'success' in monopolising the spice trade, the structure of indigenous trade in West Asia underwent a change. Along with the Arabs, Indian merchants from Gujarat had been specialising in the spice trade for centuries. The Dutch policy of controlling spice-producing regions forced them out of Southeast Asia and they had to switch their trade to the Indian subcontinent and the western Indian Ocean ports in West Asia (Santen 1991: 87).

Some merchant magnates of Gujarat, such as Virji Vora who operated from Surat, were successful in creating a web of important trading marts along the Indian Ocean seaboard through the employment of agents.[15] Vora also had considerable control over the pepper trade with Malabar and his trading connections spanned Southeast Asia (Arasaratnam 1994: 194). Virji Vora had networks of agents and allies in Calicut, Agra, Burhanpur, the interior of Gujarat and the great port cities around the Indian Ocean littoral (Pearson 2003: 166; Foster 1909, rpt. 1913: 60, 86, 107–8). In the commercial operations of the Indian merchants, kinship networks were extremely important. They utilised these networks to manage trade in distant outposts with relatives being stationed in various terminal points of the trade (Dale 1994: 112).

There are a number of references of Gujarati merchants' trade with Persia during the pre-modern period. In Persia and other parts of West Asia, the Banias functioned as moneylenders and credit providers (Matthee 1999: 44). During the sixteenth century most of the revenue of the port of Hormuz came from the Gujarat trade. Hormuz played the role of an intersection point between the Indian Ocean and the Mediterranean which were linked by the overland routes that passed through Basra, Baghdad and Aleppo (Steensgaard 1975: 37). In 1515, the Portuguese built a fort at Hormuz in an effort to control Gujarat trade in the Persian Gulf. This was an important choke point which the Portuguese tried to control very rigorously so as to enforce their spice monopoly. Yet, in spite of Portuguese control and surveillance, trade between Gujarat and Persia continued. Money was transferred from Persian ports such as Jask to Surat through bills of exchange (Gopal 1975: 39). When Hormuz was wrested from the Portuguese by the English and Persian forces in 1622, trade between Gujarat and the region was further boosted. By the mid-seventeenth century Gujaratis were carrying an enormous quantity of cotton cloth to Persia and the Dutch East India Company found it hard to compete with the Gujarati merchants there.[16] At this time Bania merchants of Surat had also come to maintain factors at Gombroon in the Persian Gulf (Habib 1990: 391).

The pearl trade between Bahrain and India was also highly lucrative for Gujarati merchants. Pearls from Bahrain had a ready market in India and were considered to be of better quality than the South Indian ones, which were said to turn pale after coming into contact with oils and perfume rubbed on the body. During the seventeenth century trade between Bahrain and India was dominated by the Bania merchants and a general profit of 30 to 40 per cent was earned on this network. It has been pointed out that about three to four million *guilders* were invested in this sector by end of the seventeenth century (Barendse 2002: 45).

Another key trading port for Gujarati traders was Mocha, which was known as the 'treasure chest' of the Mughal empire. Mocha supplied large quantities of precious metals in its trade with Gujarat. By the early seventeenth century, Mocha marked a pivotal trading destination for the Gujarati merchants in the western Indian Ocean. Many Bania merchants from Gujarat resided there on a near permanent basis and it has been pointed out that at least half of Mocha's population at this time was made up of Hindus, Jews and Christians. Banias and Jews were the principal credit suppliers at Mocha (Brouwer 1997: 228–9), while Muslim merchants from Gujarat concentrated on the vast trading opportunities available at the port. The following instance illustrates the massive amounts carried by Gujarati merchants on this trading network. In 1619 when the Dutch Company captured the English vessel *Dragon* off Ticco and Priaman, a Gujarati merchant, Mu'allim Ghanni, lost his goods worth no less than '14,000 *reals* of eight'. When he petitioned the Dutch Director at Surat, Van den Broecke, for appropriate compensation, a substantial amount of money was paid by the Dutch in 1621 to Mu'allim Ghanni 'in order not to forfeit Ghanni's sympathy' (Brouwer 1997: 316).

English Factory records also refer to the residential establishments of the Gujaratis' at Shuhair on the Arabian coast. The English merchant William Minor noted that when they went ashore with Mr Gelly, they were well received by the Governor and there were '50 howseholdes of bannians in the towne: the cheefe his name is Ramgee' (Foster 1909, rpt. 1913: 70). Sometimes Brahmins also accompanied these merchant groups to assist them in the performance of their religious rituals. Ironically, superstitions against crossing the sea seemed to have receded to the background even for the Brahmins who saw the prospects of gaining a considerable income from serving their clients settled overseas.

Conclusion

Gujarat has maintained commercial contacts with the outside world from ancient times. The tradition of sea-faring and overseas contacts goes back many centuries and the Gujarati diaspora was a logical outcome of such a tradition. The Gujarati merchant diaspora can still be found in the littoral cities of West Asia and Africa on the one hand and in Southeast Asia on the other. During the pre-modern period Gujarati merchants were involved in and managed flourishing networks of trade which spanned from East Africa to Indonesia. This vast network enabled the formation of Gujarati diasporic settlements in many parts of the Indian Ocean. From these settlements the Gujarati merchants facilitated the flow of goods by providing a number of services ranging from advancing credit, exchanging currencies and furnishing *hundis* or bills of exchange.

Gujarat's Indian Ocean trade and commerce was closely tied to the social world of its merchants. Their social and cultural lives were organised around commercial practices. Gujarati merchant society consisted of various groups of people coming from different religious and ethnic backgrounds including Hindus, Jains, Muslims, Parsis, the Armenians and the Arabs. For Banias and Muslims there was a clear division of commercial activities based on religious persuasions and canonical injunctions. For example, Muslim merchants did not deal in printed textiles with motifs of living creatures on it, while these were procured by the Bania and Jain brokers. On the other hand Bania and Jain merchants would not deal in the trade of animals while Muslims did not have any problems with such trade. Similarly, Muslim merchants dominated the shipping trade and many were big ship-owners. The *nakhudas* and the *lascars* were also primarily from the Muslim community. On the other hand, some of the Banias and the Jains were prominent merchants and they organised an extensive trade from Gujarat to other parts of Asia. Thus, two branches of trade which formed the shipping and commerce were controlled by these two major communities of Gujarati merchants. For both these communities their relationship necessitated mutual understanding and interdependence in commercial matters so that they could play a complementary role in advancing their trading interests.

Notes

1 This research was carried out at the Centre for Historical Studies, Jawaharlal Nehru University, New Delhi. I am grateful to Dr Yogesh Sharma for supervising this work. I take this opportunity to express my indebtedness to Professor Ranabir Chakrabarti and Dr Pius Malekandathil for their insightful comments.
2 The term 'Gujarati merchants' includes different merchant communities based in Gujarat, native as well as settlers, who were involved in trade and commerce of the region.
3 See Pearson (2003: 166); Levi (2002: 227). From the early decades of the seventeenth century, the Indian merchants frequented Astrakhan, established settlements and came into regular contact with Russian merchants.
4 See Carre (1990: 138). When Carre landed at Gogha, he was received by a Bania, Bhanoba, who was a broker to the Portuguese and claimed to work for all the Franks. Carre also speaks of Banias living in Persia; see Carre (1990: 97).

5 See Khan (1928: 116–17). There were 84 divisions of Banias in which *Meshris* followed the Vaishanava sect of Hinduism and *Shravaks* were the lay followers of Jainism. Though they freely dined with each other, they married only within their own sect.

6 See Khan (1928: 110). This source claims that Bohras were former Brahmans and Banias who converted to Islam.

7 See Varadarajan (1976: 227). The English Company believed that Virji Vora held a monopoly over European commodities at Surat. It seems Virji Vora had a joint family structure in which his brother also played a role and both the brothers found frequent mention in the memoirs of François Martin. One reason put forward for the decline of the famous Vora family in seventeenth-century Surat was due to the escalation of disputes within the family.

8 See Barbosa (1918: 111). Barbosa noted, 'They (Banias) dwell among the Moors with whom they carry on all their trade.'

9 Della Valle witnessed the pomp with which a Hindu marriage was celebrated in Surat. Also see Ray (1982–3: 84).

10 The Bohras living in the urban areas formed the Shia Bohras while those living in rural areas constituted Sunni ones.

11 Roques noted that the Muslim merchants did not take to the manufacture of cotton cloth, though a majority of weavers belonged to this religion. Muslim merchants considered manufacturing (or printing with motifs and designs) 'beneath them' and for a consignment of such goods they largely depended on Bania brokers. Also see, Arasaratnam (1994: 15).

12 Information on this proverb was provided by Professor Makrand Mehta when I met him in the course of my field research in Gujarat in August–September 2005.

13 At the close of the sixteenth century pepper prices rose very sharply at Bantam. Agitated Dutch traders blamed a Gujarati, who was said to have travelled to Europe and knew the price at which pepper was sold there, for this sharp inflation in pepper prices.

14 According to Arasaratnam (1994: 59), during the first two to three decades of the seventeenth century, Gujarati merchants continued trading with Aceh, Pase and the west Sumatran ports of Baros and Priaman after which they focussed more on the western Indian Ocean.

15 The English termed Virji Vora as 'the greatest banian merchant' (Foster 1909: 212). Virji Vora had trading interests in places like Mocha and Gombroon in the western part of the Indian Ocean and Malaya and Sumatra in the east. Virji Vora also used the agency of the English Company for different commercial purposes. Foster (1913: 252–3) informs of the conveyance of Virji Vora's goods from Surat to Basra on the English ship *Seahorse*.

16 See Santen (1991: 90). While the Dutch were carrying 60,000 to 80,000 pieces of cotton cloth, Gujarati merchants were carrying 555,000 to 999,000 pieces per annum during the 1640s.

References

Alpers, E.A. (1976) 'Gujarat and the Trade of East Africa, *c.*1500–1800', *International Journal of African Historical Studies*, 9(1): 22–44.

Arasaratnam, S. (1994) *Maritime India in the Seventeenth Century*, Delhi: Oxford University Press.

Arasaratnam, S. (1970) *Indians in Malaysia and Singapore*, London: Oxford University Press.

Arasaratnam, S. and A. Ray (eds) (1994) *Masulipatnam and Cambay: A History of Two Port-towns 1500–1800*, New Delhi: Oxford University Press.

Barbosa, D. (1918, rpt. 1921) *The Book of Duarte Barbosa: An Account of the Countries Bordering on the Indian Ocean and Their Inhabitants, Written by Duarte Barbosa, and*

Completed about the Year 1518, trans. and ed. M.L. Dames, Vol. I, London: Hakluyt Society.

Barendse, R.J. (2002) *The Arabian Sea: The Indian Ocean World of the Seventeenth Century*, New York: M.E. Sharpe.

Brouwer, C.G. (1997) *Al-Mukha: Profile of a Yemeni Seaport as Sketched by Servants of the Dutch East India Company (VOC) 1614–1640*, Amsterdam: D'Fluyte Rarob.

Cabral, P.A. (1937) *The Voyage of Pedro Alvares Cabral to Brazil and India*, trans. W. B. Greenlee, London: Hakluyt Society.

Carre, A. (1990) *Travels of the Abbe Carre in India and the Near East 1672 to 1674*, trans. L. Fawcett, eds C. Fawcett and R. Burn, New Delhi and Madras: Indian Reprint Asian Educational Service.

Curtin, P.D. (1984) *Cross-Cultural Trade in World History*, Cambridge: Cambridge University Press.

Dale, S.F. (1994) *Indian Merchants and Eurasian Trade, 1600–1750*, Cambridge: Cambridge University Press.

Das, B. (1957) *Ardhakathanaka*, ed. N. Premi, 2nd edition, Bombay: Hindi Grantha Ratnakara.

Forbes, A.K. (1878, rpt. 1973) *Ras Mala: Hindu Annals of Western India with Particular reference to Gujarat*, New Delhi: Heritage Publishers.

Foster, W. (ed.) (1909, rpt. 1913) *English Factories in India 1624–29*, Oxford: Clarendon Press.

Fryer, J. (1985) *A New Account of East India and Persia in Eight Letters being Nine Years Travels, Begun 1672 and Finished 1681*, ed. W. Crooke, Delhi: Periodical Experts Book Agency.

Gil, M. (2003) 'The Jewish Merchants in the Light of Eleventh-Century Geniza Documents', *Journal of the Economic and Social History of the Orient*, 46(3): 273–319.

Gopal, S. (1975) *Commerce and Crafts in Gujarat, 16th and 17th Centuries*, New Delhi: People's Pub. House.

Habib, I. (1990) 'Merchant Communities in Pre-colonial India', in J.D. Tracy (ed.) *The Rise of Merchant Empires: Long-Distance Trade in Early Modern World 1350–1750*, Cambridge: Cambridge University Press, pp. 371–99.

Haynes, D.E. (1987) 'From Tribute to Philanthropy: The Politics of Gift Giving in a Western Indian City', *Journal of Asian Studies*, 46(2): 339–60.

Hedges, W. (1888) *The Diary of William Hedges, Esq. during his Agency in Bengal: as well as on his voyage out and return overland (1681–1687)*, R. Barlow and H. Yule (Introductory notes), Vol. II, London: The Hakluyt Society.

Khan, A.M. (1928) *Mirat-i-Ahmadi Supplement*, trans. and eds S.N. Ali and C.N. Seddon, Baroda.

Levi, Scott C. (2002) *The Indian Diaspora in Central Asia and Its Trade 1550–1900*, Leiden: Brill.

Linschoten, J.H.V. (1885) *The Voyage of John Huygen van Linschoten to the East Indies*, ed. A.C. Burnell, Vol. 1, London: Hakluyt Society.

Lokhandwalla, S.T. (1967) 'Islamic Law and Ismaili Communities (Khojas and Bohras)', *Indian Economic and Social History Review*, 4(2): 155–76.

Majmudar, M.R. (1965) *Cultural History of Gujarat*, Bombay: Popular Prakashan.

Manucci, N. (1981) *Storia do Mogor or Mughal India 1653–1708*, trans. W. Irvine, Vol. I, New Delhi: Oriental Books.

Matthee, R.P. (1999) *The Politics of Trade in Safavid Iran*, Cambridge: Cambridge Studies in Islamic Civilization.

Mehta, M. (1991) *Indian Merchants and Entrepreneurs in Historical Perspective: With Special Reference to Shroffs of Gujarat: 17th to 19th Century*, Delhi: Academic Foundation.

Meilink-Roelofsz, M.A.P. (1962) *Asian Trade and European Influence in the Indonesian Archipelago between 1500 and about 1630*, The Hague: Martinus Nijhoff.

Misra, S.C. (1985) *Muslim Communities in Gujarat; Preliminary Studies in Their History and Social Organisation*, New Delhi: People's Pub. House.

Misra, S.C. (1984) 'The Medieval Trader and his Social World', in D. Tripathi (ed.) *Business Communities of India: A Historical Perspective*, New Delhi: South Asia Books, pp. 41–57.

Ovington, J. (1929) *A Voyage to Surat in the Year 1689 by J. Ovington*, ed. H.G. Rawlinson, London: Oxford University Press.

Pearson, M.N. (1976) *Merchants and Rulers in Gujarat*, Berkeley: University of California Press.

Pearson, M.N. (2003) *The Indian Ocean*, New York: Routledge.

Pelsaert, F. (1925) *Jahangir's India: The Remonstrantie of Francisco Pelsaert*, eds W. H. Moreland and P. Geyl, London: Cambridge.

Pires, T. (1944, rpt. 1967) *The Suma Oriental of Tome Pires: An account of the East, from the Red Sea to Japan, written in Malacca and India in 1512–1515*, trans. and ed. A. Cortesao, London: Hakluyt Society.

Pyrard, F. (1888, rpt. 2000) *The Voyage of Francois Pyrard of Laval to the East Indies, the Maldives, the Moluccas and Brazil*, trans. and ed. A. Gray, Delhi: Asian Educational Services.

Qaisar, A.J. (1974–5) 'The Role of Brokers in Medieval India', *Indian Economic and Social History Review*, 1(2): 220–46.

Ray, I. (July 1982–January 1983) 'Of Trade and Traders in Seventeenth Century India: An Unpublished French Memoir by Georges Roques', *Indian Historical Review (IHR)*, IX(1–2): 74–120.

Sandhu, K.S. (1969) *Indians in Malaya, Some Aspects of Their Immigration and Settlement (1786–1957)*, Cambridge: Cambridge University Press.

Santen, H.W.V. (1991) 'Trade between Mughal India and the Middle East, and Mughal Monetary Policy, c.1600–1660', in K.R. Haellquist (ed.) *Asian Trade Routes: Continental and Maritime*, New York: Routledge, pp. 87–95.

Saran, P. (1973) *The Provincial Administration of the Mughals, 1526–1658*. Bombay: Asia Publishing House.

Singh, M.P. (1970–1) 'The Custom and the Custom House at Surat in the Seventeenth Century', *Quarterly Review of Historical Studies*, X(2): 84–5.

Srivastava, S. (2001) 'Situating the Gentoo in History: European Perception of Indians in Early Phase of Colonialism', *Economic and Political Weekly*, 36(7): 576–94.

Steensgaard, N. (1975) *The Asian Trade Revolution of the Seventeenth Century*, Chicago; London: University of Chicago Press.

Tavernier, J.B. (rpt. 1977, rpt. 1989) *Jean Baptiste Tavernier's Travels in India*, trans. V. Ball, ed. W. Crooke, New Delhi: Oriental Books.

Thevenot, M.D. and Careri, J.F.G. (1949) *Indian Travels of Thevenot and Careri*, ed. S.N. Sen, New Delhi: National Archives of India.

Torri, M. (1990) 'Ethnicity and Trade in Surat during the Dual Government Era: 1759–1800', *Indian Economic and Social History Review*, 27(4): 377–404.

Valle, P.D. (ed.) (1892) *The Travels of Pietro Della Valle in India*, London: Edward Grey.

Varadarajan, L. (1976) 'The Brothers Boras and Virji Vora', *Journal of the Economic and Social History of the Orient*, 19(2): 224–7.

3 Subaltern networks in a colonial diaspora

A study of Indian migrants and Mauritius

Marina Carter

Colonial Indian labour migrants are portrayed in many historical accounts as victims of a semi-forced displacement and sojourn overseas characterised by fraud, coercion and exploitation, both in recruitment and at the workplace. The emphasis on powerful colonial forces as shaping and determining the socio-economic realities of the Indian labour migrant has sometimes served to obscure the role, nature and extent of subaltern agency in influencing and mitigating these processes. Consequently, Indian labour migrants are infrequently seen as dynamic actors in recruitment and settlement and as engaging in their adopted countries with other communities. Through a case study of Mauritius, a small Indian Ocean colony settled by the French in the eighteenth century, and under British rule from 1810, in which labour immigrants from India played a significant role, this chapter seeks to highlight the multiple and intricate networks devised by these subalterns. This chapter shows how both inter- and intra-community networks were commonly forged by contract and convict workers despite the limitations placed upon their endeavours within the colonial context.

Introduction

The island of Mauritius, settled briefly by the Dutch in the seventeenth century, and by the French between 1715 and 1810, was, until the opening of the Suez Canal, an important stop-over for sailing ships heading to and from the Indies. As such, the colony always had a close commercial relationship with India, and counted numbers of Indians among its inhabitants. During the formative period of the eighteenth century, Indians were welcomed on the island as an important source of skilled and unskilled labour, forming a relatively small but influential population on the island at the time of the British conquest, during the Napoleonic wars. From the mid-nineteenth century, the socio-economic landscape of Mauritius was permanently changed with a dramatic influx of Indian workers. Almost half a million Indian immigrants came to the island as indentured labourers during the last three-quarters of that century. The vast majority of these Indians were destined for work on the sugar estates, bound into indenture contracts that prescribed the type and duration of labour at a fixed wage for a designated employer. Within a few decades, however, a significant proportion had moved off estates into villages, and established themselves as small planters, market gardeners and landowners.

Despite the evidence of a significant drift from the semi-servile status of contract worker to that of proprietor and permanent settlement, the perception of Indian labour migration in the British Empire has been surprisingly static in the scholarly literature. While a few early attempts were made to drop the conventional distinction between 'colonisation' of the largely white Dominions and 'labour migration' to the tropical colonies (Newbury 1975: 235), the separate treatment of European and non-European labour migrants in the literature has continued, based on perceived differentials in risk and choice. A greater emphasis on single male emigrants as opposed to families and the harsher living and working conditions at the point of production are seen as factors limiting mobility and retarding the establishment of family and kin-based settlements with autonomous or semi-independent economic structures in the case of non-white colonial migrants.[1]

However, the British official gaze offers only a very limited – and sometimes misleading – version of the Indian migrant experience. The use of letters written by European migrants has helped to provide a more subaltern perspective of the experience of colonial labour: 'manuscripts of emigrant letters constitute a unique historical source material. The act of emigration led many ordinary working people to record their actions and attitudes. From such letters we can gain some knowledge of the inner social history of the nineteenth century' (Erickson 1972: 1). The letters, petitions and depositions of Indian immigrants to Mauritius will provide important source material for this chapter, in an attempt to offer new insights into the emigration experience.

Depositions taken from arriving immigrants either by police and judicial officials or by customs officers help to reveal the motives of migrants and their interactions with employers and officials.[2] Petitions, or stylised pleas for special investigations or favours, were a surprisingly common means by which immigrants would request intervention or assistance from the colonial authorities.[3] The individual and collective petitions sent by Indians reveal the presence of repeated themes or issues – for example difficulties in the procurement of licences, and conflicts over land concessions – which provide important insights into community concerns, while their focus on both individual and collective problems and ambitions, reveal a great deal about the dynamics of these groups in Mauritius.

The Mauritian context

Uninhabited before the arrival of European settlers in the seventeenth century, it was only under British rule, in the nineteenth century, that the island was developed from a mere entrepot on the trade routes with India and Southeast Asia, to become an important sugar-producer. The transformation of Mauritius into Britain's premier plantation colony was a direct result of the abolition of the slave trade and slavery in the early nineteenth century and the consequent decline of productivity in the West Indian colonies. With its proximity to India, and largely virgin soil, Mauritius was selected to be the site of an experiment in sugar production using so-called 'free labour' from the subcontinent. The result was the importation into Mauritius of tens of thousands of Indian indentured labourers in the mid-nineteenth century. This economic and demographic revolution in Mauritius brought waves of service immigration in its wake as traders and artisans rushed in from Asia to establish the necessary infrastructure for the huge new working population of the island.

The influx of indentured labour was preceded by approximately one and a half thousand convict workers, transported to Mauritius between 1815 and 1837. The disparate group, made up of Muslims, tribals and Hindus of all castes, and sentenced to criminal offences ranging from theft to murder, managed, remarkably, to represent itself as a community of sepoy exiles rather than as a body of criminals, and exercised an influence disproportionate to its size, among locals and travellers alike.[4]

The half a million Indians brought to the island over the course of the nineteenth century, mostly to serve as plantation labourers, were only nominally free, in that their progressively stricter indenture contracts required them to replace periods of sickness or agreed absences with extra duty, while unlawful absences from work – or desertion – could be punished with imprisonment. Nonetheless, those who remained relatively healthy, were able to deal effectively with the heavy labour requirements of the plantation regime, or were promoted to *sirdarships*, were able to see out their indenture contracts and to amass some wealth. They were thus able to purchase land in Mauritius and to pay for their passages back to India or to send remittances to their family and to organise the migration of kin members. By the last quarter of the nineteenth century, when the sugar industry was in crisis, Indian immigrants in Mauritius were in a position to benefit from the 'morcellement' process through which large tracts of marginal sugar land passed into their ownership enabling a class of small planters to emerge (Allen 1999).

In the wake of large-scale indentured immigration, service migrants also arrived on Mauritius. Parsees like Pestonjee and Manackjee became involved in the collection and shipment of labourers from Bombay, jewellers arrived from Tamil Nadu and Gujarat, while Sindhi and particularly Gujarati merchants quickly moved to establish an important share of the trade in rice, pulses, clothes and other goods destined for the consumption of the Indian labourers in the second half of the nineteenth century.

Social integration of migrants

The initial migration streams of Indians to Mauritius were predominantly male. This was true both for convicts and for early indentured migrants. However, within a few years of the onset of indenture, significant numbers of women were being recruited, and the skewed sex ratio was rapidly redressed. This was achieved through both official and unofficial channels. First, bounties on female immigration were introduced to stimulate recruiters to 'collect' women migrants, while male migrants were encouraged to bring their female relatives – of whatever age – to the island, with the specific promise that the women would not be required to sign the onerous indenture contracts that tied their men folk to the sugar estates. As early as the 1840s, 60–80 per cent of all arriving Indian female migrants to Mauritius were married, while the corresponding figure for men was between 20–40 per cent (Carter 1995). Single Indian women were effectively marriage migrants, since they were frequently married from the immigration depot itself. Would-be spouses petitioned the immigration authorities as the following request from Kumally testifies:

> Being in want of a wife and ... led to believe that there are many Indian women lately arrived without husbands, I beg that you will be good enough, as our Protector in Mauritius to facilitate me in getting one as I find (difficulty) in getting my breakfast cooked in the morning on acount of the distance sometimes I have to work, and to take care of my orphan children.

> (PA 22 Mauritius Archives)

The scarcity value of women in the early nineteenth century was a cause of considerable tension; however, the facility with which both convicts and indentured migrants were able to find female partners is striking. Clare Anderson's work provides numerous instances of Indian convicts entering into relationships with Creole slave women, and even, in one recorded case, with the white wife of a British soldier – a woman named Sally Collier. Anderson concludes 'the convicts transported to Mauritius were not a segregated social group. Despite their "unfree" prisoner status they integrated into Mauritian society, through intermarriage, religion and their economic activities' (Anderson 1998). Records in the Mauritius Archives also reveal instances of marriages or cohabiting relationships between indentured Indian women and convicts.

For the Indian labourers, the presence of a wealthy class of free coloured women in Mauritius provided a source of suitable partners for those ex-indentured labourers who had acquired capital in Mauritius. When the Indian immigrant Jonreesing died in 1884, his widow was named as Mme Izabella from Rodrigues (Carter and Kwong 1998). The property transactions of Jugputh Gopaul and his Creole wife Clemence illustrate the then relatively common practice for the more successful Indian immigrants to seek marriage partners from among the class of propertied Creole women to cement their economic and social status in Mauritius.[5]

Similarly, close analysis of immigration registers and statistics compiled of arrivals and departures of Indians reveal a story of circular or chain migration which is notably absent from traditional histories of indentured labour, most notoriously Hugh Tinker's *A New System of Slavery*, which have tended to over-play the coercive aspects of indentured labour mobilisation, depicting recruiters as crimps who drugged or tricked their victims, smuggled them on ships and undertook 'systematic kidnapping'. The reality of Indian indentured recruitment – in Mauritius at least – was more complex. Networks of migrant-recruiters played a significant part in the mobilisation of labour.

Indeed, within a few years of the implementation of a scheme of indentured immigration in 1834, the first networks of kin-mobilisation were in place. Thus Ramdeen deposed before the Calcutta Commission of Enquiry in 1838, that having spent three years in Mauritius as a field labourer, he was promoted to a *sirdarship*, and subsequently sent to India as a recruiter. Significantly, among those he collected were three of his own relatives (Parliamentary Papers 1841 (45): 74). Remarkably, this enquiry, conducted in Calcutta ostensibly to provide reformers with a platform to outlaw indenture, provides evidence of relatively sophisticated recruitment networks, ostensibly operating quite outside the purview of European agents.[6]

By the mid-nineteenth century, when figures began to be collected regarding the proportion of returnees re-migrating to Mauritius together with the proportion of new immigrants each had recruited, the importance of such returnee recruiters was revealed (Table 3.1). Of course, returnees, may also be seen, simply as a refinement of the trickery and exploitation exercised by an earlier generation of *arkatis*. They could, for example, by passing themselves off as examples of persons who had succeeded in the sugar islands, help colonial agents to dupe credulous villagers as to the benefits accruing from indentured migration. Conversely, returnees also acted as important disseminators of information regarding the whereabouts of kin or the advantages of a particular location. Many, as the Mauritius figures show, were indeed bona fide return migrants taking their families with them.[7] A clearer understanding of the interests and concerns of the migrants themselves can be gleaned from petitions. In a particularly revealing collective petition of a group of Telegu immigrants in Mauritius, the strong sense of community identity and a desire to remain in control of their own migration is demonstrated. In 1856, they declared to the immigration authorities on the island as follows: 'We are now returning to our respective villages and on our arrival there, we will speak to our friends who are also anxious to settle at Mauritius and fifteen or twenty thousand of them will come with their wives' (CO 167/377 UK National Archives).

Increasingly, as the above examples have shown, Indian immigrants in Mauritius instituted networks of kin and family migration and regroupment which are little different from the so-called 'chain migration' networks typically associated with other diasporas.

Economic integration of migrants

In order to explain why returnees would have wished to settle permanently abroad, and travelled to collect their families in India for remigration to sugar colonies such as Mauritius, it is vital to demonstrate that some did indeed

Table 3.1 Mauritius: returnee recruiting activities, 1857

Port of immigration	Total migrants	No. recruited by returnees	Total returnees	Returnees with wives	Average time in India (in years)	Average savings (in rupees)	Average service (in years)
Calcutta	8,246	5,416	506	381	1.6	22	5.5
Madras	3,248	2,925	188	102	1.3	10	7.5
Bombay	1,177	485	56	18	1.2	21	8.5

Source: Carter (1994).

prosper during and particularly after the term of their indenture contracts. What, then, were the avenues to economic prosperity for men purposely brought in on fixed-wage contracts, at lower than market levels, to inhibit local creole workers' attempts to negotiate a reasonable value for their labour?

The earliest opportunity for enrichment usually involved an appointment as *sirdar* – or labour overseer – which both ensured a higher wage, and provided an authority role which supported money-lending and allied activities such as gambling syndicates. Further benefits were to be derived through recruiting activities, and through job contracting. The *sirdars* often went on to play a significant role in facilitating land and property acquisitions in Mauritius, and often became landowners in their own right, and in turn employers of Indian labour. Seewoodharry Bhuguth and Gorachand Lallah offer good examples of the route to such economic prosperity. From indentured labourers in the 1850s they rose to become proprietors of extensive forests by 1873 employing hundreds of Indians in their charcoal business.[8]

A Marathi family – the Ramas – also provide an illuminating example of economic mobility of Indian immigrants in Mauritius, and demonstrates that some arrivals under the indenture system were from white-collar backgrounds. Bringing his wife to Mauritius with him from the coastal district of Ratnagiri in 1850, Kadum Rama – a former tax collector – was immediately given a *sirdarship*. The couple's four sons all grew up on and worked for the estate, and eventually obtained a plot of ten acres on which they cultivated vegetables. When an adjoining estate was put up for sale, the Ramas acquired a more substantial landholding equivalent to 300 acres, and eventually the estate itself (Carter 2002).

Indian immigrants were frequently offered a foothold to settlement by better-established members of their own community, but, ultimately, the successful integration of Indian immigrants was dependent upon support provided by cross-community networks. The indentured labourers faced discriminatory clauses in Mauritian legislation: subject to penal clauses which identified them as vagrants unless they held permits for self-employment or were engaged on a sugar estate. Once again, it was often Creole women who provided a mechanism by which they could circumvent restrictive legislation. To provide one example, an Indian, Cassy, sought to take employ in his Creole wife's shop, in order to avoid the vagrancy charges which would devolve on him as an unemployed indentured labourer. The police report on his case touched upon the wider issues it raised: 'this is a subterfuge often resorted to for the purpose of getting the immigrant population into shops, and the Creoles are paid for lending themselves to this object' (RA 1019 Mauritius Archives).

As there existed in Mauritius a wealthy class of Christianised Indian women, who had arrived during French rule in the late eighteenth century – often as slaves – and acquired wealth from cohabitation and marriage with male colonists, it is not surprising to find marital alliances between this old wealth and the new wealth of ex-indentured Indians. Thus Ramtohul, a labourer who purchased his own sugar plantation on Mauritius as early as June 1870, had a Christian wife (Carter 2002).[9]

In this manner, Indian immigrants were able to benefit from a range of intra- and inter-community networks. Not only would their time-expired co-religionists offer support, but for financing schemes such as land purchases, they could also rely on the small but wealthy and influential Gujarati and Tamil merchant communities of Mauritius. The traders used their capital to facilitate and supply credit to would-be land purchasers. The felicitous combination of merchant and *sirdari* capital and land-hungry ex-indentured workers sponsored the 'morcellements' of the mid- and late nineteenth century in Mauritius. This process saw large tracts of marginal sugar-estate land transferred from white planters to Indian smallholders in the mid- and late nineteenth century. As Richard Allen has pointed out, 'notarial acts from this era attest to the fact that the subdivision of these estates was part of a carefully planned decision in which "old immigrants" and other Indian entrepreneurs often functioned, at least indirectly, as agents for White estate owners' (Allen 1997: 107).

The creation of communities

Narratives of migration that focus only on self-contained studies of individual communities, as the foregoing has shown, inevitably portray an incomplete picture of socio-economic integration. Immigrants can rarely function without support in the receiving society, and both inter- and intra-community networks are commonly forged in order to facilitate the successful implantation of new ethnic groups. As part of this process of settlement, migrants are exposed to belief systems that they may be required to adopt wholly or partially as the needs for acceptance and integration dictate.

Indian migrants are portrayed in many historical accounts as victims of a semi-forced displacement, and hence rarely shown engaging in their countries of settlement with the wider community, or as developing a community consciousness in their own right during the indenture period. A case study of a group of Telegu migrants in Mauritius provides a useful counterbalance to the traditional depiction of the Indian labour diaspora. Telegus were amongst the first arrivals under the indenture system in early nineteenth-century Mauritius, and by 1849 a thriving community had already settled on the island, for in that year, the Calcutta Emigration Agent reported that such was the desire to go to Mauritius – to return to or rejoin kin networks already in situ – that Telegus from Ganjam had walked the coastal road all the way to Calcutta, to embark for the island, when Madras was temporarily closed as a port of embarkation (RA Mauritius Archives).

In 1856, Telegus in Mauritius complained of an ethnic bias in operation on the island which detrimentally affected their interests:

> The Calcutta men and the Tamulians are favoured and protected at Mauritius and not those of our country. When we go and make known to the police of our welfare or our grievances our words are not transmitted to the Magistrate and wherever we go to complain, we find that all the persons

employed there are Tamulians and Calcutta, they say 'poda Coringhy' or 'Diave Coringhys' [go away men of Coringhy].

(CO 167/377 UK National Archives)

The petitioners were keen to emigrate to Mauritius to improve their living standards but expressed a concern about being able to maintain contacts with family members in India: 'if we come to settle ourselves there with our wives and children, we shall meet with the difficulties of receiving tidings from our relatives in India.' The object of the petition was to secure favourable terms for the Telegus to migrate to and settle on Mauritius. They thus appealed directly to the Governor: 'if your Excellency would establish anywhere near our country a police presided by a good man of our nation, similar to that in Madras, then the people in our country and those of the neighbourhood shall all come to settle at Mauritius with their families' (CO 167/377 UK National Archives). They asked for an official in Ganjam to supervise their migration and thereby protect them from the bribery demanded of other officials. In addition they asked for legal authority over their womenfolk:

> In our country if we go and complain to the Police that our wife has been ravished or carried away, the fugitive and her ravisher are both condemned to prison and by that means they are afraid of doing so again but while at Mauritius when a woman becomes guilty of such a crime she is taken before the police and asked if she likes to return again her husband and if she says no, she is immediately dismissed and told 'aller fou moi le camp' [get out of my way] and what fear will the women have there? We therefore request that a police of our nation be established there to judge our own disputes, the same as in our country here and also that arrangements be made to enable us to receive tidings from our relatives and friends in our country.
>
> (CO 167/377 UK National Archives)

Significantly, employers in Mauritius were so impressed with the diligence and reliability of Telegu labourers that the colonial authorities quickly moved to meet their demands: a sub-recruiting agent was appointed for the Telegu districts, and an Indian Marriage Ordinance passed on the island to recognise the conjugal relationships of arriving couples – despite the lack of civil status documents.

The flexibility of the colonial state in Mauritius to meet the needs of the indentured labourers helped to ensure that the island remained popular with Indian migrants until the last quarter of the nineteenth century, when falling sugar prices, and an overstocked labour market pushed employers and the state to introduce repressive legislation which inspired the notorious 'vagrant hunts'. Here again, the evidence of effective migrant networks is revealed, insofar as preferences shifted towards the Caribbean, Fiji and Natal, with only a trickle of migrants continuing to arrive on Mauritius, largely determined by pre-existing family and kin settlements. Finally, through the 'morcellements' the plantation sector once again adapted to meet the demands of the Indo-Mauritians through the large-scale transfer of land to Indian planters. A story of continuing dependence and exploitation, as the saga of the Mauritius sugar industry shows, was mitigated through the migration and settlement networks of the Indian immigrants, which were instituted from the very first years of the establishment of the indenture system.

Conclusion

Through an examination of the processes of settlement of Indian immigrants in nineteenth-century Mauritius, this chapter has shown that the new arrivals were able to make use of inter- and intra-community networks to achieve objectives of socio-economic success. Whilst the literature on the Indian labour diaspora tends to provide an impression of forced recruitment, and emphasises an 'outsider' status that appears to be static throughout the indentured period, this chapter argues for a more refined and layered approach to the Indian labour diaspora, taking into account the evolution of legislative change, colonial attitudes and community aspirates. Through a case study of Mauritius, this chapter contends that despite being subject to discriminatory legislation and economic oppression, Indian labour migrants in many cases made effective use of local inter-ethnic and transnational intra-ethnic networks to further their settlement projects. Through the use of colonial archives, whether commissions of enquiry, petitions or judicial trials, the hidden story of the Indian labour migrant can be unwrapped from the strictures of colonial and historiographical labels that have served, and continue to serve, to dehumanise him or her, and the rich diversity of stories and experiences of the thousands of men and women who crossed *kala pani* can be unveiled.

Notes

1 See Tinker (1974); Eltis (1983). More recent studies have continued to privilege the 'exploitation' thesis: see, for example, Hoefte (1998).
2 Interviews with arriving Indian immigrants are found in the RA series of the Mauritius Archives.
3 Petitions have been sourced in the PA, PB, RA and RC Series of the Mauritius Archives.
4 Anderson (2000), has carried out a thorough study of this community.
5 Marriage alliances of wealthy ex-indentured immigrants have been painstakingly reconstructed from the nineteenth-century notarial archives of Mauritius in Allen (1999).
6 I have covered this topic in more detail in Bates and Carter (1992).
7 The complex role of returnee recruiters is explored in greater detail in Bates and Carter (1993).
8 For further details of this and similar cases see Carter (2002).
9 For further details of Indian slaves in Mauritius see Carter (2008).

References

Secondary sources

Allen, R. (1997) 'Indian Immigrants and the Legacy of Marronage: Illegal Absence, Desertion and Vagrancy in Mauritius, 1835–1900', *Itinerario*, 21(1): 98–110.

Allen, R.B. (1999) *Freedmen and Indentured Labourers in Colonial Mauritius*, Cambridge: Cambridge University Press.

Anderson, C. (1998) 'Convict Socio-Economic Autonomy in 19th Century Mauritius', in M. Carter (ed.) *Colouring the Rainbow: Mauritian Society in the Making*, Port Louis: Centre for Research on Indian Ocean Societies, pp. 61–78.

Anderson, C. (2000) *Convicts in the Indian Ocean: Transportation from South Asia to Mauritius, 1815–53*, Basingstoke: Macmillan.

Bates, C. and Carter, M. (1992) 'Tribal Migration in India and beyond', in G. Prakash (ed.) *The World of the Rural Labourer in Colonial India*, New Delhi: Oxford University Press, 205–47.

Bates, C. and Carter, M. (1993) 'Tribal and Indentured Migrants in Colonial India: Modes of Recruitment and Forms of Incorporation', in P. Robb (ed.) *Dalit Movements and the Meanings of Labour in India*, New Delhi: Oxford University Press, pp. 159–85.

Carter, M. (1994) *Servants, Sirdars and Settlers: Indians in Mauritius, 1834–1874*, Delhi and New York: Oxford University Press.

Carter, M. (1995) *Servants, Sirdars and Settlers: Indians in Mauritius, 1834–1874*, New Delhi: Oxford University Press.

Carter, M. (2002) 'Subaltern Success Stories Socio-Economic Mobility in the Indian Labour Diaspora – Some Mauritian Case Studies', *Internationales Asienforum*, 33(1–2): 91–100.

Carter, M. (2008) 'Slaves, Servants and Sugar Barons in Mauritius: Diversity and Transformation in a Historical South Asian Diaspora', in S. Koshy and R. Radakrishnan (eds) *Transnational South Asians: Identity, Culture, and Belonging in a Neo-Diaspora*, New Delhi: Oxford University Press.

Carter, M. and Kwong, J.N.F. (1998) 'Creoles and Immigrants in 19th Century Mauritius: Competition and Cooperation', in M. Carter (ed.) *Colouring the Rainbow: Mauritian Society in the Making*, Port Louis: Centre for Research on Indian Ocean Societies, pp. 41–60.

Eltis, D. (1983) 'Free and Coerced Transatlantic Migrations: Some Comparisons', *American Historical Review*, 88(2): 251–80.

Erickson, C. (1972) *Invisible Immigrants: The Adaptation of English and Scottish Immigrants in 19th Century America*, London: Weidenfeld and Nicolson.

Hoefte, R. (1998) *In Place of Slavery: A Social History of British Indian and Javanese Laborers in Suriname*, Gainsville: University Press of Florida.

Newbury, C. (1975) 'Labour Migration in the Imperial Phase: An Essay in Interpretation', *Journal of Imperial and Commonwealth History*, 3(2): 234–56.

Tinker, H. (1974) *A New System of Slavery: The Export of Indian Labour Overseas 1830–1920*, New York: Oxford University Press.

Primary sources

CO 167/377 (16 August 1856) Petition of the Telegu returnees, 1 March 1856, enclosed in Higginson to Labouchere, 16 August 1856; Higginson to Labouchere 16 August

1856; Protector of Immigrants Report, 28 April 1856, Public Record Office, UK National Archives.

PA 22 (30 Nov 1874) Petition of Kurmally, Mauritius Archives.

Parliamentary Papers 1841 (45) (27 November 1838) Calcutta Commission of Enquiry, Examination of Ramdeen, UK, p. 74.

RA (23 July 1849) Emigration Agent, Calcutta to Protector of Emigrants, Calcutta, Mauritius Archives.

RA 1019 (22 June 1849) Report of Commissary of Police, Mauritius Archives.

4 An entrepreneurial diaspora?[1]

Transnational space and India's international economic expansion

Peter Reeves

> Indian commercial migrants have long played an influential role in the development of the diaspora.... However, overshadowed by studies of indenture and by contemporary interest in professional migrants, the history of commercial migrants and their networks has received little attention.... Now, due to the substantial increase in the transnational flows of investment and trade generated by the Indian business diaspora, it is important to take note of this key aspect of the diaspora.
>
> (Rai 2006: 77)

This chapter is an exploratory contribution to research on the 'Indian business diaspora'. It begins from an hypothesis that the nature of the diaspora has been changing under the influence of the pressures built up in the processes of internationalising – 'globalising' – activities and opportunities in the world economy. It argues that the changing situation of the diaspora due to globalisation makes it possible for new forms of activity, new types of organisations and differently situated players to be accommodated within the diaspora's social and economic 'space' and that the new forms of operation which follow from that can now be sustained within 'the diaspora'.

In particular, for our present purposes, these changes have opened a 'transnational space' which could be conducive to entrepreneurial activity. Indeed Indian entrepreneurs – who were not from within an Indian community settled in the diaspora and who also did not operate from a support base or set of connections within corporate India – have already shown that they have been able to work within this transnational space, that they can develop industrial and trading operations that can successfully compete in the globalised economy – and in ways that coincide well with the efforts of Indian policy and Indian corporations' attempts to expand India's international economic position and influence. The essay will examine examples of such expansion to highlight the ways in which their presence in 'transnational space' has been an advantage for these entrepreneurs.

To do this, it will look at two case studies of international 'acquisition and merger' carried out by Indian entrepreneurs. The first of these will be Dr Sudhir Gupta's build-up of his Moscow- and Singapore-based firm Amtel into a major producer of tyres in Russia, followed by his subsequent expansion of Amtel through the acquisition of the major Dutch tyre producer Vredestein Bandan N.V., which has given him control of Russo-Dutch tyre conglomerate 'AmtelVredestein', which is highly competitive in the global tyre market. The second case is that of the much more widely known Lakshmi Narayan Mittal's creation of the worldwide network of steel plants which formed the basis of 'Mittal Steel'; and the way in which, from this base, Mittal succeeded in his hostile bid for Arcelor, Europe's leading steelmaker. The result was the creation of the world's largest steel firm, 'Arcelor-Mittal'.

Entrepreneurs in the diaspora

There is a long history of Indian merchants and financiers involved in international maritime and land-based ('caravan') trade moving out from India into neighbouring parts of Asia, where there were markets for Indian goods and sources for products from those regions which could be brought into the Indian market. Such merchant groups represented the basis of some of the earliest settled Indian communities in what, in due course, became the 'diaspora'. Such merchants operated on a circulatory mode of operation from their Indian home base to distant countries and back, often with later moves to other distant trading destinations. The settlements in which the merchants resided represented the forerunners of the later diaspora communities but before the nineteenth century these settlements were never on the scale produced by migration under indenture and the systems which followed.

Such mercantile groups became important to the economy of the regions in Asia or Africa to which they travelled and where they did business; but their activity was also significant for their home regions in India and they operated, under control from the 'firm's' headquarters in India. Some merchants were at foreign markets for long periods but others circulated between markets in different countries. This can be seen very clearly in the descriptions of both the maritime merchants from India in the Gulf, the Hadhramaut and the Red Sea; in East Africa and in Southeast Asia; as well as those involved with caravan trade in Iran, Afghanistan, Central Asia or Russia in earlier centuries (see Markovits 2000; Levi 2006a: 36–8; Levi 2006b: 214–21; McPherson 2006: 32–6; Das Gupta 1979: 121–52; 1994). Their circulation gave their trading activity significance in the economies of both the foreign markets and their home regions, a pattern which persisted in a number of areas through to early decades of the twentieth century among groups like the Sindhis and the Kutchis from western India and the Chettiar from the south.

In the nineteenth-century build-up of the diaspora, large Indian communities came into being around the world and from within these communities there developed merchant groups that operated as minority elements in the hostland's economic space and markets. The diaspora, therefore, constituted the space within which the migrants operated outside their home societies. The diaspora space clearly continued to be part of the territory of the host society, in which the migrants were minority elements; therefore, those members of the diaspora who were merchants were essentially engaged in trade that was part of the host-land's commercial operations.

In the contemporary diaspora, business people continue to be important members of the settled Indian communities. Until the period following the liberalisation of the Indian economy in 1991–2, however, economic performance in the diaspora was not given any great importance in India. This tended to be usual even in the case of those known as 'Non-Resident Indians' (NRIs), who were most often categorised as individuals who had relocated (often to advanced economies) for their own advancement and were often written off as part of a 'brain drain' which harmed India. However, the 're-discovery' of the diaspora following liberalisation and the growing importance of trade in the 'Export-Oriented Industrialisation' strategy which liberalisation and 'economic reform' prescribed, brought a new interest in the NRIs and the possibilities of what they could do to help the Indian economy. The annual gatherings at the *Pravasi Bharatiya Divas* celebrations became opportunities to recognise the importance of highly successful business people in the diaspora and, following from this recognition, incentive strategies have been developed, which are designed to encourage investment, and even resettlement, in India so that NRIs can bring their heightened skills and their money back to India. NRIs have become, as Binod Khadria, puts it, 'gain not drain' (2006a: 70).

This same period of internationalising influences in India's economic development saw the emergence of Indian entrepreneurs who looked for opportunities wherever they could be found and who operated with only minimal links with diaspora and without reference back to India. Moreover, because they operated without any base in India, they were not controlled from their former homeland and have been able to follow their own strategies and lines of development. We can think of these as diaspora-based 'entrepreneurs in transnational space' – although we need to find a way to characterise this 'transnational space' within which they operate.

India's international economic expansion

A major development, following from India's liberalisation and 'economic reforms' in the early 1990s, has been an important shift in India's approach to the international, 'globalised', world economy and, with it, international trade and investment.[2] The result, since 2000–1, has been an increasing interest in the expansion of India's place and role in the international economy by major Indian domestic industrial corporations. This has led to the adoption by India's leading industrial and trading houses of a new international strategy involving the acquisition of foreign industrial and commercial concerns to strengthen India's position in the global economy. In 2005, Indian companies purchased 118 firms at a total cost of US$2.91 billion (*Business Times*, 6 February 2006: 15). That was seven times the amount spent in 2001, when these moves were first getting under way. At these levels, Indian-led 'acquisition and merger' ('a & m') activity was small in international terms – 2005's purchases were a mere 1 per cent of global merger activity – but in terms of India's economic opening-up, it was a highly significant portent after five decades of 'ISI'-dominated economic progress. The figures for just the first three-quarters of 2006 – when 115 acquisitions were made at a cost of US$7.4 billion – was an indication of the expanding pace of acquisition activity. In 2007, a new peak was reached when Tata Steel paid US$13 billion to secure the Anglo-Dutch steelmaker Corus (Tucker and Leahy 2007: 39; Engadio 2007). In October *The Economist* (2006m: 72) reported, moreover, that this international activity had not weakened India's domestic investment since the outflow of capital almost equalled inflow. Commentators on the Indian economy predict that the acquisition strategy would see Indian firms become 'truly global' in the next 'five to seven' years (*Business Times* 2006).

While international 'a & m' became an important part of India's international economic expansion from 2000 onwards, the Indian 'entrepreneurs of transnational space' had already been moving in this direction from the late 1980s and early 1990s. What they established were not 'Indian' firms, since they have no Indian home base or connection, but international firms led by Indians. However, as we will see in the case of Mittal Steel, identification as an 'Indian firm' was often applied because situations arose when an Indian entrepreneur (even without national backing) was highly competitive and rivals had to have some 'identity' to call into question. Moreover, it was also a fact that, on occasions, the government of India treated some of these firms (Mittal Steel, in the case outlined below was a prime example) as if they *were* Indian companies.

To illustrate the nature of this entrepreneurial 'a & m', the essay outlines the acquisition programmes of the two representative Indian entrepreneurs: Dr Sudhir Gupta, a Singapore- and Moscow-based tyre manufacturer, and London-based Lakshmi Narayan Mittal, an important figure in the international steel industry. What were their objectives? How did they achieve the results which strengthened their position? And how did they deploy these results to gain further advantage?

Sudhir Gupta and Amtelvredestein[3]

In 1975, Sudhir Gupta, then a 17-year-old Delhi science student, won a USSR national scholarship to study chemistry at Moscow State University, with the aim of returning to India as a professor of chemistry. He gained a BSc in Chemical Technology in 1983, followed by a Master's degree in Agrochemistry and followed this with his doctorate in 1986. This period of study was followed, however, not by a return to an Indian university, but by four years experience as the Director of an Indian-owned store in Moscow. This change of direction was prompted by the fact that the years from 1986 to 1990 saw the enormous changes in the Soviet Union resulting from Mikhail Gorbachev's campaigns for '*Perestroika*' and '*Glasnost*'. With the collapse of Soviet communism in 1989, Sudhir Gupta found himself in a Russia that was, as he described it, opening up as 'a free-for-all capitalist economy'. This situation brought out the skills, on which his entrepreneurial career in Russia and the European Union is based.

The opening which Dr Gupta identified was in the Russian rubber goods industry. From his base in Moscow, he travelled extensively in Southeast and East Asia in the late 1980s and he saw that there was an opportunity to provide cheaper supplies of natural rubber in Russia by purchasing directly natural rubber from Southeast Asian producers and so by-passing middlemen in the London Rubber Exchange, whose supplies were much more expensive. From a base in Singapore, his firm, Amtel, was in a position to capitalise on purchases directly from producers in Malaysia, Indonesia and Thailand. In the late 1980s and early 1990s, working initially with Soviet government agencies and then directly with Russian manufacturers following the collapse of the Soviet Union, he built up an annual import trade of 100,000 tonnes through Amtel.

He then expanded Amtel's activities from the mid-1990s. He diversified it, first, in 1994 into packaging, and then into petrochemical production. Between 1997 and 1999, Sudhir Gupta acquired several Russian tyre plants at Krasnoyarsk, Kirov and Voronezh and expanded their range by developing facilities for the production of carbon black and nylon tyre cord, which were key accompaniments to tyre manufacture. These developments were brought to a new level in 2001–2 when Amtel both integrated its product supply and retail systems and then upgraded its infrastructure to provide the technological base for higher quality production. At this stage Amtel was the second or third largest Russian tyre company, specialising in middle-range products.

Dr Sudhir Gupta then began to look for collaboration with manufacturers outside Russia in order to broaden Amtel's product and trading range. This led him, in 2005, to acquire Vredestein Bandan B.V., a leading tyre producer and trader in the Netherlands, which operated at the upper end of the market, for €195.6 million in cash. Sudhir Gupta then moved, in 2006, to get greater synergies from the operations of Amtel and Vredestein. This restructuring streamlined production to three tyre plants at Enschede (in the Netherlands) and Kirov and Voronezh (in Russia) and developed a raw materials plant in Kemerovo in Russia. These plants employed 27,000 workers and staff. The new firm was then able, building on Vredestein's international trading networks, to place itself as an internationally significant 'brand' at the middle and upper ends of the market. In effect, Amtel's global operations expanded into Europe, North America, Southeast Asia and the independent nations of the former USSR. In 2006 AmtelVredestein was the fourth largest European tyre firm and was ranked 12th among world producers. The new corporation, AmtelVredestein, is managed by a representative Supervisory Board of which Dr Sudhir Gupta is the Chairman.

From 2003–4, Amtel began to attract public investment. Templeton Strategic Emerging Markets Fund first took 3.75 per cent of the stock and subsequently increased that to 5.65 per cent. In June 2005 AmtelVredestein offered shares on the London Stock Exchange. By 2006, some 10 per cent of Amtel share capital was held by institutional investors, including Citicorp International Finance Corporation which had 4.1 per cent. By private placement US$70 million were invested by Alfa-Bank (the largest private commercial bank in Russia) and by Temasek Holdings (a major investment arm of the Singapore government and its 'Government-Linked Companies'). Sudhir Gupta's 'rise and rise' – as one commentator put it – was clear for all to see.

Lakshmi Narayan Mittal and Arcelor-Mittal Steel[4]

Born in 1950 into a Marwari Agarwal family in Rajasthan, Lakshmi Narayan Mittal was brought (with the rest of the family) to Kolkata (Calcutta) by his father, who established himself as a partner in a small steel firm in the city. Lakshmi Narayan took a commerce degree in 1969 and in 1976, after experience in the Kolkata mill, he was sent to Indonesia to manage a mill, Ispat Indo, which the family had acquired. This move into the diaspora was a significant turning point and provided the experience to enable Lakshmi Narayan to set up his own operation in 1994.

Over the next decade, Lakshmi Narayan built a world-wide steel production conglomerate, which became Mittal Steel in 2004. He targeted under-producing or failing steel works, mainly in developing and unsettled areas across the globe, which could be acquired at low cost and then be turned around by Mittal's high-powered Indian management teams on an 'integrated mini-mill' model. This strategy enabled Lakshmi Narayan to consolidate a substantial position in the world steel industry with two steel-producing firms, Ispat International NV (which became a public company in 1997) and his family's privately controlled LNM Group. These two firms came to operate worldwide holdings in Trinidad & Tobago, Mexico, Canada, the USA, Ireland, the Czech Republic, Poland, Macedonia, Romania, Kazakhstan, Ukraine and South Africa.

In 2004, Mittal Steel NV emerged from a merger of Ispat International, the LNM Group and US-based International Steel, which Mittal had acquired in the US mid-west 'rust belt'. Mittal Steel NV was registered in Rotterdam but managed from London and the Mittal family held 88 per cent of its stock. Lakshmi Narayan was president of the company; his son Aditya (an accountancy graduate from the University of Pennsylvania's Wharton School) was Chief Financial Officer; and his daughter Vanisha (educated at the European Business School and the School of Oriental and African Studies) was also a member of the Board.

Arcelor, which had been formed by a merger in 2002 of three leading European steel manufacturers based n France, Spain and Luxembourg, was fully refurbished by 2005. In 2006 Lakshmi Narayan (perhaps, some think, with Aditya's prompting) identified it as an ideal target for merger with Mittal Steel. He raised this possibility of a merger on 13 January 2006 at a private dinner in his London mansion with the Arcelor CEO, Guy Dollé. Lakshmi Narayan argued that 'the rationale for merging is very strong'; but Guy Dollé flatly rejected the suggestion (Gumble 2006: 22). On 26 January 2006, therefore, Lakshmi Narayan announced that Mittal Steel would make a hostile bid for Arcelor, which would value the company at US$23.3 billion (€18.6 billion or

£12.7 billion Sterling); the offer was four Mittal Steel shares, plus a cash payment of €35.25, for every five Arcelor shares.

The immediate response by the Arcelor board and the related European governments was 'patriotic outrage' (*The Economist* 2006a: 11–12). Guy Dollé characterised Mittal Steel as 'low level businesses' and the bid as 'monkey money' (or perhaps it has been suggested, as a bid made by 'moneyed monkeys'). His exasperation with the thought that an 'Indian company' should be so presumptuous as to attempt to control a leading European firm like Arcelor was plain to see. The Prime Minister of Luxembourg, where Arcelor was headquartered, saw the bid as a 'hostile' one which needed to be met by equal hostility; and the President of France, Jacques Chirac, dismissed it as an 'unfriendly' bid with no plan behind it. The leaders of both Luxembourg and France indicated that they would put in place legislation that would prevent such a takeover. Somewhat more archly, the Arcelor management spread the word that Nippon Steel, the world's largest producer, which had linked up with Arcelor, would undermine any merger by refusing to allow a Mittal-controlled Arcelor to utilise advanced processes which it had shared with Arcelor.

The Mittals (Lakshmi Narayan and Aditya, who were now both closely involved in this operation) confronted this hostility and the attempts to denigrate the value and purpose of the bid by releasing plans for the development, from the merger, of a 'steel powerhouse', which would produce annually 130 million tonnes of steel, three times the production of Nippon Steel, the world's largest producer. It would do this, they claimed, with no redundancies. Moreover, to reassure shareholders, they would ensure that there would be a majority of independent directors on the board; and consideration would be given to moving the headquarters of the merged company to Luxembourg. Aditya, moreover, talked up the bid, which he declared 'would be settled and accepted by end June 2006' (*Business Times* 2006).

Then, having publicly declined to talk with Arcelor management, the Mittals developed a 'charm offensive' directed at several vitally important groups: journalists who dealt with these issues in the European press; politicians and officials in concerned European governments; and the Arcelor shareholders. The journalists were taken to the US to be shown the company's Midwest US operations by Aditya. Lakshmi Narayan toured western Europe talking with governments and bureaucrats. Over the same period they moved around the continent to meet and talk with two-thirds of Arcelor's shareholders, from which meetings came reassuring signs of shareholder support. A major shareholder in the Netherlands, Atticus Capital, said in a letter to the press in late February that it had no doubts that there were 'compelling industrial and financial merits in the transaction for an industry needing consolidation' (*Business Times*, 21 March 2006). By mid-March the press was reporting: 'It is clear that the shareholders want this transaction' (*Business Times*, 17 March 2006).

On 29 January, the Arcelor Board unanimously rejected the Mittal bid claiming that it was dangerous for employees, shareholders and customers. Moreover, Arcelor management continued to disparage Mittal as 'an Indian company' and, therefore, not having the strength to be a realistic bidder or competitor. Mittal, they claimed, played with 'monopoly money'; and when it came to serious steel production Mittal was second rate since, while Arcelor produced 'perfume', Mittal could only make 'eau-de-cologne'.

Besides these verbal attacks, there were other strings to the Arcelor bow. The Arcelor Board was prepared to increase dividends for shareholders from €1.2 to €1.85 and it offered €5.00 per share for a share buy-back. The Board also made overtures in a bid for Russian steelmaker Severstal, with the objective of placing an expanded Arcelor beyond Mittal's reach. The threat of European governments to legislate against a takeover continued to be discussed but increasingly against a backdrop of EU concern for such 'anti-competitive' behaviour which went against EU stated objectives; and the government of India also warned that such moves could affect its relations with EU member states.

In mid-May 2006, the arguments and counter offers assumed new importance because the bid which Mittal had put on the table in late January was finally cleared for serious discussion by the regulating authorities in the US, the EU and the most closely involved European states – the Netherlands, France, Luxembourg and Spain. The formal bid was launched on 18 May 2006. The offer for five Arcelor shares remained four Mittal shares plus €35.25; however, the total value of the bid now valued Arcelor at US$33.7 billon, which was almost a 50 per cent increase on the original bid of US$23.3 billion. The tender was opened initially to 29 June 2006; however, this was later extended to 15 July and then again to 15 August.

On 11 June 2006, the Arcelor Board formally rejected the Mittal offer. In May, Guy Dollé made a last desperate attempt to foil it with another move involving Severstal. He devised a plan whereby Arcelor would buy the whole of Russian oligarch Alexei Mordashov's 90 per cent stake in Severstal and would then sell back 30 per cent to Mordashov, with the proviso that this deal had to be met or Mordashov was to be paid €140 million. What Dollé hoped that this would do was to increase the size of Arcelor and, at the same time, introduce a major shareholder (Mordashov) with a 30 per cent stake in Arcelor, to block any takeover bid. This was seen by Dollé as a cunning move to outflank Mittal; but others saw it as a very risky strategy and there was strong shareholder opposition to it from the beginning. Shareholders basically asked: why would the company favour Mordashov, an unsafe Russian partner in a poorly regulated market, over Mittal, who was registered on both the London and the New York Stock Exchanges?

The decisive move on Severstal came on 29 June, when a major Arcelor shareholder, Romain Zaleski, who held 7.8 per cent of Arcelor decided against the move. On 30 June 2006 shareholders rejected the Severstal deal outright and the Board recommended acceptance of the Mittal bid. In fact negotiations in mid-June between Aditya Mittal and key players on the Arcelor Board (led by Roland Junck) had already paved the way for this acceptance, given that the value of Arcelor had increased 50 per cent to US$33.7 billion.

The acceptance of the bid by the shareholders opened the way for changes in management. The most obvious casualty was Guy Dollé, who left the CEO's position immediately. Roland Junck became the new CEO, with a promise to put Arcelor in good position. However, in November 2006, Junck resigned to make way for Lakshmi Narayan to take over as CEO of Arcelor-Mittal, in addition to his position as President. The 'a & m' was complete!

An entrepreneurial diaspora?

These accounts of the entrepreneurial success of Sudhir Gupta and Lakshmi Narayan Mittal suggest that the idea of an 'entrepreneurial diaspora' may be worth considering. However, these accounts that we are able to give of them lack the materials necessary for tackling that task in full. All we attempt here is to summarise what emerges on the most obvious questions:

a   What do the Gupta and Mittal experiences tell us of the special/particular features of the 'entrepreneurial diaspora'?
b   Did these entrepreneurs have advantages in operating in transnational economic space, rather than from an Indian base?
c   Can they operate more effectively than diasporic businessmen on the one hand and Indian domestic firms on the other?

It is clear that the approach and the *modus operandi* of the modern entrepreneurs broke with earlier patterns of operation. They used their diasporic position when they needed to; but they also appeared to be able to act more independently, both of the diaspora and the homeland. It is in this way that they can be seen as occupying a 'transnational' space in which they are much freer of external controllers who would be in a position to limit their freedom of action.

Operations in transnational space would have also meant, of course, greater freedom for Indian entrepreneurs from the restrictive Indian regulations and practices of the 'permit-quota-licence Raj'. Such freedom meant being able to marshal financial support from institutions such as stock exchanges and banks with broader entrepreneurial objectives than might be available in India (an example was the European Bank for Reconstruction and Development, which Lakshmi Narayan Mittal used for acquisitions in eastern Europe). Having 'freedom from regulations' necessarily meant that there was less scope for contact with governmental, bureaucratic and political elements for operations within India, but this could probably be discounted because one of the incentives of operating independently was precisely to avoid competition with established business and financial players who had already successfully established themselves in the operational world of the 'licence Raj'.

What is also clear from the accounts is that both Sudhir Gupta and Lakshmi Narayan Mittal give the impression that they do not need Indian support in terms of operating at this international level. They appear to be not thinking in terms of being 'Indian' but rather of being straightforwardly international entrepreneurs; and from this we might take the point that, in the case of such entrepreneurs, we can think less about identification with 'India' and more about the skills which they had acquired operating in transnational space and building their 'empires'.

Moreover, given the elements of racism which crept into the Mittal story, there might be good grounds for them wanting to play down their 'Indianness'. From an entrepreneurial point of view it is possible to see that they would have wished to avoid extraneous elements of this kind which could make them less effective as negotiators; while at the same time accepting support – as, for example, when India defended Mittal by invoking sanctions against France and Luxembourg when those states threatened to legislate to prevent the takeover of Arcelor; and this despite the fact that it was part of the argument that Mittal Steel was *not* an 'Indian' company!

Nonetheless, entrepreneurial activity was seen as adding to India's international economic expansion. For instance, in New Delhi in July 2006, once the bid had proved to be successful, Mittal himself talked about why Indian support – while not specific to the deal – had been important. He indicated that he believed that failure to carry through the takeover would have been 'a setback for Indian businessmen'. Subsequent events during this July visit, suggested that there might also be a sense in which these 'defensive' moves were linked to that wider agenda of encouraging the NRIs' (including in this category entrepreneurs') participation in the Indian economy. For example, Mittal, having announced that there would be 'no [more] acquisition fireworks this year' turned his attention quickly to plans for major investments in steel mills in Jharkhand and Orissa, which may well have been part of a 'deal' with India. Was the government of India thinking in terms of greater liaison with diaspora entrepreneurs coming back into India – as Indian firms moved out into international space?

Perhaps the fact is that the liberalisation of post-1991 in India opened more widely the gates for relatively independent entrepreneurial activity by Indians. When Gupta and Mittal began, perhaps those opportunities were not available except by striking out on an independent entrepreneurial path of one's own choosing. By 2006–7, however, even within India such moves could be made by corporations or individuals and the Indian state was able to accommodate such players within a general understanding of the role and scope to be allowed (even encouraged?) among NRIs. If this is the case, we will need to look at developments in the next decade of India–NRI interaction to see the full force of such a development. If such a development does take place, it will help to underline the importance, in parallel to the economic liberalising process in India, of the work and skills of the Indian entrepreneurs who chose to operate in 'transnational economic space' from the 1980s onwards.

Notes

1 The initial impetus for this essay came from work in Brij V. Lal, P. Reeves and R. Rai (eds) *The Encyclopedia of the Indian Diaspora* published in Singapore in 2006: Rajesh Rai (2006) on 'business and entrepreneurship'; Binod Khadria (2006b) on 'Lakshmi Narayan Mittal'; and Peter Reeves (2006) on Dr Sudhir Gupta, who kindly granted me an interview in Singapore. Research for the essay was based on Singapore newspapers;

especially invaluable was the *Business Times*. Some materials also came from the *Straits Times*; and some Indian and Australian papers have also been useful.

2 The discussion of India's international economic expansion draws on reporting in the *Business Times*, the *Australian*, the *Economist, Business Week* and *Time*.

3 This discussion outline of Dr Sudhir Gupta and Amtel Vredestein draws from reporting in three useful journals: by Liz White in the *European Rubber Journal*; by M. Noorani in the *Indian Rubber Journal*; and by an unnamed author in the journal *People of Indian Origin*. The website for AmtelVredestein, www.amtel-vredestein.com/amtel/ is also important.

4 This account of the Mittal–Arcelor case draws on reporting by, amongst others, Anand Giridharadas in the *Business Times* and Jonathon Fenby in the *Straits Times* in Singapore; on an invaluable series of reports in *The Economist*; and by Peter Gumble and others in *Time*. The websites for Mittal Steel, www.mittalsteel.com/index.htm and Arcelor Mittal, www.arcelormittal.com/ have also been helpful.

References

Bouquet, T. (2007a) 'Inside the World of the Men of Steel', *Evening Standard*, London, 11 September.

Bouquet, T. (2007b) 'Man of Steel', *Australian Magazine*, 24–25 November, pp. 22–3, 25–6, 29.

Bouquet, T. and Ousey, B. (2008 forthcoming) *Cold Steel: The Takeover that Defined an Era*, New York: Little Brown.

Business Times (6 February 2006) 'Indian Firms on the Hunt for Foreign Acquisitions', p. 15 (reprinted from *Agency France-Presse*).

Business Times (28 February 2006) 'Opposition to Arcelor Takeover Softening', p. 19 (reprinted from *Agency France-Presse*; *Bloomberg*).

Business Times (17 March 2006) 'Luxemburg Warned against Blocking Mittal', p. 13 (reprinted from *Agency France-Presse*; *Reuters*).

Business Times (21 March 2006) 'Mittal had Launched Without any Plan for Arcelor: Chirac', p. 13 (reprinted from *Agency France-Presse*; *Reuters*).

Das Gupta, A. (1994) *Merchants of Maritime India, 1500–1800*, Brookfield, VT: Ashgate.

Das Gupta, A. (1979) 'Gujarati Merchants and the Red Sea Trade, 1700–1725', in B. Kling and M. Pearson (eds) *The Age of Partnership: Europeans in Asia before Dominion*, Honolulu: University Press of Hawaii, pp. 123–58.

Economist, The (2006a) 'Cross-border Mergers: Heavy Mittal', 4 February, pp. 11–12.

Economist, The (2006b) 'Steel: Age of Giants', 4 February, pp. 55–6.

Economist, The (2006c) 'European Takeovers: Powerless Patriots', 4 February, pp. 56–7.

Economist, The (2006d) 'Economic Nationalism: From Karl Marx's Copybook', 4 March, p. 12.

Economist, The (2006e) 'The Nationalist Resurgence', 4 March, p. 49.

Economist, The (2006f) 'European Takeovers: To the Barricades', 4 March, pp. 55–6.

Economist, The (2006g) 'Arcelor: Up in Arms', 29 April, pp. 62–3.

Economist, The (2006h) 'Can India Fly?', 3 June, p. 11.

Economist, The (2006i) 'Treating Shareholders as Pig Iron', 3 June, pp. 68–9.

Economist, The (2006j) 'Don't Touch Taittinger', 3 June, p. 69.

Economist, The (2006k) 'Steel Takeovers: Cast Iron', 17 June, p. 13.

Economist, The (2006l) 'Arcelor Wobbles', 17 June, p. 72.

Economist, The (2006m) 'India's Acquisition Game: Circle the Wagons', 14 October, pp. 72–4.

Economist, The (2006n) 'Tata and Corus: Steely Logic', 28 October, pp. 80–1.

Engadio, P. (2007) 'The Last Rajah', *Business Week*, 13 August. Online. Available at: www.businessweek.com/magazine/content/07_33/b4046045.htm?chan=search (accessed 20 August 2007).

European Rubber Journal (2005) 'Vredestein Deal to Go Through "Soon" as Amtel's Growth Rises', *European Rubber Journal*, 187(2): 12.

Fenby, J. (2006) 'Europe's Globalisation Dilemma', *Straits Times*, 5 June, p. 17.

Girdharidas, A. (2006a) 'French Elites Raise Spectre of India Threat', *Business Times*, 6 February, p. 15 (reprinted from *International Herald Tribune*).

Giridharadas, A. (2006b) 'Following Mittal's Footsteps Overseas', *Business Times*, 15 February, p. 14 (reprinted from *International Herald Tribune*).

Gumble, P. (2006) 'Nerves of Steel', *Time*, 13 February, pp. 22–5.

Khadria, B. (2006a) The Migration of Professionals, in B.V. Lal, P. Reeves and R. Rai (eds) *The Encyclopedia of the Indian Diaspora*, pp. 70–5.

Khadria, B. (2006b) Indian Professionals Turned Entrepreneurs, in B.V. Lal, P. Reeves and R. Rai (eds) *The Encyclopedia of the Indian Diaspora*, pp. 80–1.

Lal, Brij V., P. Reeves and R. Rai (eds) (2006) *The Encyclopedia of the Indian Diaspora*, Singapore: Editions Didier Millet.

Levi, S. (2006a) 'The Indian Caravan Trade', in B.V. Lal, P. Reeves, and R. Rai (eds) *The Encyclopedia of the Indian Diaspora*, Singapore: Editions Dider Millet, pp. 36–9.

Levi, S. (2006b) 'Indians in Afghanistan, Central Asia and Iran', in B.V. Lal, P. Reeves, and R. Rai (eds) *The Encyclopedia of the Indian Diaspora*, Singapore: Editions Dider Millet, pp. 214–21.

Markovits, C. (1999) 'Indian Merchant Networks outside India in the Nineteenth and Twentieth Centuries: A Preliminary Survey', *Modern Asian Studies*, 33(4): 883–911.

Markovits, C. (2000) *The Global World of the Indian Merchants 1750–1947: Traders of Sind from Bukhara to Panama*, Cambridge: Cambridge University Press.

McPherson, K. (2006) 'Indian Maritime Communities', in B.V. Lal, P. Reeves, and R. Rai (eds) *The Encyclopedia of the Indian Diaspora*, Singapore: Editions Dider Millet, pp. 32–6.

Noorani, M. (2005a) 'Interview: Sudhir Gupta, President – Amtel Tyres', *Indian Rubber Journal*, 90(June): 10–12.

Noorani, M. (2005b) 'The Rise and Rise of Dr Sudhir Gupta's Amtel Tyres', *Indian Rubber Journal/International Rubber Journal*, 90(June): 14–20.

People of Indian Origin. (2005) 'Turning Point: The Titan of the Tyre Biz', *People of Indian Origin*, 1(3): 10–14.

Rai, R. (2006) 'Business and Entrepreneurship', in B.V. Lal, P. Reeves and R. Rai (eds) *The Encyclopedia of the Indian Diaspora*, Singapore: Editions Didier Millet, pp. 77 and 79.

Reeves, P. (2006) 'Dr Sudhir Gupta', in B.V. Lal, P. Reeves and R. Rai (eds), *The Encyclopedia of the Indian Diaspora*, Singapore: Editions Didier Millet, p. 78.

Time. (2006a) 'India Thinks Big', *Time*, 30 October, p. 10.

Time. (2006b) 'Lakshmi Mittal', *Time*, 13 November, p. 73.

Tucker, Sundeep and Joe Leahy (2007) 'Record $9bn Loan to Finance Indian Purchase of Corus', *Australian Magazine*, 5–6 May, p. 39.

White, L. (2004a) 'Amtel Invests $100m to Make 20m Tyres by 2006', *European Rubber Journal*, 186(3): 11–12.

White, L. (2004b) 'Amtel–Nokian Tyres Deal', *European Rubber Journal*, 186(3): 13.

Part II

Socio-economic identities and change

5 Indians in Southeast Asia

Migrant labour, knowledge workers and the new India

Amarjit Kaur

India's economic transformation and astounding success, particularly since the 1990s and after decades of being viewed as an unfulfilled and poverty-stricken land, has contributed to the revitalisation and augmentation of Indian diasporic communities all over the world. In Southeast Asia this trend is particularly striking in two major states, Singapore and Malaysia, which had traditionally been important destinations for Indian migrants. Current Indian immigration to these states has also assumed new patterns, though some features of the old immigration streams continue to persist. Moreover, although ethnic polarisation and fragmentation continue to be pervasive (especially in Malaysia), rapid change in these countries is also making it possible for Indian communities to acquire experience and some opportunities for new alignments with India and other Indian communities.

The Indian Diaspora has been estimated at over 20 million people worldwide. In the Southeast Asian region there are about 1.8 million Indians (7.6 per cent of the total population) in Malaysia (Kaur 2006: 156) and 293,100 Indians (8.4 per cent of the total population) in Singapore (Rai 2006: 176). Indian immigration to these countries, which had effectively stopped after the Second World War, resumed in the 1990s. Current immigration has coincided with new political and economic trends, the rise of the global market for knowledge workers and the growth of sub-continental Information and Communication Technology (ICT) firms, and changing relations between India and Southeast Asia. This chapter provides a general account of the history and development of Indian immigration to Southeast Asia and examines how politics and domestic affairs in India and the destination countries shaped, and continues to shape, policies on Indian migration. The chapter also links Indian migration trends to India's economic transformation and establishes a new basis for understanding the complexities that Indians in Southeast Asia must currently contend with.

Setting the scene

There are two major phases in Indian immigration to Southeast Asia. During the first phase (late nineteenth century to about 1940), Indian migration was linked to the expansion of British colonial rule in the region and Southeast Asia's greater integration into the international economy. Four characteristics of Indian migration trends are striking. First, labourers and auxiliaries dominated the flows but there was a steady stream of traders and merchants. Male migrants also heavily outnumbered women migrants. Second, rapid economic change led to settlement by Indians and the emergence of Indian diasporic communities in the region but Indians formed an important minority only in Malaya[1] and Burma. Third, Indian communities were not uniform in class terms, nor did the community remain so over time. There were also fewer millionaires and traders among them compared with Chinese migrants. Fourth, Indians declined in importance in Southeast Asia both in absolute and comparative standing after the Second World War, in the wake of the decolonisation process and the emergence of independent nation states.

The second phase of Indian migration to Southeast Asia (since the 1990s) has coincided with the 'new' globalisation, the expansion of the trade in services and the emergence of a global labour market. Four main features characterise this phase. First, Southeast Asian states have promoted the entry of both skilled and less-skilled Indian migrants, consistent with their development strategies. Additionally, Singapore has signed a general economic agreement with India while Malaysia has a memorandum of understanding with it for the recruitment of less-skilled workers. As before, male migrants dominate migration flows. Second, immigration is viewed as a policy measure to rectify skill imbalances in national labour markets and separate governance arrangements have been formulated for the management of skilled and less-skilled workers. Third, Singapore and Malaysia's differing recruitment policies for knowledge workers have meant that the former has been more successful than Malaysia in attracting and retaining Indian knowledge workers. Fourth, the majority of the 'new' Indian migrants generally reject the idea of settlement and integration, and view their stay as temporary. Concurrently, since migrant remittances form a valuable and stable source of income for India, the Indian government promotes closer relationships with overseas Indian communities and acknowledges their transnational identity.

Framing Indian migration in Southeast Asia in the late nineteenth and early twentieth centuries

Political and economic change in Southeast Asia, 1870–1940

European political and economic advances in Southeast Asia in the second half of the nineteenth century led to the emergence of six major Southeast Asian states, namely, Burma, Malaya, Indonesia, Indochina, the Philippines and Thailand. However, borders were kept open and intra-Asian migration facilitated labour-force growth in labour-scarce colonies. Economic change was characterised by the following trends: growth of the international economy (the demand and expansion of primary products such as tin, rice and rubber, provision of shipping and merchant services); the important role of Singapore as a trade entrepot and also as a source of capital; the role of European, Chinese and

Indian enterprise; evolving colonial economic policies; and the role of migration in economic growth.

Growth patterns were consistent with international capital mobility and nomadic global capital and had profound implications for the expansion of international labour migration in the region. Concomitantly, colonial immigration policies and mechanisms for overseas labour recruitment ensured that there was a steady movement of labour from labour-surplus countries to labour-scarce countries in the region (Kaur 2004: 3–4).

Burma and Malaya's greater integration into world commodity and capital markets under British colonial rule engendered an accelerated demand for their products and coincided with the rapid expansion of agricultural and mineral production. Since labour was scarce the British turned to another British territory, India, for their labour needs.

Indian labour migration to Burma and Malaya

The acquisition of Burma had enabled Britain to secure the eastern defences of India and the territory was administratively and politically governed as part of

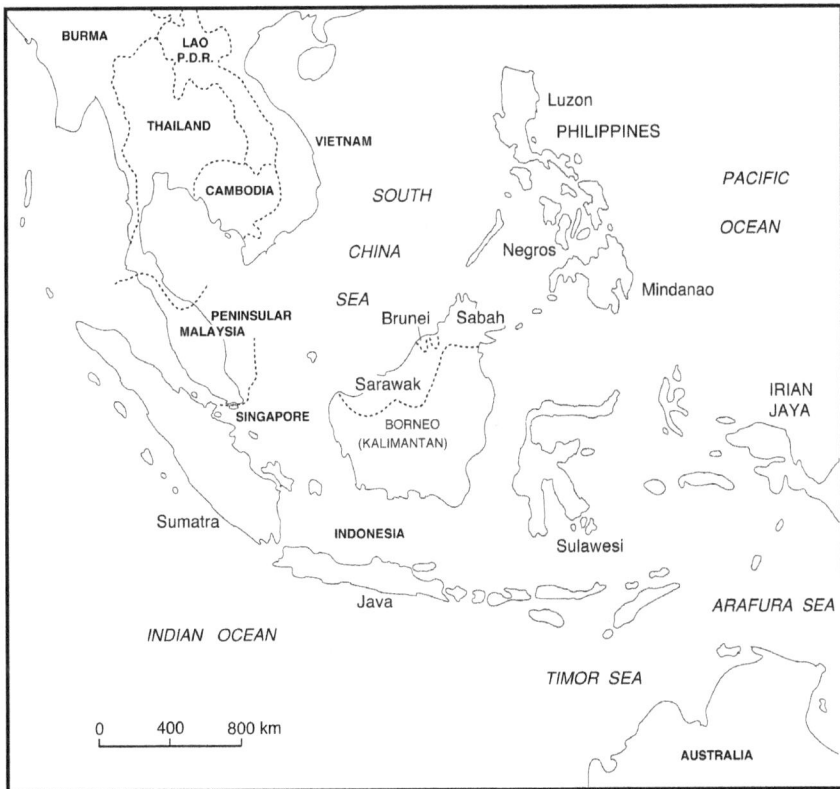

Map 5.1 Southeast Asia.

India. The subsequent export demand for Burma's rice and the rapid expansion of its rice industry coincided with the disruption of rice supplies from the United States during the American Civil War. Burma became the world's largest rice producer and expanded rice production was contingent upon labour migration from India. This labour migration was essentially viewed as an internal movement from one colonial region to another.

Malaya, on the other hand, was regarded as a strategic gateway to the Pacific. It was administered from Britain and the British preserved the myth that they governed the Malay States on behalf of the Malay rulers. Malaya emerged as the world's largest exporter of tin and rubber and migrant Chinese and Indian labour played a major role in the production of these commodities. While the Chinese dominated the mining labour force, the large-scale entry of Indian labour was associated with the development of the rubber-plantation sector. The recruitment of Indian labour involved two separate political entities and necessitated a certain degree of control and regulation by the Indian colonial government (India Office). Nevertheless, there were similarities between Malaya and Burma as well, namely, in the origins of the Indian migrants, methods of recruitment and duration of contracts.

The principal Indian migration flows by sea to Burma and Malaya are shown in Map 5.2. There was also substantial overland migration from India to Burma, especially from Bengal to Arakan.

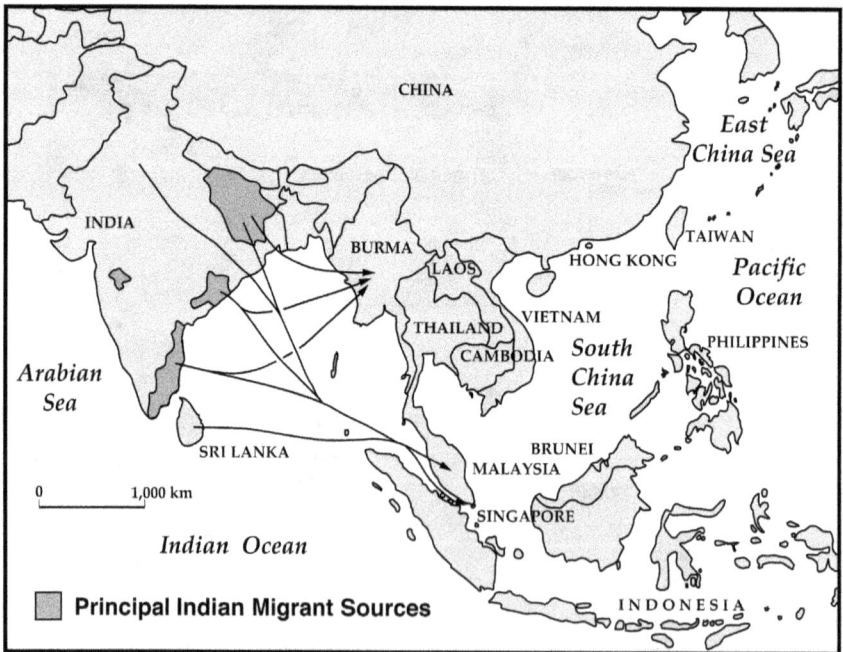

Map 5.2 Indian migration flows to Southeast Asia.

The circumstances of Indian labour migration to these territories need not detain us here. Suffice it to say that the majority of migrants from India were impoverished and were pushed into migration due to factors such as agrarian overpopulation and pressure on land, exactions by the state, natural calamities and landlord exploitation. The magnitudes involved differed, with the greater majority going to Burma. In both countries Tamil and Telegu unskilled labourers from South India dominated the migrant labour flows. The comparative flows of Indian immigrants to Burma and Malaya for the period 1910–35 are shown in Figure 5.1.

As shown in Figure 5.1, Indian migrant flows to Burma greatly exceeded migrant flows to Malaya. Burma's proximity to India and the fact that it was governed as part of India was also conducive to the greater number of Indians migrating to Burma. Indians in Burma comprised between 4.9 to 6.9 per cent of Burma's population in the period 1872–1931, as shown in Table 5.1. By 1931, there were more than one million Indians in Burma. Significantly, Indians were largely concentrated in rice production in Lower Burma where they comprised around 11 per cent of the population in 1921 and 1931 (Baxter 1941: 6). In Malaya, where the indigenous population was smaller and there were other labour sources, Indians comprised between 10 and 14 per cent of the population

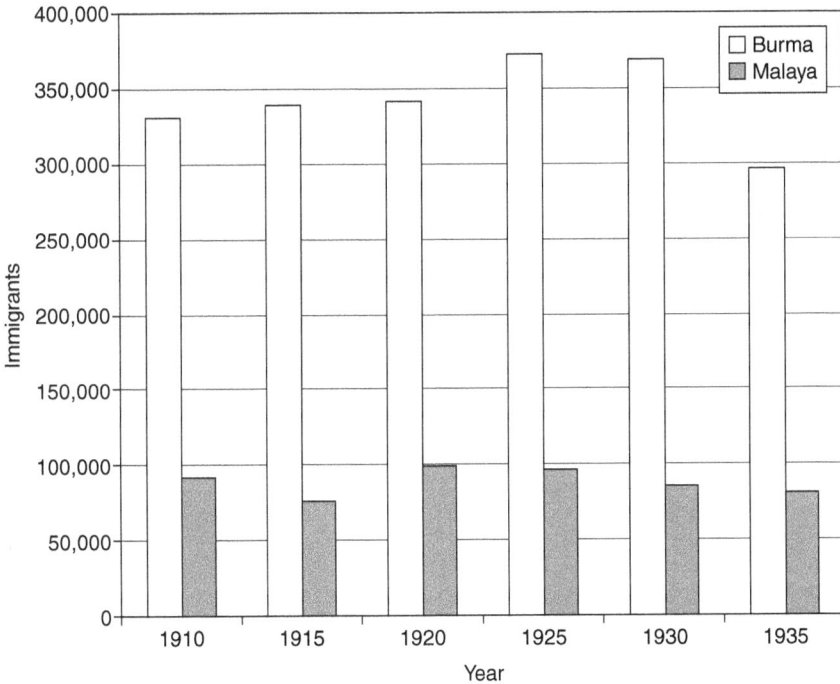

Figure 5.1 Burma and Malaya: comparative flows of Indian immigrants, 1910–35 (selected years) (source: Sandhu (1969: 157)).

between 1911 and 1947, as shown in Table 5.2, and, together with the Chinese, had outnumbered the 'Malaysians' by 1940.

Nevertheless, Indians had a lesser impact on economic and communal structures in Malaya. About 90 per cent of them were unskilled labourers and a very large number lived in isolated plantation communities. With the plantation as the 'boundary of their existence', they had fewer contacts with the indigenous Malays (Kaur 1998, 2004).

Indian workers in Burma: farm and factory labourers

There were three phases in the growth of the Burmese rice industry: the open frontier, 1870–1900; maturity and change, 1900–29; and depression and social problems, 1930–40. These phases corresponded with the fluctuating fortunes of the industry and Burma's increased dependence on world markets (Adas 1974) and migration inflows. British land policy and the transformation of rice production into 'industrial agriculture' also led to a clear division between cultivation

Table 5.1 Burma: total and Indian population, 1872–1931

Census year	Total population	Indian population	Indian % of population
1872	2,747,148	136,504	4.9
1881	3,736,771	243,123	6.5
1891	8,098,014	420,830	5.1
1901	10,490,624	568,263	5.4
1911	12,115,217	743,288	6.1
1921	13,212,192	887,077	6.7
1931	14,667,146	1,017,825	6.9

Source: Baxter (1941: 5).

Table 5.2 Malaya: population by ethnic group, 1911–47 (numbers in thousands, percentages as a proportion of total population)

Year	Malaysians[1]		Chinese		Indians[2]	
	No.	%	No.	%	No.	%
1911	1,438	54	917	34	267	10
1921	1,651	49	1,175	35	472	14
1931	1,962	45	1,709	39	624	14
1947	2,544	43	2,615	45	600	10

Source: Malaya: Census Reports 1911–47.

Notes
1 'Malaysians' include Malays and Indonesians.
2 Includes Pakistanis after 1947.
3 The table excludes 'other' races.

and processing activities and further specialisation in the cultivation, financing, processing and exporting of rice (Furnivall 1948: 116). As Burmese labour became scarce, Burmese cultivators turned to Indian labour to carry out tasks such as the construction and repair of bunds, ploughing, transplanting of seedlings, harvesting and threshing. The cultivators also increasingly became reliant on Burmese or Indian Chettiar moneylenders to finance their activities. Three main groups thus emerged in the rice industry: Burmese cultivators, who also processed some of the rice; Indian financiers, field workers and rice-mill workers; and European firms, which dominated the processing of rice and its export.

Indian rice-farm workers' employment was seasonal and regulated by the different phases of the rice season. From September to March, Indian workers carried out a range of tasks associated with the cultivation and harvesting of rice. Between March and the following September, they either departed for India, or found casual work at the rice mills in the towns or at the docks. The rice-production cycle thus determined the seasonal character of most Indians' employment, but not entirely. Although some of these workers made a return trip to India annually, they normally worked for a minimum of three years in Burma (Pillai 1947: 101).

Overseas exports of rice began in the mid-1860s, utilising the ports of Rangoon, Bassein, Akyab and Moulmein. Rangoon came to dominate the export trade in rice, and rice mills were mainly located at this port until the end of the nineteenth century. Subsequently, in the decade prior to the First World War, rice mills were increasingly established elsewhere near water and rail transportation lines. While a proportion of the padi was processed locally for domestic consumption, Indian brokers and contractors purchased large quantities that they transported to the rice mills. The manufacture of the finished product was dominated by Europeans while the mill labour force comprised mainly Indian workers, who were hired out to the European- and Indian-owned mills by labour contractors (Cheng 1968, 1989: 132–3). These workers formed the backbone of the rice mill labour force in Burmese towns.

Governance of migration

The colonial government had encouraged Indians to migrate as colonists to Burma soon after the annexation of Pegu in 1852. In the mid 1870s, consistent with the growing demand for Burmese rice, Indians were encouraged to migrate both as agriculturalists and as labourers. Subsequently, in 1876, the Indian Government enacted a Labour Act which provided for the appointment of an Emigration Agent and a Medical Inspector of Emigrants to 'regulate the methods of recruitment, transport and employment and to safeguard the welfare of emigrants' destined for Burma (Cheng 1961: 119). Migration under this scheme proved to be unsuccessful principally because mill owners found the conditions of the Labour Act onerous and preferred to obtain their labour force through the agency of the labour contractors which enabled them to both manage and control workers. Consequently, Indian labour migration was 'entirely uncontrolled' and there was no one responsible for the welfare or protection of the immigrants after they had actually landed in Burma. Ostensibly, migrants were 'free' men who landed in Burma without any debt. The reality was quite different.

The labour migrants, comprising mainly Tamils and Telegus from the poverty-stricken areas of South India, did not have the funds to move to Burma. They thus had to rely on two groups of intermediaries: the recruiting agent (who acted on behalf of the labour contractor); and the labour contractor, known as *maistry* in the Telegu districts of South India. The recruiting agents went to the villages to recruit workers who were then handed over to labour contractors. The latter transported them to the emigration depot where they underwent official migration procedures and attested that they were migrating of their own free will. They were then taken to their place of employment in Burma and remained under the charge of the *maistry*. From these simple origins the *maistry* system gradually evolved into a multi-tiered recruitment mechanism and authority system, and abuse and exploitation were enshrined at every level (Kaur 2006). According to Adapa, the relationship between the *maistry* and the labourer was of 'mutual but unequal interdependence' and relied on patronage networks (Adapa 2002: 101). Apart from the *maistry* recruitment system, shipping companies such as, for example, the British Indian Steam Navigation Company, also acted as labour recruiters, deploying a network of middlemen/intermediaries stationed at port towns in South India.

Although the *maistry* system closely resembled the *kangani* system in Malaya (see below), there were major differences between the two. The *maistry* was for all intents and purposes the de facto employer of Indian (factory) labour. In the early decades of the twentieth century he contracted out for the 'entire care' of a commodity. He arranged migration, was responsible for accommodation and travel arrangements and paid the workers. Thompson states that there was often no indication of the number of workers required and the *maistry's* contract with a firm consisted of an agreement to supply 'those needed'. He had to pay a deposit as security to the firm with whom he had contracted to supply workers, and relied on the gang *maistries* to both supply and manage the workers (Thompson 1947: 43). This enlarged function of the *maistry* in Burma can be attributed to the seasonal nature of employment in most occupations, unlike the 'permanent' employment of Indians on Malayan plantations.

Apart from the fact that Burmese peasants were unwilling to work under harsh conditions for meagre wages in towns, Indians were 'preferred' for three main reasons. They were considered a 'fluid' labour supply; they cost less to hire and manage compared with Burmese workers; and their accommodation costs were also cheaper since they could be housed in sub-standard tenement housing. Unregulated labour migration also meant that there was a general lack of supervision of Indian labour immigration into Burma.

The making of a community?

The preference for male migrants, diverse occupational categories, harsh work regimes and seasonality of employment impacted on Indian sex ratios in Burma and the making of an Indian community. According to Kondapi, the sex ratio varied from 8.2 males to one female to as high as 250 males to one female (1951: 92). This wide divergence was due to occupational and caste (or class) differentiation. High caste/class men left their families behind in India since they travelled frequently between the two countries. Workers employed on ships as engine room and deck crew also left their families behind due to the nature of their occupations. Moreover, the living conditions of urban factory workers – cramped quarters and a lack of privacy – discouraged workers on short-term contracts from taking their spouses with them. Thus, with the exception of Arakan province, the number of Indians who settled permanently in Burma formed only a small proportion of those who arrived as workers.

Indian workers in Malaya: the rubber-plantation industry

The spread of plantation agriculture in Malaya was consistent with the economic penetration that accompanied the diversification of economic activity, changing production technologies and the emergence of new markets for tropical products in the West. By the second decade of the twentieth century, Malaya had emerged as the world's largest rubber producer. Much of the development was concentrated in the western half of Malaya in areas already well provided with roads and railways (Kaur 1985: 3).

Governance of migration

Plantations were established in sparsely populated areas in the western half of the country and planters had to look overseas for workers willing to work under frontier conditions. The colonial government, itself a major employer, favoured a regulated migrant labour supply and the avoidance of excessive dependence on any one racial group. The European companies also recruited workers from three racial groups – Indians, Chinese and Javanese. Of these, (South) Indians were the preferred workforce. A major drawback was that the South Indians lacked the funds for spontaneous mass migration, and consequently, from the start, the recruitment of Indian plantation labour was both regulated and sponsored by the Malayan administration.

Until 1923, Indian immigration to Malaya was regulated first by the Indian government, and then by the Straits Settlement and the Federated Malay States governments. In 1923, following enactment of the Indian Emigration Act of 1922, the Indian government took over the management of Indian emigration to Malaya. Labour regulations were framed that defined hours of work, working conditions and welfare provisions for Indian workers. Moreover, an Agent of the Government of India was appointed in Malaya to ensure that these regulations were honoured in the workplace. Thus, unlike Burma, Malaya's 'independent' political status vis-à-vis India enabled the Indian government to station an Agent who had some measure of authority to investigate Indian labour's working conditions on estates and other places of employment in Malaya. The Agent could also make recommendations to the Malayan government in cases of perceived infringement of the regulations. Nevertheless, employers could not be compelled to accept the Agent's recommendations. Crucially, workers remained chained to their workplaces by their contracts and the powers of the state.

The main mechanism for recruiting Indian migrant labour was the indenture contract whereby employers used sanctions to enforce wage-labour agreements. The workers were contracted to a single employer for between one and three years. The contract was normally a written one and a breach of the contract was regarded as a criminal rather than a civil offence. At the end of the contract, the worker had to repay the travel and associated costs (or these were paid through deductions) before he was released from his contract. Since most workers were too poor (they earned very low wages), they were re-indentured for a further period (Kaur 2004; Parmer 1960).

Another important mechanism for the recruitment of Indian labour was the *kangani* system, whereby planters sent established labourers to India to recruit other labourers from their villages or home districts (Sandhu 1969: 89). The *kangani* was paid a commission for each labourer recruited and acted as a plantation foreman for the labourers recruited by him. The contractual position of workers recruited under this system was less harsh than that under indenture. The contract was usually an oral contract, the worker had the right to terminate his contract and desertion was regarded as a civil rather than as a criminal offence. Nevertheless, this system too was open to abuse since the *kangani* usually had a vested interest in ensuring that the labourers did not abscond – he received 'head money' for every day worked by each labourer. The colonial government subsequently introduced legislation for the licensing of *kanganies* in 1901 to reduce worker abuse by the *kangani*.

Between 1844 and 1910, about 250,000 indentured labourers came to Malaya (Sandhu 1969: 81). The peak of *kangani*-assisted recruitment occurred in the 1910s, when about 50,000 to 80,000 Indian workers arrived per annum. *Kangani*-assisted recruitment began to decline in the late 1920s associated with the global economic downturn, was suspended during the Great Depression and formally abolished in 1938. As in Burma, improvements in workers' living and working conditions in Malaya were conditional on global economic conditions, government policy and the goodwill of employers and intermediaries. The specific political relationship between the India office, the Colonial Office in London, and government in Burma and Malaya was equally significant. As Tinker reminds us, the conditions of Indian factory workers in Burma were 'infinitely worse' and on 'the doorstep of India, Indian labourers were treated as harshly as in the most distant colony' (Tinker 1974: 373).

The making of a community

The Indian plantation labour force comprised predominantly single adult males, hired as individuals. Married men were discouraged from emigrating because they could not bring their families since wages were low; the norm of payment was a single-person wage; working conditions were harsh; and accommodation was available for single men only. Nevertheless, there was a small stream of women migrant workers during the period. In the nineteenth century, approximately one in ten Indian migrants were female. Women's work was also considered less important than men's, and this impacted on the gender division of labour on the plantations, resulting in differential wage scales, with women paid lower wages than men.

Workers had to carry out a wide range of tasks on plantations, which included tapping, weeding, sorting of seeds and general maintenance. This diversity of tasks and agitation for a more stable Indian society on the plantation frontier led to increasing calls for more female labour recruitment in the twentieth century. From the 1920s the Indian government began to focus on the gender imbalance among emigrants and its concerns were embodied in subsequent legislation. By far the most important legislation in this regard was the Indian Emigration Act of 1922 and the Indian Emigration Rules of 1923 that stipulated that there should be at least one female emigrant for every 1.5 males (Ramasamy 1994: 27).

Notwithstanding the fact that Malaya was repeatedly exempted from the gender-ratio provisions of the above legislation (it was cheaper to rely on a constant supply of new workers), a striking feature of the *kangani*-assisted recruitment system was the emigration of families. Female emigration was encouraged through the reduction of the assessment paid on women workers, in order to improve the sex ratio and reproduce the workforce. The *kangani* also earned a higher commission for women migrant workers as well as for married couples. Furthermore, amendments to the Labour Code in Malaya stipulated the provision of rooms for married couples as well as childcare and educational facilities. On arrival in Malaya, voluntary or non-recruited assisted migrants and their families and dependents were provided with free transport to their place of employment and other facilities.

Indian women workers' participation rate in the formal sector (principally rubber cultivation) was proportionately higher than that of the more numerous Malay and Chinese women in the country. This was largely due to the type of economic activity Indians were engaged in, rather than the cultural attitudes or values of Indians. Since wages paid to plantation workers were low, almost all working-age members of families sought employment on the plantation. The provision of childcare centres of some sort facilitated women's participation in the paid workforce. During the period 1911–47, women workers (principally Indian) formed between 9.4 per cent and 32 per cent of the total commercial agricultural workforce (Kaur 1986: 5–6).

Increased female recruitment and the migration of families are reflected in the census statistics for 1901, 1911, 1921, 1931 and 1947. The proportion of Indian women in these census years for every 1,000 Indian men was: 171 in 1901; 308 in 1911; 406 in 1921; 482 in 1931; and 637 in 1947 (Ramachandran 1994: 32). These statistics also explain the increasing trend towards permanent settlement by Indian labour by the 1930s. With increased female migration, more children also arrived in Malaya, and by the 1920s women accounted for 30 per cent of all arrivals from India. More children were also born in Malaya and raised locally, contributing to the transition towards permanent settlement, and the availability of a pool of workers. Hence, job possibilities for women on plantations and elsewhere, the provisions of the 1922 Emigration Act, the Emigration Rules 1923, and the establishment and reconstitution of families led to greater permanent Indian settlement in Malaya.

Indian auxiliaries and the Indian business community

Apart from the rural (rice-farm and rubber-plantation) workers and urban labouring class, Indian auxiliaries in colonial employment (predominantly in Malaya) and Indian commercial migrants formed a distinct urban community. These migrant groups exercised a monopoly of political, economic and social influence in the Indian community that was disproportionate to their numbers.

The auxiliaries in Malaya comprised predominantly North Indians (particularly Sikhs), who were first hired as policemen in the Straits Settlements in the 1880s. They were also employed as a paramilitary force, namely the Malay States Guides, which was formed in 1896, following the creation of the Federated Malay States. They were also much sought after as security guards, 'watchmen' and caretakers by the colonial state and the private sector. Whether in the public or private sector, the majority of the Sikhs migrated as single adult males, and there was little family movement until the late 1930s and after the Second World War. Apart from the security personnel, Sikhs migrated as free men (and women), utilising their own or family resources and Sikh *gurdwaras* (temples) played a key role in their migration and settlement in Malaya. The *gurdwaras* were guesthouses for travellers, places of worship and community centres and enabled Malayan Sikhs to connect with other Sikhs and the larger Sikh 'nation'. This distinctiveness was acknowledged by the appointment of specific Sikh community leaders, as opposed to Indian community leaders, in colonial society. Other North Indians were predominantly merchants, traders, shopkeepers and pedlars (Kaur 1974).

Of the traders, the Gujaratis were the most widespread and important Indian group and conducted international trade throughout Southeast Asia. From their base in Gujarat on the west coast of India, these skilled shippers and traders formed part of the vast trading network that linked western Indian ports with ports on the eastern shores of the Bay of Bengal. These included the Burmese ports of the Irrawaddy delta, Thai ports and Malay ports. The Gujaratis plied routes linking West Asia, the Mediterranean, Southeast Asia, Japan and China. They were specialist textile traders, distributing silk and cotton textiles from

Ahmedabad and Baroda to the Southeast Asian region in exchange for rice and teak from Burma, pepper and tin from western Indonesia and Malaya, and spices gathered in the Straits of Melaka from the neighbouring regions. Gujarati ship owners controlled the inter-island trade and parts of the international trade with western Asia and Europe.

Like the Chettiars, the Gujaratis also developed a financial trading system throughout the region. They operated as bankers and merchant bankers and their letters of credit (*hundi*) issued in one region could be cashed in another. The arrival of the Europeans in the sixteenth century resulted in the dispersal of the spice trade and forced the Gujarati and Malabar Muslim networks to expand into other areas as well. In the nineteenth and twentieth centuries the Gujaratis became increasingly important as compradors (shroffs) to Western banks in Southeast Asia, securing credit for large urban textile firms or opium traders, with networks extending from Persia (Iran) and China. The Gujaratis also provided short-term credit to the Chettiars. Their dominance in the Indian textile trade in the urban areas of Singapore, Malaya, Sabah and Sarawak, Indonesia and Bangkok continues to this day.

Among the Indian financiers, the South Indian Chettiar money-lending caste played a major role as regional suppliers of credit in the expansion of export production in Burma and Malaya. The Chettiar financial networks were based on a complex structure of independent family firms that undertook money lending and commodity trading activities. In this flexible partnership structure, members of a particular family could hold partnerships in many different firms. Each partnership operated through a system of overseas agents who were usually younger partners. In Burma they were the wealthiest of the Indian groups and it is alleged that by 1937 they had taken over about one-quarter of Burma's best rice-land. The Chettiars also handled the remittances of the overseas Indian communities and during the interwar period, they made the transition from primarily short-term moneylenders to bankers, long-term creditors of trade and manufacturing, and land and property owners in both countries. They fled Burma in early 1942 when the Japanese invaded the country.

Indians in Burma and Malaya: needed, not wanted

Though acknowledged as British subjects, both the British and the indigenous inhabitants regarded Indians in Burma and Malaya as contract workers/sojourners. After the Second World War they were no longer welcome in either territory. The ending of colonial rule in Burma and Malaya was thus noteworthy for two major reasons. First, in the domain of immigration policy, more restrictive legislation was implemented to reduce Indian immigration and this was largely dictated by economic and socio-political considerations. Second, new border control regimes and internal enforcement measures were enforced by the 'modern' nation state, devised primarily to differentiate between the indigenous inhabitants and the resident 'aliens' particularly with respect to economic and political rights. In Burma, for example, as tension increased between the

Rohingya, a Bengali Muslim minority and the local Rakhine population in Arakan state in the 1970s, the Burmese government announced that the Rohingya did not qualify for citizenship and denied them access to basic social, educational and health services. Subsequently, in March 1978, the Burmese government arrested large numbers of the Rohingya community and expelled them from Burma. This forced migration created the Rohingya refugee community, with many fleeing to Bangladesh, Thailand and Malaysia (Kaur 2007). In Malaysia, Indians became the most marginalised community in the country.

The 'new' globalisation, the global labour market and Indians in Southeast Asia since the 1990s

International labour migration, which had virtually ceased after the Second World War, expanded rapidly in Southeast Asia across sovereign national borders in the 1980s and again became associated with growth and development in countries like Singapore and Malaysia. This has enabled them to overcome labour shortages and ease skill imbalances. Three important features characterise this labour migration. First, the migration intake comprises both skilled and less-skilled workers. Second, conditions of work and employment contracts favour skilled migrants. While less-skilled workers are recruited as temporary guest workers on a rotating basis from a range of countries, knowledge workers and skilled migrants are a privileged group (especially in Singapore). Third, India has once again emerged as an important source of knowledge workers and migrant labour. Indian knowledge workers in particular move easily between India and Southeast Asia, and are successfully promoting India's image in the host countries. Although they utilise Indian networks and rely on local contacts with Indian communities in the region, they have multiple identities and present challenges for integration in these countries. The following discussion focuses on Singapore and Malaysia, the main destination countries for Indian migrants in Southeast Asia.

Singapore

At present, migrant Indian labour in Singapore is employed under two distinct categories. The first includes various labour-intensive sectors such as construction and shipping where workers are hired on two-year work permits. These contract workers are expected to return home after a contractual period, unless they have acquired further training or obtained trade certificates in Singapore's vocational and technical institutes. The training enables them to be re-classified as skilled workers who may subsequently continue to work in the country over the longer term. The second comprises skilled workers who work mainly in tertiary institutions and in the engineering, information technology, business, banking and financial sectors. A large majority in this category comprise professionals who hold tertiary qualifications and are employed as senior executives in local and multinational companies, or are engaged in specialist research work, or manage their own firms in the ICT, engineering and accountancy sectors. These knowledge workers are encouraged to take up permanent residency (and ultimately citizenship), depending on the skill requirements of the country.

Both categories of Indian workers contribute to the progress of the Singaporean economy but only the second, larger group is privileged. Moreover, whilst Singapore regards India as an important source for upgrading its human resources, Singapore in turn holds an attraction for Indian knowledge workers due to its proximity to India, a congenial socio-cultural environment, world-class infrastructure in terms of housing and educational facilities, and competitive taxation rates. Singapore has also emerged as a major investor in India. Thus complementarities between Singapore and India have facilitated skilled Indian migration to Singapore.

The Singapore government has also facilitated the migration of Indian knowledge workers through several initiatives. For example, it established a 'Contact Singapore' centre in Chennai that provides information on employment and settlement policies. Moreover, it organised the recruitment of Indian professionals through tie-ups with the private sector and, in 2000, for example, the Infocomm Development Authority of Singapore (IDA) signed an agreement with an Indian firm to recruit a thousand Indian ICT professionals within a year. In 2005 Singapore and India also signed a Comprehensive Economic Cooperation Agreement (CECA), covering labour migration in addition to trade in goods, services and investment. Under CECA, both India and Singapore have recognised ICT professionals in 18 areas of computer related services that include systems design and analysis, software engineering and programming, database analysis, information technology quality assurance and computer engineering. Professional bodies are encouraged to negotiate Mutual Recognition Agreements. This agreement is expected to increase the number of Indian ICT professionals in Singapore (Gaur 2006).

The arrival of Indian knowledge workers has resulted in a further stratification of the Indian community. Although a sizeable group occupies the middle and higher sectors of Singaporean society, the Indian community is also well represented at the bottom of the social hierarchy. Additionally, in recent years many well-qualified Indians have migrated to developed countries like Australia and New Zealand, as part of the secondary migration from Southeast Asia.

Malaysia

As in Singapore, Indian migrants are employed in both the less-skilled and skilled categories. Under the first, unskilled and semi-skilled workers are recruited on temporary rotating contracts in a selected range of occupations. The recruitment of this group of Indian workers corresponds with the recruitment of other less-skilled workers from other parts of the world. This category of Indian workers is restricted to specific occupations as shown in Table 5.3.

Unlike Singapore, Malaysia utilises Memoranda of Understanding (MoUs) with neighbouring countries as instruments for negotiating rules governing the employment of less-skilled migrants. The MoUs are 'elaborate systems' for the temporary employment of the nationals of one country in the other and require

Table 5.3 Malaysia: sectors permitted to recruit foreign workers, 2006

Sector	Source country
Construction	Philippines (male), Indonesia, Cambodia, Kazakhstan, Laos, Myanmar, Nepal, Thailand, Turkmenistan, Uzbekistan and Vietnam, Bangladesh (Effective 1 August 2006)
Manufacturing	Philippines (male), Indonesia (female), Cambodia, Kazakhstan, Laos, Myanmar, Nepal, Thailand, Turkmenistan, Uzbekistan and Vietnam, Bangladesh (Effective 1 August 2006)
Plantation/agriculture	Philippines (male), Indonesia, India, Cambodia, Kazakhstan, Laos, Myanmar, Nepal, Thailand, Turkmenistan, Uzbekistan and Vietnam, Bangladesh (Effective 1 August 2006)
Service	
Restaurant	All source countries for general worker posts (except India – cooks only). Restaurants in major towns in Peninsular Malaysia.
Laundry	All source countries except India.
Cleaning/sanitation	All source countries except India.
Caddy	All source countries except India.
Resort islands	All source countries except India.
Welfare homes	All source countries except India.
Cargo	All source countries except India.
High tension cable	India only.
Domestic workers	Sri Lanka, Indonesia, Thailand, Philippines and Cambodia.
Foreign nurses	Albania, India, Bangladesh, Philippines, Pakistan, Indonesia and Myanmar.

Source: Ministry of Home Affairs, Malaysia. Online. Available at: www.moha.gov.my/opencms/export/KHEDN/BhgB/dasarpekerja.html (accessed 4 September 2007).

active participation and oversight by both countries. These MoUs specify the terms and conditions of workers and both governments are required to ensure the return of workers to their countries upon completion of their employment contracts. The MoUs are also revised as the situation requires in either country. The MoUs are thus a governance structure for recruitment and repatriation policies and also for the protection of workers in host countries. In March 2005 the Indian and Malaysian governments took the first steps towards a formal agreement on manpower recruitment from India on a contract basis. It is estimated that Indians comprised about 4 per cent of work permit/temporary contract workers in 2003 (Kassim 2005, Table 4).

Indian professional (expatriate) workers play a premier role in the ICT industry and in the higher education, engineering and health sectors. Unlike Singapore, however, permanent residency is not offered on the same basis in Malaysia. Singapore is thus the preferred destination for Indian knowledge workers and skilled migrants. Indian dominance in the knowledge workers/professionals category is shown in Figure 5.2.

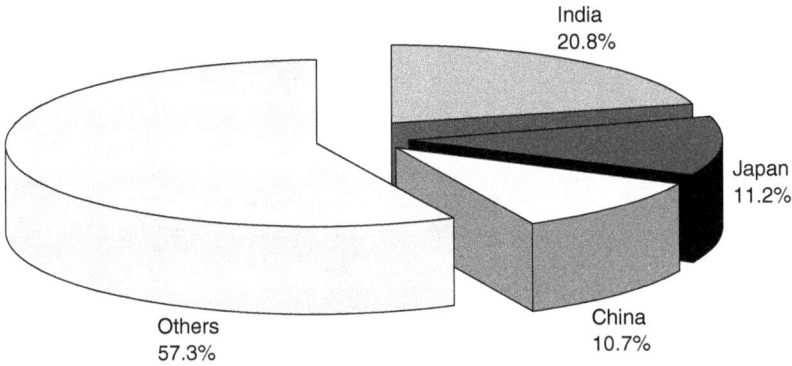

Figure 5.2 Malaysia: expatriates by country of origin, 2006 (as a percentage) (source: *Malaysia: Economic Report* 2006/7, p. 7.)

Note
As in Singapore, therefore, the position of the 'new' Indian migrants highlights issues arising from the challenge of transnationalisation of the Indian community.

Indians in Southeast Asia: prospect and retrospect

The declining importance of Southeast Asia's Indian minorities since the mid-1950s appears to have been arrested by the current demand for Indian professional migrants and contract workers. India is also considered less daunting than China by Malaysia. Moreover, Indian communities in Malaysia and Singapore have strengthened social, religious and cultural bonds with India in an increasingly globalised Asia. The Indian Government's current policy of developing links with wealthy and successful overseas Indian communities and its celebration of *Pravasi Bharatiya Divas* – Day of the Persons of Indian origin and Non-resident Indians – has also played a role in this process. In 2003, for example, the president of Malaysia's Malaysian Indian Congress, Datuk Seri Samy Velu, was awarded the Indian Diaspora Award. Notwithstanding this, India's neglect of the poorer Indian overseas communities has come under increasing criticism by social commentators in Malaysia and Singapore.

Note

1 Prior to 1940 Malaya included both Singapore and Peninsular Malaysia.

References

Adapa, S. (2002) '"Birds of Passage": Migration of South Indian Laborers to Southeast Asia', *Critical Asian Studies*, 34(1): 89–115.
Adas, M. (1974) *The Burma Delta: Economic Development and Social Change on an Asian Rice Frontier, 1852–1941*, Madison, WI: University of Wisconsin Press.
Baxter, J. (1941) *Report on Indian Immigration*, Rangoon: Government Printer.

Cheng, S.H. (1968) *The Rice Industry of Burma, 1852–1940*, Kuala Lumpur: University of Malaya Press.

Furnivall, J.S. (1956) *Colonial Policy and Practice: A Comparative Study of Burma and Netherlands India*, New York: New York University Press.

Kaur, A. (2007) Refugees and Refugee Policy in Malaysia, in A. Kaur and I. Metcalfe (eds) *UNEAC Asia Papers* (No 18), Special Issue on 'Refugees and Refugee Policies in the Asia-Pacific region', pp. 77–90. Online. Available at: www.une.edu.au/asiacenter/UNEAC_Asia_Papers_12–19.html (accessed 4 September 2007).

—— (2006) 'Indian Labour, Labour Standards, and Workers' Health in Burma and Malaya, 1900–1940', *Modern Asian Studies*, 40(2): 393–444.

—— (2004) *Wage Labour in Southeast Asia: Globalisation. The International Division of Labour and Labour Transformations*, Basingstoke: Palgrave Macmillan.

—— (1998) 'Tappers and Weeders: South Indian Plantation Workers in Malaysia, 1880–1970', *South Asia* (Special Volume, L. Brennan and B.V. Lal (eds) *Across the Kala Pani*) XXI: 73–102.

—— (1986) 'Women at Work in Malaysia', in H.A. Yun and R. Talib (eds) *Women and Employment in Malaysia*, special issue of *Jurnal Manusia dan Masyarakat* Kuala Lumpur: University of Malaya, pp. 1–16.

—— (1985) *Bridge and Barrier: Transport and Communications in Colonial Malaya*, Singapore: Oxford University Press.

—— (1973/74) 'North Indians in Malaya: A Study of their Economic, Social and Political Activities, 1870–1940s', Thesis (MA), University of Malaya.

Kondapi, C. (1951) *Indians Overseas, 1838–1949*, New Delhi: Indian Council of World Affairs.

Ministry of Home Affairs, Malaysia. Online. Available at: www.moha.gov.my/opencms/export/KHEDN/BhgB/dasarpekerja.html (accessed 4 September 2007).

Parmer, N.J. (1960) *Colonial Labour Policy and Administration: A History of Labour in the Rubber Plantation Industry in Malaya*, New York: J.J. Augustin for the Association for Asian Studies.

Pillai, P.P. (1947) *Labour in South East Asia*, New Delhi: Indian Council of World Affairs.

Rai, R. (2006) 'Indians in Singapore', in B.V. Lal, P. Reeves and R. Rai (eds), *The Encyclopedia of the Indian Diaspora*, Singapore: Editions Didier Millet, pp. 176–88.

Ramachandran, S. (1994) *Indian Plantation Labour in Malaya*, Kuala Lumpur: S. Abdul Majeed & Co. for Institute of Social Analysis (INSAN).

Ramasamy, P. (1996) *Plantation Labour: Unions, Capital and the State*, Basingstoke: Macmillan.

Sandhu, K.S. (1969) *Indians in Malaya: Some Aspects of their Immigration and Settlement*, Cambridge: Cambridge University Press.

Thompson, V.T. (1947) *Labour Problems in South-east Asia*, New Haven, CT: Yale University Press.

—— (1945) *Notes on Labour Problems in Burma and Thailand*, Secretariat Paper No. 8, typescript, New York: Institute of Pacific Relations.

—— (1943) *Post-Mortem on Malaya*, New York: Macmillan.

Tinker, H. (1974) *A New System of Slavery: The Export of Indian Labour Overseas, 1830–1920*, London: Oxford University Press.

6 Indo-Fijians

Roots and routes

Brij V. Lal

Florida, Utah, Montana, Louisiana, Gladstone, Victoria, Eve, Plato, Jacob. Names of esoteric places and famous people, you might say. That they are. But they are also the names of the first Indian children born in Fiji. They were born not in Rewa or Rakiraki or Raralevu, later to become important centres of Indo-Fijian settlement on Fiji's main island of Viti Levu, but on the remote, tiny, island of Rabi, on planter John Hill's estate, the largest employer of the first batch of Indian indentured labourers to arrive in Fiji. The new migrants were sent there because other European planters who were expected to recruit them were angry with the government for prohibiting the employment of Fijian labour and so they sullenly refused to have anything to do with the new comers. Sir Arthur Gordon, Fiji's first governor and the chief architect of the indenture scheme – he had seen its operation in Mauritius and Trinidad where he had been governor before coming to Fiji – was disappointed, but not despairing. By the early 1880s, the prospects brightened considerably with the expansion of the sugar industry under the – recently arrived – Australian-owned Colonial Sugar Refining Company (CSR), which would go on to dominate not only the industry but also Fiji's economy for nearly a century until its departure in 1973.

Between *Leonidas'* inaugural voyage in 1879 and *Sutlej V*'s last in 1916, 87 ships, specially designed to carry human cargo in difficult conditions over interminably long distances, ferried 60,000 men, women and children from Calcutta and Madras to Fiji. They had such magical names, after great rivers and classical figures: *Danube, Elbe, Ganges, Jamuna, Rhine, Avon, Syria, Pericles, Leonidas*. Remarkably, only one of the 87 ships, the *Syria* in 1884, perished through negligent navigation, on the reefs at Nasilai, claiming 59 lives, though the long journey itself – three months by sailing ship and one by steamship – broke many land-locked lives and disrupted irreparably the settled habits, practices and thoughts of ancient village India. The voyage across the *kala pani*, the dark, dreaded seas, was a great leveller of hierarchy and protocol. But the destruction also contained within it seeds for rejuvenation, for from the fragments of a common past and a mutual predicament, a shared destiny and a common destination, emerged other bonds. None was more emotionally powerful than the bond of the *jahajibhai*, brotherhood of the crossing, as intimate and comforting as real blood kinship which men cherished well into their twilight as a mark of solidarity against the asperities and alienations of the strange outside world.

In the end, some 24,000 of the indentured migrants and their families (some born in Fiji) returned to India, but the majority stayed on, attracted by the promise of possibilities in their new homeland and the fear of the reception they might receive in India having broken taboos – marrying across caste lines, eating food cooked by unknown hands, doing work considered ritually polluting – taboos still held sacrosanct at home. Many talked, and continued to talk, until well into old age of returning one day, but the day of decision never came as memories of the past frayed and faded and the realities of life in a new place took hold. That new life was fraught. Ancestral wisdom had to be adapted. New pragmatic, cross-caste relationships had to be established. A new geography had to be understood, a new vocabulary mastered.

This the *girmitiyas* and their descendants did with resilience and resignation, often on their own, without a helping hand. In time, their labour laid the foundation of the Fijian economy, illiterate thumb-prints seen most visibly in the undulating seas of green cane fields across vast, often inhospitable, stretches of previously untamed terrain, in the damp paddy fields of the Rewa and Navua deltas, in the slowly emerging market towns in the cane belts, precursors to modern urban centres, in rudimentary structures on the way to becoming ground-breaking primary and secondary schools, in the steady stream of school children leaving the village environment to enter the world of the professions beyond even the imagined horizons of their parents.

There are many ways of narrating the complex and fascinating story of the Indo-Fijian experience – through fiction, for instance, or through detached historical narrative. I choose the device of autobiography for this essay, convinced of the truth of the great Australian historian K.S. Inglis' contention that a 'lot of history is concealed autobiography'. I use personal experience to humanise a story whose broad features are well known but whose inner configurations remain largely unexplored. Autobiography, I find, facilitates the excavation of worlds hidden from the public gaze. My experience is not exceptional. In it many of my generation in Fiji will, I hope, hear the echoes of their own footsteps, markers of their own special moments.

My direct link with Fiji begins in 1908. That was the year my grandfather came to Fiji as a *girmitiya*. *Aja* (grandfather) was lucky in one respect: he arrived in Fiji when the worst abuses of *girmit* were over – the heart-rending infant-mortality rates of the 1890s, the excessive over-tasking, the physical violence on the plantations, an uncertain life on the raw edges of extreme vulnerability.[1] In 1907, there were 30,920 Indians living in Fiji, of whom only 11,689 were under indenture. The freed population – *Khula* – was cultivating 17,204 acres of land on their own, 5,586 devoted to cane and 9,347 planted with rice. In time, sugar cane cultivation would become the principal occupation of the Indian population (Coulter 1967: 90–1). By 1911, of the 40,286 Indians, 27 per cent had been born in the colony, the Fiji-born proportion of the population increasing rapidly with time, until, by 1946, they became the outright majority of the population, spawning the threat of 'Indian domination' that would bedevil the country's complex political negotiations as it lurched towards independence in the 1960s.

As young children, we heard stories about indenture from *Aja* and other grizzled, *dhoti*-wearing *girmitiyas* – the hard work at the first light of dawn, about overseers good and bad and indifferent, the fraught family life in the estate lines, the cultural confusions and transgressions that pervaded plantation life, the peculiar ways in which they attempted to make sense of their predicament. I heard these stories long before I read scholarly accounts of the indenture experience at university. These accounts, most famously Hugh Tinker's *A New System of Slavery* (1974), captured our imagination. I read it in the final year of my undergraduate degree at university. That book, with its catchy, memorable title, emotionally appealing but intellectually suspect, set the tone of the new historiography.[2] *Girmit* was slavery by another name, nothing more, the book informed us. The indentured labourers themselves were gullible simpletons from impoverished rural backgrounds, hoodwinked into migrating by unscrupulous recruiters (*arkatis*), and brutalised by the unrelenting pace of work on the plantations, their sufferings ignored, their women molested by the overseers and *sirdars* (Indian foremen), their families separated, their dignity in tatters.

The 'whips-and-chains' story is still a dominant part of the public discourse and understanding of *girmit* even though the new indenture historiography casts serious doubts about its explanatory value.[3] There is of course undeniable truth in the indenture-as-slavery thesis. Many *girmitiyas* were broken by work, claimed by disease or wrecked by human violence and greed. Suffering and pain were an integral part of indenture. All this is abundantly clear from the historical record (Lal 2000). But it is not the whole story. It cannot be. It is possible to acknowledge hardship while granting *girmitiyas* agency as a people who had a hand in shaping their destiny.

A central plank of the slavery thesis is that deception and fraudulence played a key role in the recruitment process. Migration was not an integral part of Indian society or psyche, the argument goes, and no one in their right minds would therefore ever leave their home for places unknown or unheard of. The Indian peasant was a landlubber, bound to the soil by strict codes of ritually authorised behaviour, not an intrepid explorer of unknown, pollution-threatening worlds. But that's not how things actually were. In the nineteenth century, rural India was in the throes of profound change caused by the introduction of new notions of private ownership of property, increasing fragmentation of land holdings, deepening indebtedness among the peasantry, the effects of natural calamities. Places in eastern Uttar Pradesh, which furnished 45,000 of Fiji's 60,000 migrants – the remainder came from South India after 1903 when sources in the North had begun to dry up – were particularly adversely affected. As employment opportunities there diminished, people moved about in search of a better life elsewhere. It was the natural thing to do.

And so, large numbers left – for the Assam tea gardens, the Calcutta jute mills and factories, the Bihar coal mines and the Bombay textile mills. Between

1891 and 1911, many districts in the Indo-Gangetic plain – Faizabad, Gonda, Allahabad, Azamgarh, Benares – experienced population decline, which officials attributed partly to emigration. In Sultanpur migration was being used to restore 'fallen fortunes or ease off a redundant population which have long been familiar to the inhabitants of the district' (Brownrigg 1898: 6); and in Ghazipur,

> immense numbers of people leave their homes every year to find employment in or near Calcutta and in the various centres of industry in Bengal and Assam, while many weavers and others report to the mills of Bombay. The extent of this migration is astonishing and its economic influence is of the highest importance since these labourers earn high wages and remit or bring back with them large sums of money to their homes.
>
> (Neville 1908: 79)

The claim about high wages is open to contention – how high was high? The point about the importance of migration, however, is clear.

The indentured labourers to Fiji and to other places came from this uprooted mass of peasantry. Most of them were registered in their own provinces rather than in large distant cities as critics alleged. But not all those who registered migrated. In Gonda and Basti, two of the largest indentured emigration districts, nearly 50 per cent did not migrate, while elsewhere, nearly a third remained behind, either because they were rejected or because they refused to enlist. The high failure rate gives some agency to the recruited. This is not to say by any means that the unscrupulous recruiters did not snare the gullible and the needy and the unwary into their nets. They did, but perhaps not to the extent the slavery thesis alleges. Migration to the colonies was an extension of the massive internal movement of people.

I vividly remember *Aja* telling us how he happened to come to Fiji. He was up and about, a young man in his early 20s, when a friend told him about golden opportunities awaiting him in the *tapus* (islands). What opportunities? He did not ask: he was footloose and free, and the lure of adventure attracted him. He eventually ended up in Calcutta, in the batch bound for Guyana (Demerara). That ship was full, so he took – or was put on – the next one to Fiji. I have no doubt that he had no idea what or where Fiji was, but that somehow did not seem to matter to him. He knew that he would be back one day soon, after he had earned enough. But enough was never quite enough. The day of decision never came – for him and for most of his fellow *girmitiyas*.

Fiji was spared the massive cultural dislocation that accompanied slavery (and even indenture) in the Caribbean and elsewhere. Fiji was, after Suriname, the last major importer of Indian indentured labour. By the late 1870s, the darkest period of indentured emigration was over, the period of almost complete break from India a thing of the past. Fiji was lucky to escape the horrors of its sister colonies in the Caribbean. The *girmitiyas* never completely lost touch with their cultural roots. As early as the 1890s, only a decade after the beginning of indentured emigration, the basic texts of popular Hinduism and folk culture were circulating in the main areas of Indian settlement in the sugar belts of Fiji (Lal 1995: 99–110). These included *Ramchritramanas, Satya Narayan ki Katha, Surya Purana, Devi Bhagat, Danlila, Durga Saptshati* and *Indra Sabha* as well as stories from *Baital Pachisi, Salinga Sadabrij* and *Alaha Khand*. The texts were recited communally at social functions and other occasions when people got together to celebrate life or mourn its passing. From very early on, *Holi* (*Phagua*) and *Tazia* (*Mohurram*) were observed as public holidays on most plantations. Religious leaders, both Hindu and Muslim, established centres for spiritual instruction (*kutis, dharamshalas* and *madarasas*). Informal gatherings of like-minded men later materialised as cultural and social associations which made enduring contribution to the growth and development of the Indo-Fijian community.

Religion became both an instrument of survival as well as a tool of resistance. Despite their best efforts, Christian missionaries, associated in the *girmitiya* minds with the excesses of the CSR overseers and the racially discriminatory practices of the colonial government, never made much headway among Indo-Fijians. J.W. Burton in his *Fiji of Today* (1910) and *The Call of the Pacific* (1912), recalls his experience in trying to convert Indians to Christianity. They refused to convert because they saw their own religion as superior. This contrasted with the Indian experience in the Caribbean where Christian missions, especially Presbyterians, enjoyed far greater success, providing the migrants, through education, a powerful vehicle for self-improvement and upward mobility.[4] In the Caribbean, an immigrant culture weakened by long separation from its ancestral roots and almost total dependence on the plantation system, fell easy prey to external temptations; in Fiji the roots, though frayed and planted in a shallower soil, were allowed – through indifference as much as anything else – to nurture themselves unhindered.

There was another important contrast with the Caribbean. Whereas the indentured labourers and their descendants there lived on the plantations for generations – and reminders of the dominant influence of the plantation system are still visible in Guyana – in Fiji, the period of dependence was limited to five, or at most ten, years.[5] In Fiji, *girmit* was a limited detention, not a life sentence for several generations, which it was in the Caribbean and in the case of slavery. Those freed from indenture from the mid-1880s onwards began to establish free settlements, mostly around the sugar mills on the two main islands of Viti Levu and Vanua Levu (Gillion 1962: 136–64; Ahmed 1976). These places remain the principal centres of Indian settlement in Fiji even today, still dependent in one way or another on the sugar industry as growers, casual labourers, mill workers. Besides giving the former *girmitiyas* individual opportunities, the free settlements were also symbolically important as beacons of hope for those still under indenture, a palpable reminder of the reality of freedom just across the plantation boundary. The rapid growth of free settlements on the fringes of the plantations meant that the period of complete isolation for those under indenture was limited, and with time the boundaries, both physical as well as emotional between the indentured and the free, became porous (Weller 1968: 65).

For many immigrants, indenture, for all its hardships, must have represented an improvement over their condition in India. This was particularly so for the lower castes who were permanently consigned to the unlovely fringes of rural Indian society as untouchables, tenants-at-will, and landless labourers with little hope of betterment in this life – or the next. The routine of relentless work on the plantations was nothing new to them as strenuous physical labour was their permanent lot in India. In Fiji, at least, their individual worth as human beings in their own right was recognised and their effort rewarded on the basis of achievement rather than ascription. For them, the levelling tendencies of the plantation system must have heralded a welcome change from an oppressive past and promised a future in which they and their children had a chance. Others who were victims of natural calamities, such as famines, floods and droughts, or of exploitative landlords, welcomed the peace and security that the new environment offered them. So, at one level, the *girmitiyas* were all peas in the same pod, beasts of burden, but they were also a socially differentiated group from diverse backgrounds and with divergent experiences and expectations of what life was about, what it had to offer. *Girmit*, then, was a simultaneously enslaving as well as a liberating experience.

Aja became a free man in 1913, after serving his indenture as a stable hand for the CSR in Labasa. Like most other freed *girmitiyas*, he continued as a mill hand for the CSR for a few years more before eloping with his best friend's wife, leasing a ten acre piece of land and starting on his own in the newly opened settlement at Tabia. He planted rice, lentils, maize, beans, eggplants, watermelon, pumpkin, and peanuts until sugar cane arrived in the late 1930s. It was on that sugar cane farm, raw, without paved roads, running water or electricity, that we were all born and raised. Now the farm is gone, taken back by the Fijian landowners. This has ruptured my sense of the place of my birth, dimmed the intensity of my association with it.

Aja went to Tabia not because he had friends or family or fellow caste members or *jahajibhais* there, but because a new settlement was being opened up and land was available for lease. Geography, the availability of productive agricultural land and its proximity to markets and roads and other facilities, determined the pattern of territorially and socially scattered Indian settlements in Fiji, rather than caste brotherhood or religious affiliation or even government edict; although, within a settlement, sub-cultural groups – South Indians, for example – could be found clustered in one part. This meant that the pattern of village India, with socially ranked clusters of houses with clear caste-based rules defining access to common facilities, formulating and enforcing rules of appropriate behaviour, could not be reproduced in Fiji (Mayer 1953: 1–3; Mayer 1963: 28). The fragmentation of the Indian village world, begun in the depots of Calcutta and Madras, and accelerated on the plantations, was completed in the post-indenture period.

I knew *Aja* as an old man of perhaps around 80, although he reckoned he was well over 100 in the way most old men do. Some things I can say about his life with absolute certainty, from personal experience, while others I deduce from my own reading and research. *Aja* spoke his own language (a mixture of *Bhojpuri* and *Awadhi*) with other surviving *girmitiyas*. He spoke Fiji Hindi with a distinct provincial Indian accent. My Fiji Hindi, incorporating more English and Fijian words, would be incomprehensible to him. He always wore Indian clothes – *dhoti* and *kurta* and *pagri*. The Indian garment would disappear with him and his generation, replaced by western clothes of shorts and shirt that became the standard for my father's generation. Women's jewellery and finery – *bichwa* (toe-ring), *payal* (anklet), *jhumka* (earring), *nathini* (nose-ring), *bajuband* (armlet) would also disappear with the *girmitiya* women, replaced by a single string of gold sovereigns – *mohur* – which women displayed as a sign of status and prosperity. In rural areas of Fiji, they still do.

Aja's world was full of ghosts and demons and evil forces – *bhoot pichas*, and *jadu tona* – which had to be pacified through a variety of precise ritual performances, that would disappear with him (see Vertovec 1996: 108–30). He continued to invoke, in (to me) incomprehensible language, the names of village and clan or caste deities – *gram devtas* and *kul devtas* – for some blessing or to ward off an evil or impending misfortune. To cure headache, jaundice, fever or a dog bite, he consulted the local sandalwood paste-covered *pujari*. He had faith in him; that, after all, was how things were done in India. He knew nothing about western medicine, which was expensive and inaccessible anyway. And although caste as a basis or determinant of social relationship had been jolted in the crowded depots of Calcutta and in the crowded cabins of the immigrant ships, finally crashing on the plantations (Jayawardena 1971: 88–119; Schwartz 1967), *Aja* continued to practise some minor, harmless customs from his childhood, perhaps to retain a vanishing connection with the remembered world of his youth. The practice of playing at caste died gradually as the *girmitiyas* moved on and as new forces of change (education, improved communication) entered the community. So, too, did the practice of seeking marriage partners for children from roughly comparable castes (Klass 1961: 121; Smith and Jayawardena 1967: 50).

Life in Fiji must have been very different for *Aja* and others like him, a complete contrast to what they had left behind. The physical landscape of an island surrounded by sea, criss-crossed by rivers and streams, full of forbidding forests and brooding mountains, and inhabited by a people who looked strange, must have been alien to a land-locked people from the flat, densely settled Indo-Gangetic plains. Perhaps the pace of work on the plantations may not have been new to those who came from labouring and farming backgrounds, though its relentless pace, in the absence of a vibrant, organic community, must have taken its toll. Within the domestic sphere, traditional notions of proper relations between men and women were re-negotiated, as they had to be, as women worked alongside men in the fields and assumed other responsibilities they would not have countenanced in India. Caste, minus its minor ritualistic aspects, had gone, and boundaries of social and cultural inclusion and exclusion were drawn more flexibly. New, pragmatic, cross-caste and cross-religious relationships had to be established in a new environment. In that new environment, the *girmitiyas* were more on their own, more alone, making their way by adapting the metaphors and strategies of a remembered, evanescent, past.

My enduring memory of *Aja* is of an old man lying on a string bed in the shade of the mandarin tree behind the thatched house where he slept, looking vacantly into the distance, his near-blind eyes focussed on some imaginary point, always talking about the world of his childhood, sometimes crying, wondering aloud about what his friends and family might be doing back home, hankering hopelessly for a past that was truly past, but unable – perhaps not knowing how – to embrace the new world that was his home. He died in 1962.

My father was born around 1918. No one knew the precise date; that did not seem to matter – that was the way things were done then. Whenever asked about it, he would say he was born during the *Badi Beemari*, the Influenza Epidemic of 1918. That rough approximation served the purpose. His generation grew up in the shadow of indenture. They were formed and deformed by the experience of poverty and uncertainty on the unformed edges of a slowly evolving community, still uncertain of its identity and character but making strenuous efforts to establish and enforce standards recalled from a remembered past. They grew up in a largely enclosed and culturally self-sufficient world. Once indentures had expired, Indians had ceased to be of concern to the colonial administration.

Left to their own devices, the Indo-Fijian community developed its own voluntary associations and self-help projects – forming settlement committees to harvest cane, establish temples and mosques, build schools, construct cemeteries, start annual festivals and organise *Ramayan* recitals through village *mandalis*. *Panchayats* – a council of five male village elders – were started in the early 1930s with official encouragement to maintain a semblance of order in village life. They resolved petty issues and enforced community standards – settling land boundary disputes, adjudicating fines for damage caused by stray cattle, intervening in family quarrels, punishing extra-marital relationships. Suspicion of alien legal institutions and practices, the cost of court cases, fear of social disapproval and ostracism – a mixture of all these – forced people to resort to time-tested ways. The *panchayats* worked effectively when the village world was still isolated, but lost their authority and rationale in the post-war years as joint families cracked, education and income increased, and improved communication connected the village to the outside world. Now, they are a distant memory. Litigation became a prominent, fractious feature of Indo-Fijian life, as it still is.

The self-absorption of the Indo-Fijian community came from the particular circumstances it encountered in the post-indenture period – the scattered settlements, the hard struggle on the cane farm, the absence of outside helping hands, the indifference of the colonial state. But it also resulted from a colonial policy which restricted contact with others, most notably and damagingly, with the indigenous community. Gordon's 'Native Policy', as it came to be known, created a separate system of administration – in effect a state within a state – which restricted Fijian mobility and limited opportunities for employment outside the authorised chief-dominated order in order ostensibly to shield the indigenous community from the corrosive effect of contact with the outside world (Chapman 1964; Legge 1958). When Indians transgressed village boundaries and established de facto relationships, Fijians were reprimanded and often fined, and Indians expelled from the vicinity of the *koros* (villages).

Colonial policy designed to keep the two communities in separate compartments compounded the problem of disrespect and suspicion that came from racial prejudice and cultural difference. There were some exceptions in parts of Fiji where the two groups shared contiguous space, but separate development and compartmentalised existence for the two communities became the norm. There was a Fijian *koro* on the outer fringes of our settlement: a row of brooding thatched bures with dark doors and tiny windows surrounding a neatly manicured *rara* (open green), but we never entered it for fear – of what I cannot now say. There was a Fijian woman who had somehow adopted my father as her younger brother and was openly playful with my mother, her *bhauji*. We called her *phua*, father's sister, and treated her like a member of the extended family. But that was about it. We children had no Fijian friends. In the absence of any meaningful contact, we continued to view things Fijian through the prism of prejudice. The Fijians reciprocated our ignorance. Things were different where the two communities lived closer to each other.

My father's world, like that of most of his contemporaries, centred upon a ten acre plot of land leased from the Native Land Trust Board, a statutory organisation which leased land to Indo-Fijians and others on behalf of the indigenous landowners. It was only a lease, so obvious in hindsight; but we never thought that the land wasn't our own, that it wouldn't always remain our own. The notion that it might revert to the owners – as it has now done – never once entered our minds. The ten-acre plot was the CSR's idea when, facing labour shortage after the end of indenture, it decided to get out of cane growing to concentrate on milling (Moynagh 1981). The CSR was clever. It wanted to relinquish cane farming, but not control over the industry. On that ten-acre farm, we grew sugar cane and rice, had a cow or two, some goats and chicken for meat and vegetables for domestic use or for selling to neighbours to raise cash. That was about it. Like other people in the village, we did not get anywhere very far, but we got by. J.W. Coulter, the American geographer who carried out field research in Laqere, the village across the river from our own, captures the daily routine of farm life in the late 1930s and early 1940s accurately:

> The regular work of Indian farmers in Fiji is in contrast to the irregular, easy going life of the Fijians. The Oriental rises at half-past five, harnesses his oxen, and plows from six to eight. He breakfasts at home or in the field on roti and milk and tea (roti is bread made from flour and fried in ghee). He resumes plowing until ten; at that time his oxen are unhitched to lie in the shade during the heat of the day. Shortly after ten he milks his cow, and from ten-thirty to twelve hoes weeds or cuts fodder along the ditches or road-side. At noon he lunches on rice, dal or rice curry, and milk. In the early afternoon he hoes again, cuts more grass, or does odd jobs about the

house. From three to five he plows. Supper at six consists of rice curry and chutney and milk. There is smoking and conversation by a kerosene lamp until bedtime at eight. In the evenings groups of Indians who have been working in the fields all day trudge home in the dusk, carrying lunch pails.

(Coulter 1942: 93)

The precise details might vary from place to place and from time to time, but the overall picture will be familiar to anyone of my generation growing up on an Indo-Fijian farm in the post-war years.

Anthropologist W.E.H. Stanner, who closely observed the Indo-Fijian community in the mid-1940s, also captures their problems and aspirations. Thousands of families suffered 'under a crushing burden of private debt', he wrote. 'Peasants and labourers lived frugally, worked long hours for extremely low wages or incomes, and saved with desperate application to keep alive, to repay loans and mortgages, to buy freehold land, to remit funds to India, to discharge customary social obligations requiring expensive outlays, and to acquire a competence for old age or return to India' (Stanner 1953: 179). On the cultural side, caste barriers had almost disappeared. 'High and low castes might sit together at school or in other assemblies or live together in unsegregated neighbourhoods. Restriction on vocation and occupation had greatly modified. European dress was widespread among men except in rural areas. Women no longer veiled and their costume, too, had altered. The *purdah* was unknown. Religious ceremonials had been simplified and shortened, especially the ritual purification, Hindu–Muslim separatism had so far weakened that members of the two religious communities sat together in amity on public committees, often took the same line of policy, co-operated politically on (especially on educational matters) and mingled fairly freely socially (Stanner 1953: 179–80).

Some old customs, observed by our grandparents' generation, were on the way out. Stanner noted the diminishing relevance of caste in everyday life. There were others. Polyandrous relationships, common during indenture because women were few and competition for them was intense, were also a thing of the past as the sex-ratio improved and the community stabilised. Monogamous marriage became the strict rule, the breach of which often led to violence, occasionally murders. During indenture, again because of the shortage of women, Hindu–Muslim marriages were not uncommon – and tolerated – but this practice, too, ended in the post-indenture period as the two groups began to establish 'morally correct' behaviour for their followers and as debates about religious identity engulfed the community. Inter-religious marriages are rare today.

The practice of child marriage, common at the beginning of my grandfather's generation, and continued from village India, also ceased. The legal age of marriage for boys was increased in 1961 from 16 to 18, and for girls from 13 to 14, though in practice most marriages took place later than the stipulated legal age. Girls' education was still frowned upon. In 1940, only 11 per cent of girls (1,430) – compared with 20 per cent of boys (3,607) attended primary school (Coulter 1967: 107). This situation changed within a decade. In 1959, for example, of the 77,000 pupils in primary schools, 20,000 were Indian boys and 15,000 Indian girls. The remaining gender barriers would crumble soon as the value of education, even if it was not for a career, became entrenched in the community and as the expectations of the women's role in the home and in the community at large expanded.

The leased farm was the only property our parents had, but it was clear that there was no future on it for all the children, six boys and two girls. We were encouraged to seek alternatives. Education was the key to that quest (Gillion 1977: 118–29). Our parents started community schools – nothing fancy, just rudimentary structures of thatched bures of bamboo walls and cow dung-plastered floor on a piece of land donated by some generous villager. By 1956, there were 154 Indian schools in Fiji, of which 129 were run by non-denominational settlement committees (Mayer 1963: 9). Some partially literate village elders assumed the role of instructors in Hindi and elementary arithmetic in return for help with house- and farm-work. The spectacle of poor parents with nothing, unlettered, making sure that the life of their children was better than theirs had been, is moving. Things improved with time and government assistance. By the early 1970s, over 500 primary and secondary schools were run by Indo-Fijian settlement and denominational bodies.

I have for some years been interested in the colonial texts which instructed our fathers' generation, to see the kinds of ideals and ethos that colonial official-dom tried to instill in them, its conception of the ideal colonial subject. I recently came across a copy of texts which were used in Fiji Indian primary schools in the 1930s. They are instructive. Here is just one example from the *School Journal, 1930*.[6] There are stories and anecdotes in it from Indian history: about Siddhartha, Rama, Harish Chandra, Tulsi Das, Guru Nanak and other figures of legend and myth. The emphasis on things Indian is important; it was a marker of our collective cultural reference point.

The government was keen for the Indo-Fijians to retain links with their cultural heritage (and then complained that they did not assimilate into the mainstream colonial society!). The *Journal* also carried stories about Fiji, excerpts from the governor's addresses, announcements about coming events, but these were brief, dry and uninteresting. Much more interesting were the stories about the Empire, Our Empire, marked by red patches on the *Clarion* atlas. The geography of Samoa and Hawaii featured in some of the texts as did items on Casablanca and the Ford Motor Factory at Detroit, the White Cockatoo. And then there were tips on how to be good citizens, law abiding, respectful of authority, appreciative of the great things that the 'Mother Country' was doing for its children in the colonies. Items on the best way to cultivate maize, banana and tobacco, the precautions to take during hurricanes and floods, the importance of keeping wells clean, were designed to teach people about clean, healthy, hygienic living.

If you were training to be an Indian primary school teacher in 1930, you would be expected to know, among other things, two virtues for which the Chinese are famous, why ANZAC was celebrated, what things the people of

Nigeria and Fiji had in common, how the Union Jack came into existence, the names of some of the finest buildings in Auckland, where the missionary John Williams was born, what religious festivals Rumanians enjoyed most and how they celebrated it, how David Livingstone got his education, what Florence Nightingale's favourite game as a child was, what pupils knew about the children of Labrador, the importance of the Chrysler Building in New York, the number of talons or claws a cat had.

Students sitting their Primary School Leaving Certificate Examination in 1936 would be expected to know the name of the governor of Roman Britain who encouraged the building of houses, towns and markets, the name of the British General who captured Jerusalem in 1917, the name of the brave French Commander who was killed in the same battle as General Wolfe, the name of the Roman Empire revived by Charles the Great, the name of the highest mountain in Australia, the chief export of New Zealand, the capital of Fiji before Suva, two ways in which disease could be spread.

The idea was not to 'educate' but to train cogs for the colonial bureaucratic wheel. Apart from the court clerks and assistants and interpreters in the district administration, primary-school teachers were people of respect and status in the community. Most people of my father's generation aspired to know just enough to read and write letters or sign their names on official documents.

Besides education, the earlier generations devised other ingenious means to erase barriers to social mobility and obliterate marks of social differentiation based on caste. One way of doing this was the names people gave to their children. *Girmitiyas* had names which a careful observer could use to decipher a person's social status. The lower and middle castes were named after objects, days and months, a particular emotion or event or state of affairs in the household or the village at the time the child was born.[7] Thus such names as Dukhia and Bipati (sadness/hardship), Gendia and Phulbasia (after flowers), Hansa (a mythical bird), Bhola, Bhullar and Jokhu (simple ones), Mangal, Budhai, Sanicharee, Mangru, Somai, Sukkhu (after days of the week), Gulab and Gulabi (after a colour), Bahadur, Shera (brave one), Sundar (pretty one). Other names with no particular connotation that I can decipher included Kalpi, Bisun, Tahull, Jaitoo, Jhinul, Chagun, Aleemoolah, Ulfat, Chaitu and Umrai.

The *girmitiyas* named their children after gods and goddesses and great mythical figures, which threw the old patterns into confusion, making it difficult to establish one's caste from the names. These names were common in my father's generation: Ram Prasad, Ram Saran, Ram Autar, Arjun, Hari Prasad, Ram Piyari, Bhola Nath, Bihari Prasad, Ganga Din, Jamuna Prasad, Sukh Raji, Suruj Pati, Shiv Lal, Mata Prasad, Tota Ram. No one could tell whether Ram Prasad was a *Chamar* (a tanner) or a *Kurmi* (cultivator). The higher castes maintained their caste surnames – Sharma, Singh, Mishra, although these were sometimes appropriated by those below them in social hierarchy. Sanskritisation was clearly at work here. Our parents named their children after film stars and famous personalities – Rajendra Prasad, Raj Kumar, Jawahar Lal, Vijay Singh, Rajesh Chandra, Mahendra Kumar, Satish Chand, Surendra Prasad, Sunil

Kumar, Biman Prasad – thus obliterating the last vestiges of caste distinction. Children now have names – Akilekshwari, Ravineshwar, Shikashni – which would be completely unrecognisable to our parents and grandparents.

In some areas, though, distinctions and differences were being institution-alised. This was particularly so in the fields of culture and religion. With the end of indenture in 1920, a number of religious and cultural associations emerged to provide a semblance of order and regularity to a rapidly stabilising Indo-Fijian community. Arya Samaj and Sanatan Dharam had been established at the begin-ning of the twentieth century, and the Muslim League and Sangam, the umbrella organisation of the South Indians, came in 1926. As the community began to set down roots, the different groups sought to 'define' the proper code of religious conduct, the proper observance of rituals and ceremonies. Conflict erupted. Samajis, followers of Swami Dayanand Saraswati's reformist branch of Hin-duism, clashed with the more orthodox, ritual-observing, idol-worshipping Sanatanis.[8] Shia and Sunni Muslims clashed over whether the appropriate suc-cessor to Prophet Mohammed were members of his own family (his son-in-law Ali and his sons Hussein and Hassan) or the Caliphs.[9]

Hindu–Muslim tensions, reflecting the political developments on the subcon-tinent in the inter-war period, were visible but restrained, though as the divisions hardened and pressure mounted to conform to strictly prescribed codes in food and dress and prayer and worship – not least because of the arrival of religious teachers from India – the more relaxed interaction and easy friendships of earlier years 'when we were all brothers' suffered. Faith became an important marker of identity in time, erasing and superseding other markers such as regional origin. And so it has remained.

The enclosed and socially isolated world of my father's generation began to fracture when we arrived in the post-war period. The things which had enthralled my father's generation, embroiled them in acrimonious debates with other sections of the community, defined their sense of identity and place, gave them meaning and purpose, had less relevance for us. Arranged marriages were, for us, a rapidly vanishing thing of the past, as were large families (a baker's dozen was not uncommon before our time). Daylight marriages of short duration became the norm for us, but were unheard of in the past. Our conceptions of women's role in public and private life would have been alien to the earlier gen-erations. Compulsory shaving of head and facial hair as a public sign of bereave-ment was observed, but not enforced. Strict rules about diet – little beer but definitely no beef – were beginning to be observed in the breach. Village moneylenders – *mahajans* – who had exercised such a baleful influence in the past became a distant memory for us as banks spread their tentacles around the country.

The great, wrenching debates of the late 1940s about whether prohibition should continue to be imposed on the Indo-Fijian community – an issue that deeply polarised people and wrecked political careers – meant nothing to us. Whether the meat you ate was *halal* or *jhatka*, an issue that had strained Hindu–Muslim relations in the past, had little relevance for us. Similarly, whether Sanatanis greeting Arya Samajis with a *Namaste* rather than the customary *Ram-Ram* would be seen as a sign of defeat or subservience seemed a petty issue to my generation. Christmas – *Bada Din* (Big Day) – became for us a convenient excuse for exuberant, drunken celebration, eating fresh goat meat and drinking rum – only the poorest of the poor ate chicken or duck on that day – a much anticipated feature of our annual calendar.

We spoke a 'new language'. Words and concepts used during my father's generation were forgotten: *kakkus* (toilet), *bhuccahd* (silly, stupid), *chachundar* (loose woman, a flirt), *bhong* (dumb), *behuda* (fool), *jahua* (con man), *lokum* (gaol), *bailup* (place for cattle), *Black Maria* (police van), *bagrap* (buggered up), *lifafa* (envelope). We had no idea what *tanzeb*, *nainsukh*, *motia*, once the pride of female jewellery, looked like. *Lehanga naach* (male dancers dressed as female) which was performed during marriage ceremonies to lighten the mood, *gutka* (stick dance) done during festivals, *tassa*, *hudda*, *nagara* (all folk musical instruments) were for us a part of a vanished past.

Unlike our parents' generation, we did not require permission from the colonial officialdom to drink alcohol. Aubrey Parke, who was district commissioner in Labasa when I was completing my primary schooling in the 1960s, tells me about the distinct categories of permission you required: one which allowed you to drink beer only, one which permitted the consumption of both beer and spirit in a pub, one which entitled you to buy a dozen bottles of beer a month and, if you were really somebody, you had the permission to buy a dozen bottles of beer and a bottle of spirit – Dozen and One – a month. That world was gone when we were teenagers. The older generation mourned the passing of a culturally ordered world which had been built from the memory of a remembered past, but there was little they could do about it.

Improving communication – better roads, bridges and regular public transport – joined us to an expanding world beyond the village horizon. Radio came in the 1950s and Hindi newspapers – *Jagriti, Jai Fiji, Shanti Dut, Kisan Mitra*. And films: *Alam Ara, Anarkali, Baiju Bawra, Awara, Shree 420, Jagte Raho, Pyasa, Mother India, Ganga Jamuna*. (Subramani, 1995: 111ff.; Mishra 2002: Preface). Films had been coming to Fiji since the late 1930s – eight of the ten cinema houses were run by Indo-Fijians in the 1940s – but they were viewed mostly by people in the urban areas. Going to the movies was a major social event of the week, an occasion to display the latest fashion in clothes and jewellery, to meet the elite of society, to know who was who in the community. The Hindi newspapers, Hindi movies, the religious functions we performed with mundane regularity, kept us intact as a community, gave us purpose and cohesion. We in the villages, closer to our cultural roots, thought ourselves superior to the urban dwellers who had, so it appeared to us, drifted away and embraced western ways.

Expectation of what life was – or what it could be – had risen for our generation. By the early 1960s, for instance, primary education was within the reach of most children who wanted it, and secondary education, too, for those who passed the entrance examination. We now could, if we were any good – and our 'goodness' was judged solely on the basis of our performance in external examinations – contemplate a lowly career in the public service, in the banking sector, in the sugar industry as trainee overseers and in the teaching profession, possibilities that were beyond even the imagined horizon of our parents. In the early 1960s, university education was restricted to a select few – perhaps ten a year – who were sent on government scholarship to New Zealand (rarely to Australia) to train as high-school teachers, administrators and economists. They were the cream of the crop, who returned from overseas after a few years, proclaiming themselves culturally disoriented, social misfits, unable to speak their language, ill at ease among their own people, even embarrassed about their past. For all their idiosyncrasies, though, they made a huge impression on your youthful minds, representing possibilities that could be ours if only we tried hard enough. Many became our role models.

But all this changed with the founding of the University of the South Pacific in 1968. That event must be counted as one of the turning points in the modern history of the Pacific islands.[10] It opened up opportunities for higher education to thousands of children from poor homes who would almost certainly have otherwise missed out. It brought us into contact with people from other parts of Fiji and from other parts of the Pacific, which had, until then, remained forbidding names on paper, nothing more. A new generation had come of age at a critical time in the region's history as islands were on the eve of independence. We were trained – and destined – to play an important part in our countries' and our region's future.

Our world was more diverse than our parents'. Those who went to Christian or urban schools lost the Hindi language, were more exposed to modern influences, were more at home in cross-cultural friendships. Those of us who went to rural schools or schools run by various Indo-Fijian cultural organisations retained firmer links with our culture and language. This, I now realise, had its obvious advantages, but it also imposed limitations that dawned upon me much later. Just as we went to predominantly Indian schools, Fijian children went to predominantly Fijian schools – Queen Victoria and Ratu Kadavulevu. In 1960, when I was in grade two, there were only 88 non-Fijians in the colony's 325 Fijian primary schools, and only 53 non-Indians in Indian primary schools (Burns 1963: 230). We thus grew up engrossed in the ethos of our own community, untouched by cross-cultural influences, completely ignorant of the values, interests and concerns of the Fijians, blind to the complex, inner impulses of their society. And yet, we were a part of the generation which was called upon to play an important role in national life in the post-colonial era – as teachers, administrators, politicians. No wonder Fiji has faltered so often in its recent journeys.

For us, education became a profound agent of social change, just as indenture had been for the *girmitiyas*. The classroom was a great leveller of hierarchy. Before the Second World War, education, especially higher education, was largely the prerogative of the wealthy and the well-connected in the Indo-Fijian community. Wealth, status and power came from owning property or proximity to officialdom. The early generation of leaders came from this privileged background: lawyers, landowners, businessmen such as Badri Maharaj, the Grants, the Deokis, the Ramrakhas, the Mishras, the Singhs of Ba, the Sahu Khans, the Tikarams. But the expansion of educational opportunities opened up the field to children from poor, nondescript backgrounds. Talent and merit became the markers of success and ladders to power, and that has remained the case. The old, well-established families, whose names were once synonymous with status and sophistication and fame and fortune, have gone and are now largely forgotten.

As we grew up, the world of our parents began to recede into a vanishing past – joint families, proper and periodic observance of rituals and ceremonies, the comforting bonds of a cohesive community, family solidarity, respect for age and authority, politeness in the presence of *pandits*, extreme carefulness in the management of money, a healthy fear of the unknown. The gap widened with time in much the same way as it had done when our parents moved away from their parents' world. The change was inevitable – and liberating. And it continues. As mobility increases and modernity touches nearly every aspect of life, Indo-Fijians are becoming more aware of their complex and conflicting identity. Living in a society corroded by the ravages of racial politics, they continue to nurture the roots of the Indian cultural heritage as a matter of pride and choice, though perhaps not with the ritualistic reverence and understanding of their parents and grandparents. Indian music, dress, food and art are being interpreted and re-interpreted through a different and distinct sense of lenses, touched by modernity and the inevitable forces of globalisation that would have been feared and forbidding to the earlier generation. Western cultural values, alien and alienating to our forebears, also continue to be embraced and incorporated, not the least because it opens up doors to other opportunities.

Aja would be surprised, as he peers down the corridors of time, to see the way in which his children and grandchildren have accommodated themselves to the ethos and mores of a land to which he had come by accident but which he could not, or was perhaps unable to, comprehend. He will also, sadly, recognise that the uncertainties and anxieties that attended his experience in Fiji still continue. He will be saddened to see the cane farms which he and his compatriots had created from nothing, with so much hard labour under the most trying of conditions, turning to bush as leases expire and people are forced off the land. Generations of effort ending just like that. He will be perplexed to see his grand and great-grandchildren, leaving for the land of the sahibs, embarking on the second crossing, forming the diaspora of the 'Twice Banished'. He will wonder whether their presence in the islands was a temporary stopover for a people condemned by fate to wander the world. Whether immigration to emigration might not form the ultimate epitaph for his people. He will ask the questions his grandchildren are asking now: how many generations do a people have to live in a place to be allowed to call it home? He will probably talk about Florida, Utah, Montana, Gladstone, Victoria, Plato and Pompey and wonder what happened to them. And their children.

Notes

1 This history is treated at length in Lal (2000). For an earlier account, see Gillion (1962).
2 For an application of the slavery thesis to Fiji, see Ahmed (1979).
3 Among others, the works of Seecharan (1997); Dabydeen and Samaroo (eds) (1987); Carter (1994); Bhana and Brain (eds) (1990).
4 See Bisnauth (1977: 490); See also Niehoff and Niehoff (1960: 136ff.). They argue that Hindus had little difficulty accepting Christ as an *avatar* of God, like Ram and Krishna. Fewer Muslims converted because of their belief that Prophet Mohammed was the last messenger of God. Samaroo (1996) has a number of important case studies.
5 For the Caribbean, see among other studies: Jayawardena (1963); Dabydeen and Samaroo (1987); La Guerre (1985).
6 The text was produced by A.W. Macmillan, a LMS missionary and an inspector of Indian Schools in Fiji, who had served in India for many years.
7 I use only Hindu names here as I am not familiar with the etymology of Muslim names.
8 Arya Samajis can be likened to the Protestants and the Sanatanis to the Catholics. For more discussion, see Kelly (1991); Gillion (1977: 102–29).
9 A short history of the Muslim community is given in Ahmed (2004).
10 More discussion of this is in Lal (2004).

References

Ahmed, A. (1976) *Society in Transition: Aspects of Fiji Indian History, 1879–1937*, Suva: USP.
Ahmed, A. (1979) *Girmit: The Indenture Experience in Fiji*, Suva: Fiji Museum.
Ahmed, A. (2004) 'Remembering', in B.V. Lal (ed.) *Bittersweet: The Indo-Fijian Experience*, Canberra: Pandanus Books, pp. 71–87.
Bhana, S. and J. Brain (eds) (1990) *Setting Down Roots: Indian Migrants in South Africa, 1860–1911*, Johannesburg: Witwaters-rand University Press.
Bisnauth, D. (1977) 'The East Indian Immigrant Society in British Guiana, 1891–1930', Thesis (PhD), University of the West Indies, Mona, Jamaica.
Brownrigg, F.W. (1898) *Sultanpur Settlement Report*, Allahabad: North-Western Provinces and Oudh Government Press.
Burns, A. (1963) *Fiji*, London: HMSO.
Burton, J.W. (1910) *The Fiji of Today*, London: Charles H. Kelly.
Burton, J.W. (1912) *The Call of the Pacific*, London: Charles H. Kelly.
Carter, M. (1994) *Lakshmi's Legacy: The Testimonies of Indian Women in 19th Century Mauritius*, Stanley-Rose Hill, Mauritius: Editions de l'Ocean Indien.
Chapman, J.K. (1964) *The Career of Arthur Hamilton Gordon: First Lord Stanmore, 1829–1912*, Toronto: University of Toronto Press.
Coulter, J.W. (1942) *Fiji: Little India of the Pacific*, Chicago: Chicago University Press.
Coulter, J.W. (1967) *The Drama of Fiji: A Contemporary History*, Rutland, Vermont: Charles E. Tuttle.
Crawford, C.E. (1898) *Azamgarh Settlement Report*, Allahabad: North-Western Provinces and Oudh Government Press.
Dabydeen, D. and B. Samaroo (eds) (1987) *Indians in the Caribbean*, London: Macmillan.
Dabydeen, D. and B. Samaroo (eds) (1996) *Across the Dark Waters: Ethnicity and Indian Identity in the Caribbean*, London: Macmillan.

Gillion, K.L. (1962) *Fiji's Indian Migrants: A History to the End of Indenture in 1920*, Melbourne: Oxford University Press.

Gillion, K.L. (1977) *The Fiji Indians: Challenge to European Dominance, 1920–1946*, Canberra: Australian National University Press.

Hiatt, L.R. and C. Jayawardena (eds) (1971) *Anthropology in Oceania*, Sydney: Angus & Robertson.

Jayawardena, C. (1963) *Conflict and Solidarity in a Guianese Plantation*, London: The Athlone Press.

Jayawardena, C. (1971) 'The Disintegration of Caste in Fiji Indian Rural Society', in L.R. Hiatt and C.J. Jayawardena (eds) *Anthropology in Oceania*, Sydney: Angus & Robertson, pp. 88–119.

Kelly, J.D. (1991) *A Politics of Virtue: Hinduism, Sexuality, and Countercolonial Discourse in Fiji*, Chicago: University of Chicago Press.

Klass, M. (1961) *East Indians in Trinidad: A Study in Cultural Persistence*, New York: Columbia University Press.

La Guerre, J. (ed.) (1985) *Calcutta to Caroni*, St Augustine: Institute of Caribbean Studies.

Lal, B.V. (1995) 'Hinduism Under Indenture: Totaram Sanadhya's Account of Fiji', in *Journal of Pacific History*, 30(1): 99–111.

Lal, B.V. (2000) *Chalo Jahaji: On a Journey of Indenture through Fiji*, Canberra and Suva: Fiji Museum.

Lal, B.V. (ed.) (2004) *Pacific Places, Pacific Histories*, Honolulu: University of Hawaii Press.

Legge, J.D. (1958) *Britain in Fiji, 1858–1880*, London: Macmillan.

Mayer, A.C. (1953) 'The Organisation of Indian Settlement in Fiji', *Man*, 53(284): 182–5.

Mayer, A.C. (1963) *Indians in Fiji*, London: Oxford University Press.

Mishra, V. (2002) *Bollywood Cinema: Temples of Desire*, New York: Routledge.

Moynagh, M. (1981) *Brown or White? A History of the Fiji Sugar Industry, 1873–1973*, Canberra: Australian National University Press.

Neville, H.R. (1908) *Ghazipur District Gazetteer*, Naini Tal: United Provinces of Agra and Oudh Government Press.

Niehoff, A. and J. Niehoff (1960) *East Indians in the West Indies*, Milwaukee: Milwaukee Public Museum.

Samaroo, B. (1996) *Pioneer Presbyterians: Origins of Presbyterian Work in Trinidad*, St Augustine: Institute of Caribbean Studies.

Sanders, J.T. (1963) 'Interlude', in B. Allen (1963) *Fiji*, London: HMSO, pp. 149–76.

Schwartz, B. (ed.) (1967) *Caste in Overseas Indian Communities*, San Francisco: Chandler Publishing Co.

Seecharan, C. (1997) *Tiger in the Stars: the Anatomy of Indian Achievement in British Guiana, 1919–1929*, London: Macmillan.

Smith, R.T. and C. Jayawardena (1967) 'Caste and Social Status Among the Indians in Guyana', in B. Schwartz (ed.) *Caste in Overseas Indian Communities*, San Francisco: Chandler Publishing Co., pp. 43–92.

Stanner, W.E.H. (1953) *South Seas in Transition. A Study of Post-War Rehabilitation and Reconstruction in Three British Pacific Dependencies*, Sydney: Australasian Publishing Co.

Subramani (1995) *Altering Imagination*, Suva: Fiji Writers' Association.

Tinker, H. (1974) *A New System of Slavery: The Export of Indian Labour Abroad, 1834–1920*, London: Oxford University Press.

Vertovec, S. (1996) 'Official and Popular Hinduism in the Caribbean: Historical and Contemporary Trends in Suriname, Trinidad and Guyana', in D. Dabydeen, and B. Samaroo (eds) *Across the Dark Waters: Ethnicity and Indian Identity in the Caribbean*, London: Macmillan, pp. 108–30.

Weller, J. (1968) *The East Indian Indenture in Trinidad*, Rio Piedras: University of Puerto Rico.

7 From Bharat to Sri Ram Desh

The emigration of Indian indentured labourers to Suriname

Chan E.S. Choenni

In 2004, descendants of the 24,000 Indian indentured emigrants who originally settled in Suriname numbered over 300,000 more than half of whom have come to reside in the Netherlands. This more than ten-fold increase compares favourably with other parts of the Caribbean such as Trinidad and Guyana where their number has grown by three to four times the original number. This substantial increase in number is even more startling when one takes into account the fact that the recruitment of Indians to Suriname through indenture occurred much later here when compared with other parts of the Caribbean. In addition, Indians in Suriname have displayed considerable socio-economic mobility, while sustaining their Indian cultural and linguistic heritage.

This chapter will explore the nature of the indenture experience for Indian labourers of Suriname particularly in terms of the emigration process. It argues that the specific features of the indenture system in the former Dutch colony to some extent provide an explanation for the remarkable demographic growth, and the sustenance of their cultural and linguistic heritage in Suriname. As British subjects in a foreign country Indian indentured labourers not only received special protection, but also profited as relative latecomers from the enhancements made to the system, particularly in terms of better methods of recruitment, a greater proportion of women indentured labourers, and improved medical care. In exploring these issues, the chapter will study the recruitment of Indian emigrants, their voyage, the conditions they faced in Suriname, and the reasons that led to the abolition of the indenture system.

Introduction

Following the abolition of slavery in Suriname on 1 July 1863, the necessity to find an alternative source of labour was a matter of great urgency for plantation owners. To prevent the exodus of slaves from the profitable sugar and coffee plantations, a policy of *Staatstoezicht* (State supervision) was employed after the abolition of slavery; this effectively obliged 'former' slaves to work ten years after their 'liberation'. With the *Staatstoezicht* scheduled to end in 1873, concerned plantation owners lobbied the Dutch government, and the colonial parliament of Suriname, to allow the procurement of indentured labour from British

India. In 1868, G.J.A. Bosch Reitz, a member of the colonial parliament of Suriname, prepared a brochure arguing that the import of indentured Indian labour was crucial in preventing an 'imminent miserable situation' ('*uit den treurigen toestand*').

This was not the first time that planters in Suriname had turned to indenture as a replacement for slave labour. Prior to 1863, indentured labourers from China and Madeira had been recruited to work in Suriname. This experiment was not a success. In 1864 only 353 Chinese workers were procured through this method. Moreover, labourers from China and Madeira were found to be unsuitable for hard plantation labour, with many Chinese workers using every opportunity to set up retail shops. A system of recruiting free labourers for Suriname from 1863 also failed due to an inability to gather sufficient recruits. These failures led to stronger calls for the recruitment of indentured labour from British India, a system that had proven to be successful in neighbouring British Guyana.

In 1862, the Dutch government contacted the British government for permission to recruit Indian labourers for Suriname, and while the British responded positively, there was considerable delay in implementing this request. After considerable debate, the Suriname immigration treaty was drafted on 8 September 1870, although it took almost three years before the actual emigration of Indian labourers took place.

The immigration treaty

The Suriname immigration treaty was based on an earlier convention between France and Britain, dating from 1860, that regulated the emigration of Indian labourers to French colonies. The Indian indentured labourers signed a contract for five years. A close reading of the 27 articles in the treaty reveals that at least on paper, humane conditions – measured by the standards of that time – prevailed in the requirements for recruitment, shipping, boarding and treatment. Article 6 of the treaty states:

> No immigrant shall be embarked unless the Agent described in the preceding article shall have been enabled to satisfy himself that his engagement is voluntary, that he has a perfect knowledge of the nature of his contract, of the place of his destination, of the probable length of his voyage, and of the different obligations and advantages connected with his engagement.

Article 8 of the treaty also regulated the salary, working hours and days of indentured labourers, the right of a free return ticket to British India at the end of the contract of five years and free medical treatment.

Admittedly those involved in implementing regulations did not always apply these humane regulations strictly, yet emigrants to Suriname had a more favourable treaty than Indian indentured labourers who had emigrated to British plantation colonies. For example, article 9 of the treaty posited that the duration of the engagement between an emigrant and the Dutch government was five years, although it could be extended annually or for another five years. Furthermore the British government itself acted as a pressure group for their 'subjects' (the emigrants to Suriname were British subjects till 1927) who were employed in a foreign country, demanding that the regulations be strictly observed. Moreover since Indian emigrants to Suriname were recruited much later than in British Guyana (1838) and Trinidad (1845) – the earliest arrived in Suriname on the *Lalla Rookh* on 5 June 1873 – they benefited from the changes that had taken place in the system, including stricter health checks at the time of recruitment, better health facilities, a larger proportion of women migrants and a better regulation of working hours amongst others.

The Suriname immigration treaty stated that the recruitment, embarking and shipping of Indian emigrants to Suriname was the responsibility of the Dutch government. A specific agency was created for this operation. The enrolment and recruitment in India was put under the management of an emigration agent. He was appointed by the governor of Suriname and was the superintendent of the main barrack in Calcutta known as *dipu* (a corruption of the Dutch word *depot* meaning barrack) among the Indians. Important emigration agents for Suriname included W. Durham (serving 1872–5), E. Van Cutsem (serving 1875–88) and L. Gommers (serving 1901–22). The emigration agent appointed medical practitioners, interpreters and sub-agents (often Indians) who were named *sirdars*. The sub-agents in turn appointed recruiters, the so-called *arkatis* (recruiters). The British government also appointed a 'protector of emigrants', responsible for the interests of the Indian indentured labourers. Dr W. Comins and Mr I. Grant became well-known protectors of emigrants.

The highest authority of this operation was the Agent-General who resided in Paramaribo, the capital of Suriname. Appointed by the Dutch government and the head of the immigration department, he managed the staff in the main barrack in Paramaribo. The emigration agent in Calcutta recruited Indian labourers based on the instructions of the Agent-General who in turn received annual applications for Indian indentured labourers by plantation owners based on which a quota for the enrolment of Indian labourers was fixed. When the labourers arrived in Suriname the Agent-General allocated them to the plantations. He was required to report regularly to the British government on the conditions of indentured Indian labourers. Furthermore Indian labourers could claim juridical assistance from the British representative appointed to assist and protect the Indian labourers in Paramaribo.

Early British checks on Indian emigration to Suriname

Between 1873 and 1874, six batches of Indian indentured labourers arrived in Suriname. It was found, however, that in spite of the preparations that had been made to safeguard the health of recruits, there was a high incidence of disease and a relatively high death toll amongst the recruits. The British government held the view that the relief and care given to indentured labourers on the journey and in Suriname was inadequate and that the health-checks conducted on potential recruits in Calcutta were not sufficiently meticulous.

Without informing the Dutch government, the British government postponed the emigration of Indians to Suriname indefinitely. The great need for labourers in Suriname resulted in the Dutch government taking measures to improve the living conditions of the Indian immigrants. A medical institution[1] was founded to provide medical care for immigrants. The main barrack in Paramaribo was refurbished, as were the toilets and the bathing area where new showers were installed. In 1877, the British government, after an inspection of these improvements, agreed to resume the emigration of its subjects to Suriname.

The initial check undertaken by the British government went a long way in improving the condition of indentured labourers to Suriname. Plantation owners were required to ensure that labourers were free after working hours, on Sundays and on religious festivals, which included 32 holidays for Hindu and 16 holidays for Muslim religious festivals in a year (Emmer 1984: 259). Labourers also had the right to re-migration to British India upon the completion of their contracts. The Agent-General, appointed by the Dutch government as the protector of recruits, became an important institution in upholding the legal rights of labourers as he had a considerable hold on the plantation owners. If a plantation owner acquired a bad reputation for mistreating labourers, the Agent-General could restrict or bar that owner from recruiting new Indian labourers.

The first Agent-General Cateau van Roosevelt (served 1872–91), known commonly as *Koelie-papa (father of the coolies)*, was so popular amongst indentured labourers that his funeral attracted a mass audience of Indians.[2] His successor Agent-General Barnet Lyon (serving 1891–1902) was also well liked and the Indian community in appreciation erected a bust for him that was placed at a prominent spot in Paramaribo, near the presidential palace. Others such as the Agent-General C. Van Drimmelen (serving 1902–21) were less popular because he and his aide, the Indian interpreter Sital Persad, were perceived as authoritarian by the labourers.

Although the juridical protection of the emigrants was improved, they continued to be subject to strict penal sanctions (*poenale sanctie*) in cases where they were found guilty of breaking the law. To allay plantation owners' fears of desertion by Indian labourers, emigrants were not allowed to leave their plantation without a permit. Where labourers were found guilty of indecent and improper behaviour, absenteeism and desertion, strong penalties were meted out by the commissioner of the district who was authorised to penalise emigrants.

Recruitment

After the emigration agent in Calcutta received applications for labourers from Paramaribo through telegram, he ordered sub-agents to begin the recruitment process. The sub-agents in turn mobilised the *arkatis*. Sub-agents were paid 25 *rupees* for every male and 35 *rupees* for every female recruited. *Arkatis* in turn received their remuneration from sub-agents and were only paid for those persons who were deemed fit for labour. The average number of enrolments for an *arkati* for Suriname was 35 persons annually. If the *arkati* was not sufficiently diligent in performing his duties, his recruitment licence, which was valid only for one year, was not renewed.

The main recruitment areas were West Bihar and the United Provinces (now Uttar Pradesh). Sub-barracks, where preliminary medical checks were conducted, were situated in Benaras, Allahabad, Ghazipur, Muttra (Mathura), Basti, Gorakpur, Fyzabad (in the United Provinces), Patna and Muzaffarpur (in Bihar). *Arkatis* usually sought potential recruits from crowded areas such as bazaars, markets and train stations (Bhagwanbali 1996: 87). Potential emigrants were asked if they wanted employment: *'Naukari loge?'* ('You want to work?') *Naukari* (meaning delivering service in lieu of money) had an honourable meaning. As far as possible, only those that were perceived to be strong and healthy were approached because sub-agents and *arkatis* had to pay the costs of transport to Calcutta and a possible return passage for those who were rejected.

In general, *arkatis* informed potential emigrants that they had to work in another country, although they did not define exactly where this country was. Names of the colonies were sometimes mentioned. Mauritius was known as *Mirchdesh* (Country of peppers), Trinidad was *Chinidad* (Country of sugar) and British Guyana was named Damra or *Damraila* (corruption of Demerara). Suriname was associated with the country *Sri Ram*. The passage to Suriname was thus depicted by many *arkatis* as a pilgrimage to the holy country of the god Ram, named Sri Ram or *sarnam* ('famous') or *srinam* ('sublime name'). Occasionally, *arkatis* would say that the area of work was simply located on the other side of the Ganges but their ability to falsify the location of work was somewhat constrained by the fact that they would not receive payment if recruits deserted upon arrival in Calcutta.

The *arkati* was better placed, however, to provide false information as to the nature of work. This was usually represented as relatively simple, just *chini chale* (cutting and transporting of sugarcane). When the potential recruits were policemen or were from a higher caste and unwilling to perform manual work, they were often [mis]informed that they would be given service-orientated jobs and not plantation work. An important element in winning over potential recruits was the *arkati's* promise that they would be protected by the *Sarkar* (the British government), and that their work was somehow linked to the army. This was particularly crucial in recruiting emigrants with a martial background from the *chatri* caste (Kolff 1999: 18–22), many of whom had lost their livelihoods in the army following the Indian mutiny in 1857.

However, the most important factor in recruitment was the opportunity to earn money. *Arkatis* portrayed Suriname as an affluent country where food was served in gold *thalis* (plates) and gold *lotas* (bowls) were used for drinking. The *arkati* told stories of returned emigrants who had made a fortune and had even become *zamindars* (landlords). The *arkati's* myths did not go uncontested. There was resistance especially from orthodox Hindus who argued that by crossing the so-called *kala pani* ('dark waters') the emigrant would lose his caste and be subject to the anger of God. In addition there were stories of macabre practices in the colonies. One was that oil was withdrawn from the head of emigrants, and pamphlets were distributed showing Indians hung upside down to extract oil from their bodies.

In spite of such resistance, the severe economic conditions in the region did result in many turning to emigration. The Gangetic plain was (and remains) a very densely populated area, and it had witnessed numerous famines in the second half of the nineteenth century. Between 1873 and 1875 acute famines prevailed in Bihar, Oudh and other provinces. Period of famines and bad harvests corresponded with high numbers of emigrants and likewise during periods of good harvest as in 1902 and in 1904 it was more difficult to procure emigrants. A decrease in the availability of jobs in the construction of railway tracks in the region after 1870 and the decline of the local cotton and textile industry due to the popularity of ready-made textiles from England led to an increase in unemployment. Besides economic reasons, personal motivations like family feuds, escape from legal penalties, fear of blame (of unmarried mothers and fathers), a spirit of adventure and the restrictive caste system were some of the other reasons for emigration.

If push and pull factors did not work sufficiently, the *arkati* was not averse to employing more forceful means. The kidnapping of people, though not common, was used. Also, the *arkatis* employed other methods such as money-lending to procure recruits. When a person in debt to the *arkati* defaulted on his loan, he was asked to emigrate and repay the debt following his return. *Tohar namak khaili, girmit katib* ('because I have eaten your salt, I shall perform agreement labour'), was a well-known phrase at the time.

Gender and the socio-economic profile of emigrants

The overwhelming majority of the Indian emigrants to Suriname were recruited from eastern United Provinces while a minority came from western Bihar. Speakers of *Bhojpuri* and *Awadhi*, the interaction between these migrants led to these two languages gradually merging into Sarnami-Hindi, which remains an important language in Suriname. The emigrants to Suriname were not exclusively farmers. In one shipment, the majority consisted of domestic servants, soldiers, policemen, barbers, shopkeepers, street vendors and persons with a profession other than agriculture. Artists, in particular musicians, were also recruited. A group of *nautch* (dancing) girls and male actors were also known to have been recruited to entertain the emigrants during the long passage. Other emigrants recruited included wrestlers and persons who could fight with sticks (*gutka*) (Tinker 1977: 52).

Some 82 per cent of the emigrants to Suriname were Hindus, the majority belonging to the Sanatan Dharma and a small number to the reformist group, Arya Samaj. The caste profile of emigrants was also diverse including those from the higher castes. Small numbers of Kabir Panthis, Jains, Sikhs and Parsis also emigrated to Suriname. However, these groups are not recognisable anymore, and many have integrated into the Hindu community in Suriname. Muslims, comprising Sunnis, Shias and Ahmadiyas, formed 17.5 per cent of emigrants.

The British and Dutch governments had agreed that for every 100 men, 40 women were to emigrate.[3] In particular in the later period of emigration – between 1880 and 1916 – the 100:40 rule was strictly applied, because in the colonies the sex imbalance among the Indian emigrants was known to have lead to killings, rape and social unrest. As a result the departure of ships to Suriname was sometimes postponed until the 100:40 quota was achieved. The strict application of this rule resulted in a higher percentage of (unmarried) women emigrating to Suriname when compared to other colonies (see Table 7.1). It is plausible that this is an important reason for the higher growth of the Indian population in Suriname compared with British Guyana, Trinidad and Jamaica.

The 100:40 quota for the recruitment of women was a matter of concern for both the authorities and the *arkatis*, since there were few women available for emigration. This explains why the *arkatis* received more money for females than for male emigrants and were known to have deceived and even kidnapped widows and unmarried women and registered them as emigrants. According to the Indian emigration expert De Klerk (1998), however, the kidnapping of women was an exception. He argues that it is unthinkable that large groups of emigrants could forcefully be locked up in the sub-barracks while the British government controlled these places. The British emigration expert Tinker states that, in particular, young widows who did not have children were more agreeable to emigration because they were often rejected by their community. Many were recruited from Mathura, a place of pilgrimage in the United Provinces (Tinker 1977: 195). For the salvation of their husband's soul – and often with no real home to which to return – these widows were, after their pilgrimage, willing to undertake the journey to Suriname, known to them as *Sri Ram Desh* (land of lord Ram).

The need to fulfil quota requirements for female emigrants meant that sometimes the *arkati* recruited prostitutes. As Emmer (1984: 250) points out,

Table 7.1 Married and unmarried women as a proportion of Indian emigrants in some colonies (1893)

Colony	Men	Women	Total	Percentage of women	Percentage of unmarried women
Suriname	682	275	903	30.5	66.7
Guyana	3,298	1,395	4,693	29.8	45.0
Trinidad	1,181	507	1,688	30.0	51.3
Jamaica	323	130	453	28.7	35.5
Fiji	513	206	719	28.7	46.1
Mauritius	247	130	377	34.5	43.1
South Africa	361	154	515	29.9	46.1

Source: Based on I.O.R.E.4.viiA (1)1893 available in Shepherd (1992: 51).

however, the word prostitute in the Indian context at the time must be interpreted broadly. Women who had sexual relations with a man before marriage, or
had been adulterous, or did not live with their husbands because they were dis-
satisfied with their arranged marriages, were considered prostitutes. The authori-
tative report of McNeill and Chimman Lal concludes that in Suriname

> approximately one third consists of married women that migrated with their
> husbands, others are often widows and women who left their men … a
> small percentage are ordinary prostitutes … the large majority however are
> not as often is stated shameless immoral. They are women who had faced
> trouble and emigrate to prevent that they would live their life in India as
> prostitute.
>
> (Tinker 1974: 205)

Final selection and the journey from Calcutta

The potential emigrant travelled from the sub-barrack under the attendance of a
chaprasi (an attendant in uniform) to the main barrack in Calcutta. Usually
recruited labourers arrived by train to the Howrah station in Calcutta. From
Howrah, they were brought to different barracks situated at the banks of the
Hooghly River. Four main barracks served the different colonies. Those bound
for Suriname went either to the barracks at Ballygunj or at Chitpur. After their
arrival in the main barrack in Calcutta the emigrants obtained new clothing.
Most emigrants took some of their own possessions with them, particularly jewellery carried on their body. Women were often heavily dressed with jewellery
and some emigrants were known to have brought musical instruments and religious books (Bakker 2002).

The barracks had high walls meant to exclude undesirable immigrants and to
prevent desertion. They were also well guarded by *durwans* (gatekeepers). In
spite of these restrictions, there are stories of immigrants who did not qualify for
indentured labour – for health or other reasons – succeeding in embarking as
stowaways to the colonies. Similarly there were cases of desertion. For example,
between 1 August and 17 September 1902, 26 recruits managed to escape from
the main barracks for indentured labourers bound for Suriname (Weller 1968).

At the main barracks, the final selection took place on the basis of a stringent
medical examination in the presence of the British protector of emigrants and
under the attendance of the medical inspector. The emigrants had to be deemed
fit to survive an arduous sea journey of almost three months and to undertake
hard plantation labour in a strange tropical country. There was also a need to
ensure that they were free from diseases so as to prevent epidemics on board the
ship. In registers of the characteristics of the emigrants distinctive physical
marks like stains and scars were mentioned. Potential contract labourers would
be rejected if they showed signs of internal bleeding or fracture.

According to Emmer (1984: 255) the emigrants were also selected on their
'relative superior physical condition' which involved meeting the demands of a

medical and 'mental' abilities test, and meeting height requirements. While statistics of the average height of Indians are unavailable, it is highly plausible that the Indian emigrant to Suriname was quite tall by Indian standards at the time. Half of the emigrants averaged 1.60 metres, a quarter averaged 1.50 metres and the remainder 1.70 metres. In comparison, in 1890, the average height of young men (18/19 years) in the Netherlands was 1.69 metres (Hira 2000: 27). Almost two-thirds of emigrants were aged between 20 and 30, a quarter under 20 years, and less than 2 per cent of emigrants to Suriname were aged above 40 years. Few children emigrated to Suriname because it was not stipulated that children should emigrate. No payment was given for children under 12 years, as they were deemed unfit for plantation work. Families with more than two children were not encouraged to embark because this would raise the risk of epidemics like measles. All in all it can be surmised that there was a rigorous selection process for contract labourers bound to Suriname. Of the 52,330 Indians originally enlisted for emigration to Suriname only 34,395 Indian emigrants finally left. More than one-third of these potential emigrants were excluded (Bhagwanbali 1996).

After the (medical) examination, all approved emigrants had to meet the protector of emigrants in accordance to article 6 of the treaty of 1870. Emigrants were required to sign the agreement voluntarily. To ascertain their voluntary accord, the conditions of the agreement, which bound them to a period of indenture for five years, were read in the Hindustani language. If there were no protests, the emigrant would 'sign' the agreement usually by marking a cross on the agreement form because the majority could not write (Bhagwanbali 1996: 120). The emigrants were then required to further testify that the agreement was voluntarily signed. The labour agreement between the Indian labourer and the Dutch government came to be known among the Indian labourers as *girmit*, a corruption of the word agreement. Serving the agreement period was called *girmit kate*. The Indian indentured labourers were known as *girmitwallah or kontraki*, the latter term a corruption of the Dutch word *kontrakt* meaning agreement.

After signing the agreement, the indentured labourers received a tin plate with their embarkation number marked upon it. The tin plate was carried around their necks. When a sufficient number of approved emigrants were available in the main barrack in Calcutta and all the administrative formalities had been conducted, embarkation began.

The voyage

Only British ships were used for the transportation of Indians to Suriname. Between 1873 and 1916, 64 ships with names like *Ganges*, *Sheila*, *Sutlej*, *Dewa*, *Zhenab* and *Zanzibar* transported more than 34,000 Indian emigrants to Suriname. Up to 1907, 38 batches of indentured labourers were transported by sailing ships, and from 1907, 26 batches arrived by steamship. Amongst these the *Laleham* and *Peshwa* made two journeys (De Klerk 1998: 71–3). The number of emigrants that each ship carried varied from 350 to 800 persons. Emigrants received an identification number that corresponded with the number of the departing ship. Thus the emigrant could be traced through this identification number to the ship, the date of departure from British India and the year of arrival in Suriname.[4]

The journey to Suriname, via the Bay of Bengal to the Indian Ocean and around the Cape of Good Hope (South Africa) to South America lasted three months for sailing ships depending on sailing conditions. On steamships the journey was shorter, usually five to eight weeks. These ships tended to call at the island of St Helena in the Atlantic Ocean to stock up on fresh drinking water and fruits. According to article 14 of the Suriname immigration treaty, emigrants could depart on sailing ships from 15 August until 11 March. If ships departed between 11 March and 15 September, there was a requirement that emigrants receive at least a double blanket because of the cold weather conditions in the Southern hemisphere.

Indian emigrants were divided into groups of 25 and a headman (*sirdar*) was appointed who was responsible for his group. Some emigrants were appointed as barbers, cooks (*bandaras*), cleaners and nurses. It was compulsory that on every ship one or more interpreters be appointed. To prevent men from visiting women at night, women's quarters were guarded. The cabins of unmarried women were situated at the front of the ship and the cabins of unmarried men at the back, with the cabins of families in between. Entertainment on the upper deck ended at eight in the evening and by 10 pm all had to return to their sleeping cabin.

Article 15 of the immigration treaty provided detailed prescriptions on the living conditions of emigrants on board. The cabin had to be fully covered and not less than six feet high (1.80 metres). A surface area of six square metres (two by three metres) was to be made available for every person. Ships were constructed according to these guidelines. While space was limited, very few complaints about living space and life on the ships were registered. The hospital was situated on the lower deck, and the surgeon was required to make regular inspections of cabins particularly to ensure that they were properly ventilated. Emigrants were encouraged to stay as long as possible on the upper decks to get fresh air. Although flammable material was forbidden in the cabin, smoking was allowed in a separate area. Emigrants, however, were not allowed to consume alcoholic beverages and drugs (like *ganja*).

Provisions were acquired and stocked in accordance with the number of emigrants on board. Water and other amenities were distributed daily at six in the morning. The daily ration for an emigrant was: 20 ounces of rice, four ounces of lentils (*dhal*), two ounces of tobacco, two pounds of salted fish and one gallon of water. The ration further included clarified butter (*ghee*), salt, pepper, onions, turmeric and garlic. Once a week, sheep or goat meat was served. For 100 persons, about six sheep or goats were carried on the ship. Vegetables were provided twice a week and sometimes pumpkin and yams or potatoes were included in the menu. When bad weather hampered cooking, emigrants were fed more basic rations (Geoghegan 1874: 25; cited in Weller 1968: 143). In the distribution of provisions and food, children above ten years were considered adults, while for those under ten, two counted as one adult.

The captain, the surgeon and the crew of the ship received pro-rata payment on the basis of emigrants that completed the voyage, and an extra payment for every immigrant that arrived in good health in the colony. If mortality rates or the number of patients suffering illnesses was high, the company that owned the ship could refrain from the service of the captain and the surgeon in the future. Thus it was in the interest of the captain and surgeon to ensure the health of emigrants. The surgeon on board was usually European although on occasion Indian surgeons were used, as in the case of one who demanded better conditions for the indentured labourers on board. Labelled an agitator, he was forced to disembark on the island of St Helena (Tinker 1974). Surgeons were required to ensure that a strict hygiene and nutrition regime prevailed. At the upper deck, breakfast was served at 9 am, lunch at 1 pm and dinner at 5 pm. The surgeon ensured that the meals were hygienically prepared. For children under seven years, there was milk daily. After each meal, the upper deck was cleaned thoroughly. Inspection of the food supply took place periodically. To maintain a healthy appearance, especially at the time of their arrival, the emigrants also had to be massaged twice a week with coconut oil. During the voyages, surgeons occasionally had to deal with child-birth and during one journey, on the ship *Elbe* in 1889, as many as 15 children were born. An extensive report of all aspects of life on board was maintained and all surgeons were required to write a medical report of the journey, which was then delivered to the Agent-General in Paramaribo. Sometimes rapes and suicides occurred, but these were exceptions (Shepherd 1995).

Because of high mortality rates in the initial period of emigration to Suriname, continuous improvements were made on ships. Professional cleaners (*topaz*) were appointed, the hospital was moved to the upper deck, and extra care was given to ensure the cleanliness of water on board. Later water distillery equipment was included. These improvements went a long way in ensuring a reduction of mortality rates especially in the latter period of Indian emigration to Suriname.

On the voyage, no special arrangements were made for emigrants of different castes or classes. The harsh weather conditions, the spatial restrictions of life at sea, and the inability to cater for specific food restrictions had an impact of breaking down caste divisions. Religious obligations, such as prayers five times a day amongst Muslims, or regular Hindu prayers (*puja*), could also not be properly observed.

To alleviate boredom during the long voyage, emigrants partook in various forms of entertainment such as dancing and singing, drumming, wrestling, swordsmanship competitions and stick fighting (*latimar*). Sometimes professional dancers and wrestlers were recruited as emigrants for entertainment purposes. Some such as the wrestler Hari Sing and the dancer Alarakhi would later become well known in Suriname. *Birhas* (elegies) were also sung of their departure from homes, the loss of families and their uncertain future. Life on board ship also included its fair share of quarrels with occasional accusations of theft such as stealing one's *lota* (bowl) or *thali* (plate).

In spite of these arrangements, the voyage to the Caribbean was a dangerous enterprise and most emigrants had ambivalent feelings towards their journey. Dr De Wolfe, a surgeon on an emigrant's ship sailing in 1883 wrote: 'most of the coolies are very homesick after they have left India. They arrived in a strange world.... Fear has taken them while from their nature they are timid' (Tinker 1974: 157). Most emigrants suffered from sea-sickness at the beginning of the voyage and diarrhoea was a common ailment.

Over 40 years of indentured emigration to Suriname, the average mortality rate on the sea voyage was 1.2 per cent, slightly less than the average death rate of 1.3 per cent on sea voyages to all the colonies (Bhagwanbali 1996: 150–1). Of the 34,395 Indian emigrants leaving British India 34,011 arrived in Suriname alive. The number of deaths recorded was quite high especially on the sailing 42 of the 748 emigrants on board perished, amongst whom 32 were children. Most perished in the Bay of Bengal, when high waves shook the *Elbe* heavily. On other ships which recorded high mortality rates, the usual cause was the outbreak of contagious disease. An outbreak of measles on the sailing ship *Ailsa II* in 1880 led to the death of 83 of the 461 emigrants. Similarly on the sailing ship *Sheila* in 1882, 49 of the 452 emigrants succumbed to cholera, and another 14 perished shortly after their arrival in Suriname. On average, however, usually between five to ten emigrants perished on board, and the mortality rate on steamships was lower than on the sailing ships. Only one of the 64 transports to Suriname was shipwrecked: this was the *Laleham*, which was stranded in 1884 off the east coast of Sri Lanka. The *Laleham* emigrants were shipped to Suriname on the next ship, *Peshwa*. In May 1916 the *Dewa* brought the last 303 Indian emigrants to Suriname.

Through the common experience of dangers, and the considerable interaction in small quarters, a bond was formed amongst emigrants during the voyage traversing the *kala pani*. Eating the same food and drinking water from the same tank strengthened this bond. Friendships and relationships were made for life. They became *jahaji bhai* and *jahaji bahin* (ship brothers and sisters), a relationship that to some was so sacred that even marriages between children of those who became brethren during the ship journey was not allowed.

After their arrival in Suriname, emigrants were hosted for 48 hours at the expense of the immigration department in the Coolie barrack in Paramaribo. After further medical checks, the emigrants were allocated to the plantation owners and transported to their plantations, where they were met earlier settled indentured labourers who saw them as an important source of information on developments in British India.

The end of Indian indentured emigration to Suriname

In the early twentieth century, the indenture system came under sustained attack from Indian nationalists. In 1912, G.K. Gokhale introduced a resolution in the

Indian Legislative Assembly to prohibit indentured labour, arguing that the system deprived people of their freedom. His views were supported by the renowned female poet Sarojini Naidu. Besides apprehensions that indenture marked a transitional stage between slave labour and 'free' labour, there were also concerns about the recruitment and departure of strong and healthy Indians from British India. Following the organisation of an agitation and Pandit Madan Mohan Malaviya's and Mahatma Gandhi's insistence on the abolishment of the system, the British government finally relented. On 12 March 1917, the emigration of labourers under indenture from British India officially ceased.

Both the Surinamese government as well as the Indian community in Suriname were disappointed with this decision to end indentured emigration. In 1920, a delegation left Suriname, on the steamer *Madioen*, to plead for the re-opening of indentured emigration. Members of the delegation included H.N. Hajari, an official of the immigration department, interpreter Sital Persad, businessman (and son-in-law of Sital Persad) Lutchman Singh and J.B. Singh, a prominent Indian from Suriname. Using the report of McNeill and Chimman Lal (1915), they argued that emigration and the indenture system held more advantages than disadvantages for immigrants. They met Pandit Madan Mohan Malaviya in Varanasi, Mahatma Gandhi and Shaukat Ali in Ahmedabad and Chimman Lal, the writer of the report on emigration to Suriname, who was then mayor of the city of Meerut. According to Hajari, while the Indian leaders were impressed by the good treatment and position of Indians in Suriname, with the exception of Chimman Lal, they all rejected a re-opening of emigration.

Between 1922 and 1924 the emigration agency and the main barrack in Calcutta for indentured emigration was liquidated. In 1927, the Indians in Suriname, who were till then British subjects, became Dutch subjects thus bringing to an end protection from the British government. The immigration department in Paramaribo was shut down in 1932.

Conclusion

It is clear that in general, Indian emigrants to Suriname were selected stringently and not, as is often portrayed, picked up against their will from the streets and transported to Suriname and other colonies. Many were eager to emigrate to the colonies to earn money. Because Indian emigrants to Suriname arrived at the end of the nineteenth and the beginning of the twentieth century they were able to profit from the improvements in the indenture system especially with regards to provisions on ships and medical care. These emigrants were also provided protection on the basis of the rules of the immigration treaty between the British and the Dutch. The fact that two-thirds of the more than 34,000 Indian emigrants later settled in Suriname and gave up their free passage back to British India is to some extent proof that, for them, life in Suriname was better than in British India. Many returnees to India, in fact, regretted their decision and tried, in vain, to obtain a new agreement for Suriname.

The emigration of Indians to Suriname can be considered a 'success story'.

The relatively good medical treatment that was provided to these emigrants and the fact that the gender ratio for indenture was strictly adhered to led to a huge and rapid growth of the Indian population in Suriname which compares favourably with other Indian diasporic communities in the Caribbean. Similarly, when compared to other parts of the Caribbean, Indians in Suriname have been better able to conserve their Indian culture and heritage.[5] Indians in Suriname also benefited from government policies that introduced obligatory education for boys from 1875 and encouraged educational activities for girls from early on.[6]

Through their diligence and their perseverance Indian emigrants were able to sustain the plantation economy until competition from beet sugar, and other innovations and circumstances, destroyed the labour-intensive plantation system. Building on the crown land they got in the settlement after indenture, many sent money to their families or relatives in British India. Additionally, Indians fostered the cultivation of large parts of Suriname introducing the farming of rice and a wide variety of vegetables and developing cattle-breeding. Furthermore they indirectly aided in the establishment of high quality of medical care and the medical institute in Suriname (Van der Kuyp 1973).

In commemoration of the 75th anniversary of the Indian emigration in 1948, governor Brons addressed the Indians in the former coolie barrack as 'Citizens of Suriname'. Within two decades following this monumental statement, Indians had become the largest, most influential and prosperous ethnic group in Suriname. Many would re-migrate to the Netherlands prior to the independence of Suriname in 1975 - mainly because they wanted to keep their Dutch nationality and felt insecure about the economic and social prospects of Suriname. Notwithstanding this re-migration, or possibly also because of it, the emigration of Indians to Suriname should in the final analysis be seen as a positive journey from Bharat to *Sri Ram Desh*.

Notes

1 For a long time, this college was the only higher educational institute in Suriname. It was founded because of the high mortality rate amongst Indian emigrants in 1873 and 1874.
2 The passing of van Roosevelt in 1891 at the age of 68 was deeply regretted by the Indian emigrants. A large crowd of Indians was said to have attended his funeral. See Fontaine (1980: 114).
3 See Emmer (1984: 240, 250).
4 See database Amrit (1998).
5 According to Tinker, most Indians in the Caribbean, after three or four generations, lost the ability to speak or write in their mother tongue. In drawing this conclusion, it is possible that Tinker did not account for Suriname where Indian languages remain vibrant. See H. Tinker (1974: 13).
6 The spread of education amongst Indians in Trinidad and other British colonies in the Caribbean was more gradual when compared with Suriname. For example, even in 1953, half of the Indian adults in Trinidad were illiterate. Part of the reason why education did not spread as quickly amongst Indians in the British colonies in the Caribbean was due to concerns of conversion to Christianity. In Trinidad, the Sanatana Dharma Maha Sabha had to fund Hindu schools to educate the children, mainly due to these

concerns. In Suriname there was less pressure to become a Christian if you wanted to be educated. In addition there were non-religious coolie schools for children. Such schools were largely absent in the British colonies in the Caribbean.

References

Adhin, J.H. (1998) *Cultuur en maatschappij: veertig artikelen van Jnan Adhin*, Paramaribo: Prakashan.

Adhin, J.H. (1973) *100 jaar Suriname: gedenkboek in verband met een eeuw immigratie (1873–5 Juni 1973)*, Paramaribo: Nationale Stichting Hindostaanse Immigratie.

Amrit (consultancy) (1998) *Hindostaanse immigratie*, database, Den Haag.

Angel, W.H. Captain (1995) *A Return to the Middle Passage, the Clipper Ship 'Sheila'*, Trinidad: CIS.

Bakker, F. (2002) 'Nieuwe groei en ontwikkeling op vreemde bodem: De religies van de Hindostanen in Suriname en de andere Caraïben', *Oso*, 21(1): 58–75.

Bhagwanbali, R. (1996) *Contracten voor Suriname: Arbeidsmigratie vanuit Brits-Indië onder het intendured-labourstelsel 1873–1916*, PhD thesis, Nijmegen.

Buddingh, H. (1999) *Geschiedenis van Suriname*, Utrecht: Het Spectrum.

Choenni, C.E.S. (1982) *Hindoestanen in de politiek*, Rotterdam: Futile.

Choenni, C.E.S. and K. Adhin (2003) *Hindostanen, van Brits Indisch emigrant via Suriname tot burger van Nderland*, Den Haag: Sampreshan.

De Klerk, C.J.M. (1998) *De immigratie van Hindostanen in Suriname*, 2nd edition, first published in 1953, Den Haag: Amrit.

Emmer, P.C. (2000) 'A Spirit of Independence or Lack of Education for the Market? Freedman and Asian Labourers in the Post-emancipation Caribbean 1834–1917', *Slavery & Abolition*, 21(2): 150–68.

Emmer, P.C. (1990) 'Immigration into the Caribbean; the Introduction of Chinese and East Indian Indentured Labourers between 1839 and 1917', *Itinerario*, 14(1): 61–96.

Emmer, P.C. (1987) 'Asians Compared, some Observations regarding Indian and Indonesian Indentured Labourers in Suriname, 1873–1939', *Itinerario*, 11(1): 149–54.

Emmer, P.C. (1986) 'The Meek Hindu: The Recruitment of Indian Labourers for Service Overseas, 1870–1916', in P.C. Emmer (ed.) *Colonialism and Migration; Indentured Labour Force and after Slavery*, Dordrecht: Martinus Nijhoff, pp. 187–207.

Emmer, P.C. (1984) 'The Great Escape: The Migration of Female Indentured Servants from British India to Suriname 1873–1916', in D. Richardson (ed.) *Abolition and its Aftermath: The Historical Context, 1790–1916*, London: Frank Cass, pp. 245–66.

Fontaine, J. (1980) (ed.) *Uit Surinames historie: Fragmenten uit een bewogen verleden*, Zutphen: Walburg.

Gandhi, M.K. (1958) *The Collected Works of Mahatma Gandhi*, vol. 1, New Delhi: Publications Division of the Government of India.

Hira, S. (ed.) (2003) *Het dagboek van Munshi Rahman Khan*, Den Haag: Amrit.

Hira, S. (2000) *Terug naar Uttar Pradesh, op zoek naar de wortels van Surinaamse Hindostanen*, Den Haag: Amrit.

Hira, S. (1982) *Van priari toten met de Kom*, Rotterdam: Futile.

Hoefte, R. (1998) *In Place of Slavery: A Social History of British Indian and Javanese Laborers in Suriname*, Gainesville: University Press of Florida.

Kolff, D.M.A. (1999) 'Het Hindoestaanse erfgoed uit de emigratietijd', *OHM Vani*, 5(4): 18–22.

Laxmi, M. and Mansingh, A. (1999) *Home Away from Home: 150 Years of Indian Presence in Jamaica, 1845–1995*, Kingston: Ian Randle.

McNeill, J. and C. Lal (1915) *Report to the Government of India on the Condition of Indian Immigrants in the Four British Colonies and Suriname*, London: HMSO.

Naipaul, V.S. (1996) *The Middle Passage*, London: Penguin.

Ramdin, R. (2002) *Arising from Bondage: A History of the Indo-Caribbean People*, New York: New York University Press.

Shepherd, V.A. (1992) *Transients to Settlers; The Experience of Indians in Jamaica, 1845–1950*, Kingston: Peepal Tree.

Shepherd, V.A. (2000) 'Maharani's Misery: Narratives of a Passage from India', Migration Conference Paper, UWI St Augustine, Trinidad.

Singhvi, L.M. (2002) *Report of the High Level Committee on the Indian Diaspora*, Delhi: Government of India.

Tinker, H. (1974) *A New System of Slavery*, Oxford: Oxford University Press.

Tinker, H. (1977) *The Banyan Tree, People on the Move*, Oxford: Oxford University Press.

Traktaat Staatsblad van het Koninkrijk der Nederlanden (The Official Gazette of the Kingdom of Netherlands), 17 March 1872, Den Haag: Staatsdrukkerij en Uitgeverij.

Van der Kuyp, E. (1973) *Een eeuw wetenschappelijk onderzoek, medisch wetenschappelijk onderzoek*, Paramaribo.

Van Lier, R. (1977) *Samenleving in een grensgebied, een sociaal historische studie van Suriname*, Amsterdam: Emmering.

Varma, O.F.H.R. (1993) *De slavernij van Hindustanen in Suriname*, Paramaribo: Eigen Beheer.

Waltmans, H. (2002) *Suriname 1650–2000, een politieke studie*, Oosrterhout: Waltmans.

Weller, J.A. (1968) *The East Indian Indenture in Trinidad*, Rio Pedras: University of Puerto Rico.

8 Sociological reflections on the diasporic Bangladeshis in Singapore and USA

Habibul Haque Khondker

Just a few years before his death Nirad C. Chaudhuri (1992) wrote an article, *'Ami Keno Bilate Achi'* ('Why am I living in England') explaining in great detail his reasons for self-exile. Mr Chaudhuri, then in his matured age of 95, was responding to an innocent letter from a Kolkata woman who wanted to know why someone as famous as Nirad Chaudhuri does not want to return to his native land. Chaudhuri provides a long justification as to why he left India and makes other points, such as that he left before he was famous and so on. In that long essay, it is evident that after quarter of a century of self-exile, this well-known 'unknown Indian' is still nostalgic and yet bitter about India. An India he hates, an India he loves; an ambivalence that describes many diasporic Indians and for that matter Bengalis. Needless to say, the late Mr Chaudhuri was a Bengali.

Apart from the setbacks, frustrations and financial difficulties he had had in India, Mr Chaudhuri even picked on such day to day banalities as the difficulty of walking along the night-soil infested bank of the river Jamuna in Delhi. His critical stance on India revealed in his famous *Autobiography of an Unknown Indian* published in 1951 did not endear himself to his fellow Indians. Many of his critics are patriotic Indians and Bengalis who never forgave him for presenting India in an unfavourable light. As far as Chaudhuri was concerned, he was trying to tell the truth and nothing but the truth. Truth – as he saw fit. He wanted to say it as it was, with warts and all. This is what a commentator observed about Chaudhuri following his death on 1 August 1999 at Oxford where he spent the second half-century of his life:

> What a journey Nirad Chaudhuri made, from the Bengali village where he was born in 1897 to Oxford where he just died, still writing and publishing after turning 100. The entire culture and history of Asia and Europe seemed to be in the head of this last eminent Victorian. His knowledge served truth, not flattery. The people of India in his opinion had been fortunate: British rule had rescued them from decadence. Once independent, the whole continent of India heedlessly squandered a civilizing and universal legacy. Several of his books tell the story in the form of autobiography, and they are masterpieces all. Settling in England, he discovered a country turning its

back on everything it once stood for. This was decadence. With supreme energy and humor, he savaged the tragicomedy of the permissive society and its mass-produced political correctness. A free spirit, a great man.

(*National Review* 1999)

Yet at the same time it is interesting to observe that many in the diaspora are overly critical of their homeland. Such criticism is not unrelated to the much-needed justification for self-exile. Surely, all Bengalis in the diaspora are not in self-exile, yet exile as a metaphor captures an important aspect of their experience. Their longing for return is the obverse of their sense of exile.

Bengalis, and by implication, Bangladeshis, have a reputation for being homebound. In fact, a BBC survey conducted in 2006 revealed that a very large number of Bangladeshis are happy to remain homebound. The aftermath of the independence of Bangladesh in 1971 was a trying time for many Bangladeshis as a combination of forces, the ravages of the war, the unfavourable global economic situation and an inexperienced – though well-meaning – administration, led to an economic decline. A sense of hopelessness and a wide gap between the high expectations and dismal achievements created frustrations and many Bangladeshis sought an exit option.

In the mid-1970s, some parts of the Middle East – awash with petro-dollars – attracted large numbers of migrant workers and professionals from Bangladesh. Young Bangladeshis, mostly men, showed up in France, Germany and Italy; some made their way to the western part of Europe from various erstwhile socialist countries in East Europe where they went to study on scholarships. North American and Southeast Asian destinations were added too in the 1980s and 1990s. I have observed Bangladeshis in diaspora from Sweden to Canada and Singapore to Abu Dhabi.

In this chapter, I look at the Bengali-speaking community from the state of Bangladesh; they are not all in self-exile but they have scattered – in search of a good life for some, in search of mere survival for others. I look at two communities one in Singapore and one in the United States. The majority of the Bengali-speaking communities in Bangladesh are Muslims (88 per cent). Some of them are quite secular; others are fairly religious; and there are several shades in between. This diversity is well reflected in the diasporic Bangladeshis. Bangladeshis began to trickle out of Bangladesh from the early 1970s – some out of desperation, others bitten by the bug of *wanderlust*. A number of young Bangladeshi students were given scholarships to study in the USSR and other Soviet-bloc countries. I met a young Bangladeshi in Michigan State University in the mid-1980s who taught Russian literature and language. In the aftermath of the liberation of Bangladesh, the USSR offered scholarships to Bangladesh and hundreds of meritorious Bangladeshis went to various parts of the Soviet Union to study. The young man I met had studied Russian language and literature at Moscow State University, where most of his compatriots studied science and engineering subjects. Globalisation, like God, works in such mysterious ways.

In this chapter, I want to talk about identity, especially the transient nature of identity, drawing on a study which is empirical, rather than theoretical. My research strategy here is in the vein of ethnographic research; my presentation follows the style that Geertz calls 'thick description'. I have interviewed some diasporic Bengalis; many of whom like to identify themselves as Bangladeshis rather than Bengalis, in order to draw a line of difference between themselves and the Bengali-speakers from West Bengal, which is now a state in India. I have tried to elicit their biographical experiences as members of the diasporic Bengali/Bangladeshi community. I observe everyday life; I chat both with people I know and others who I do not know and I reflect on the conversations and encounters and try to narrate these experiences under some sociological rubrics so that the stories of everyday life gain some coherence and sociological standing, so that the snap-shots become a composite picture rather than a mere collection of images. The observations in Singapore were made between 1985 and 2005 and in the United States between the early 1980s and the present.

A framework for discussion

Globalisation is the template through which I approach this flow of people which results in intercultural encounters, building or re-building of community and maintenance of culture. Globalisation is a process which has some superficial resemblance to modernisation writ large but it is not a linear expansion of Western modernisation. Non-linearity, complexity and uncertainty are essential features of globalisation (Khondker 2000). It is somewhat akin to the notion of multiple modernities but these different traditions of modernity do not stand side by side as pillars; under the rubric of globalisation they coalesce, intermingle and generate new forms – often captured by such terms as hybridity, pastiche, mosaic and melange (Pieterse 1995, 2004). Globalisation has been defined by Bartelson (2000) in terms of three Ts: 'transference', 'transformation' and 'transcendence'. Globalisation has intensified transference or exchange of things. Globalisation can also be understood as transformation or changes of systems, ideas, values and so on. The third 'T' in Bartelson's discussion is 'transcendence' which suggests that the old divisions and dichotomous categories such as 'inside' and 'outside' or even 'local' and 'global' are increasingly becoming inadequate to describe issues. Global is as much constructed as local. Robertson (1995) has coined the term 'glocalisation' which attempts to transcend the time-honoured polarities.

Three more Ts can be added: 'transmigration', 'translation' and 'transience'. Migration reiterates the need for translation of culture and values and emphasises the importance of the category of transience. I use globalisation in this sense as my framework. Migration is both a symptom and a defining feature of globalisation. If we view globalisation as an historical process in the making for centuries rather than a post-Second World War economic grid connecting the world, we will recognise the significance of the movement of people along with the movement of capital as a key element in the processes of globalisation. The transatlantic slave trade; the system of indentured labour; enforced or 'encouraged' systems of population movement during colonial rule; all these constitute important episodes in the making of a globalised world with implications for multiculturalism and identity politics today. It is hard to separate or ignore the historical antecedents if we want a clearer understanding of contemporary migrations, be it temporary or contract labour migration or the migration of the aspiring and socially mobile middle classes.

In 2005, according to the United Nations Department of Economic and Social Affairs (UNDESA), 191 million persons representing 3 per cent of the world's population lived outside their country of birth. The equivalent figure in 1960 amounted to 75 million persons or 2.5 per cent of the world's population. Almost one in every ten persons living in more developed regions is a migrant (UNDESA 2006). Transnational movement of people is a fundamental feature of globalisation: 'Diaspora populations in many locations ... are engaged in complex interpersonal and intercultural relationships with both their host societies and their societies of origin' (Thambiah 2000: 163).

Why do I compare Bangladeshi communities in Singapore and USA? I look at these two locales, primarily because of my familiarity with these two places and also because of the contrasts they present. The United States is still the most attractive destination of migrants from Bangladesh. It is also a liberal society, a society that promotes tolerance and multiculturalism based on the recognition of the rights of individuals and communities from distant lands. Singapore is officially a multi-ethnic and, by and large, tolerant society; but here, compliance with rules and laws which are strictly enforced keep the society integrated and peaceful. The divergent social and political milieu of the host societies exert differential impact on diasporic Bangladeshis. The USA is a terminus, an end point in a long journey. Singapore, for some is a terminus but for many Bangladeshis it is a transit point in their migratory movement to USA, Canada or Australia; and only a handful who move on yearn for a return to Bangladesh (although some do at retirement age).

Diversity

In early 2004 a Bangladeshi businessman in Singapore, whose enterprise had a turnover of around three million Singapore dollars in the first year of his business, hosted a party to celebrate the first anniversary of his company. Ironically, the word anniversary was misspelt in the colourful banner that bedecked the ballroom of a Singapore hotel, where well-dressed Bangladeshi men and colourful, sari-clad women feasted on Indian cuisine. It was a manifestation of a contradiction that characterises the life-stories of many Bangladeshis: some of them are making it in a competitive environment. It was a display of the success of a promising Bangladeshi businessman, but it was also a story of his failure. His success is related to two processes in Bangladesh: an outgoing business culture – Bangladesh's business with Singapore stands at over one billion Singapore dollars in 2003 – and a failed education system in Bangladesh, which is just one aspect of a weak state. With the exception of a handful of elite

English-medium schools and small number of private universities, public education in Bangladesh is in a shamble, the victim of a social malaise. The function in question was attended by the elite of the Bangladeshi diaspora in Singapore and some of them had the best of overseas education. A common language, Bengali, unites the successful businessman and the rest of the community, as English, the language of the world at the moment, divides them and works as a yardstick for measuring cosmopolitanism.

The diversity and the pluralities amongst the migrant communities can sometimes be greater than the differences between the host and the migrant groups. In order to minimise my task and to give this chapter some focus, I deal with the Bangladeshis and not Bengalis as such. The difference, needless to say, is political. By which I mean that this invented difference reflecting the constructed geopolitical history of political division in India has gained a life of its own. The territory that comprises present Bangladesh joined Pakistan in 1947 on the grounds that it was a Muslim-dominated region. The Muslim political leadership whipped up the religious sentiment among the Muslim peasantry and other Bengali Muslims, who joined in this demand for a separate 'homeland' of their own. Since a large number of landed gentry and the overlords were Hindus and the vast majority of small peasants and agricultural labourers were Muslims, a class antagonism helped fuel that division. However, by 1971, the people of Bangladesh (then called East Pakistan) had had enough of Islamic solidarity, which barely camouflaged regional exploitation.

It was a combination of economic exploitation, political domination and cultural hegemony of the military-dominated Punjabi elites of Pakistan that alienated the people of the then East Pakistan. Bengalis in East Pakistan launched a movement for defending their language and culture which graduated to a full-scale political movement of the rights of self-determination. In March 1971, when Pakistan's army launched a military crackdown to stem the growing political unrest, an armed struggle began which led to the creation of Bangladesh. In the armed conflict, the Indian government provided both military and moral help and gave sanctuary to the Bengalis who crossed over into the bordering states of India. Although the refugees and escapees from East Bengal were received with care and sympathy by the Bengalis of West Bengal and other Indians in the areas where they took shelter, the friendship did not last long. After Bangladesh became independent, the newly installed government did not last long. A military coup removed the nationalist government and they began to capitalise on wedging a difference and unfriendly relations with India.

In cyberspace there is a 'soc.culture Bengal', which, in principle, deals with issues of interest to Bengali-speaking people as a whole. In reality, however, 'soc.culture Bengal' is a platform for the Bengalis from West Bengal. There is also a 'soc.culture Bangladesh' which deals primarily with events and issues affecting the nation-state of Bangladesh. The division has, thus, become official.

Bengali community organisations in Singapore and USA

In Singapore there are three separate social or civic organisations of broadly Bengali people registered with the Registry of Societies. The oldest is known as the Bengali Association of Singapore set up in 1956 by the Bengali-speaking people from India comprising both recent and earlier migrants. One of the main functions of that organisation was to hold *Puja* ceremonies and other cultural events in the Bengali calendar. However membership was not limited to Bengali-speaking community members from the Indian state of West Bengal. Some Bangladeshis joined this organisation and some of them even held offices.

Chronologically, the second organisation was set up in 1981 by migrant professionals from Bangladesh who came to Singapore after the country's independence in 1971. In 1977, an attempt was made by a local Bangladeshi businessman, Mr Kader, to set up an organisation. The Registry of Societies turned down his request apparently on the grounds that there was already an organisation for the Bengalis.[1] The successful application was lodged by a group of Bangladeshi professionals mainly academics under the leadership of Dr M.A. Aziz to set up an association called Singapore–Bangladesh Society (SBS). Dr Aziz served as the President of Singapore–Bangladesh Society for the first five years.

The third organisation called the Bangla Language and Literary Society was set up in 1994 and this organisation has members drawn both from Bangladesh and the Indian state of West Bengal. The main function of Bangla Language and Literary Society (Singapore) or BLLS, as it is commonly known, is to run a Bangla School with over 300 students. The school meets on Saturdays for three and a half hours, where teachers from both Bangladesh and West Bengal teach students who also display a similar diversity of background.

In addition to the three community associations, there are such specialised associations as the Tagore society of Singapore which is limited to the educated *bhadralok* class at the moment but has the potential to become a community organisation. There is also an association of Bangladeshi engineers in Singapore whose numbers have swelled in the early twenty-first century. Many promising Bangladeshi engineering students, who under normal circumstances would have ended up in the United States, came to universities in Singapore after the debacle of 9/11. As the State Department of the US government imposed strict control of visas for Bangladeshi students as part of an overall increase in stringent measures to prevent potential terrorists from entering the United States, they found alternative destinations to pursue higher education and employment. This coincided with Singapore's policy of targeted immigration of young professionals to increase her talent pool.

An overall increase in immigration and employment visa holders in Singapore, among other things, popularised cricket in Singapore. There is a cricket club set up by Bangladeshi professionals and students known as Bengal Cricket Club which taps players from the pool of cricket enthusiasts from India, Pakistan, Sri Lanka and Bangladesh.

In the early 1980s when we – mainly students drawn from the British Commonwealth countries – played cricket at the Carnegie Mellon University, some Americans would stop their cars to watch this game which they thought was a slow-speed version of baseball. Now, in 2007, cricket is more visible with increased Indian migrants. Interestingly, both the USA and Singapore are united by a common historical legacy of British rule where, unlike other former British colonies, cricket failed to emerge as a popular sport.

There has been a mushrooming of Bangladeshi and Bengali community organisations in North America. In the major cities, there are Bangladeshi organisations, organised around locality, i.e. districts of origin in Bangladesh, such as Feni Foundation or Noakhali Society; occupation-based, for example the Bangladesh Medical Association, Engineers Association; or alumni associations of various educational institutions. These associations are primarily support groups which also become sites of intense political activities.

There are also associations created for the preservation of the memories of the founding politicians of Bangladesh, such as *Bangabandhu Parishad* or *Zia Parishad*. The most important of all such associations are the political organisations which work as branches of the political parties in Bangladesh, with excellent links with their respective political patrons in Bangladesh. Then, of course, there are mosques which become the nucleus of community organisations. Even the mosques, often clearly, albeit unofficially, bear the identity of the district of origin of the faithful. There are mosques for the Sylheties (those from the district of Sylhet), a mosque for the migrants from Noakhali and one for those from Chittagong.

A number of Bengali weeklies are published in New York which cover, in great detail, political news from Bangladesh. *Thikana*, a weekly, has been in circulation since 1990; *Akhon Samay, The Weekly Darpan, The Kagoj Bangla, The Weekly Bengalee, Bangla Barta and New Probashi* are some of the Bengali language newspapers in New York. All in all, the political scene among Bangladeshi organisations is vibrant. During election season, the local newspapers carry advertisements of various local associations. Electronic media too plays an important role in maintaining a close link between Bangladeshis in USA with their families and friends back home. There are several Bangladeshi artists in USA who left Bangladesh for various reasons. Hence Bangladeshi cultural events in USA often host these émigré artists which draw big audiences. In Singapore, the strict control on media and stringent regulations keep satellite-television out of reach for the Bangladeshis. This is, however, compensated for by the availability of Bangladeshi newspapers and magazines in shops that line certain Serangoon streets.

In the USA, an umbrella organisation, the Federation of Bangladeshi Associations in North America, draws a large number of local Bangladeshi associations into a national convention once a year. This gathering, now popularly known by its acronym FOBANA, takes place on the Labour Day weekend, the first Monday of September, every year in one of the big cities. Since 1987 it has met 21 times. The 21st meeting took place in Kansas city. The first meeting in 1987 took place in Washington DC. Although its mission statement indicates that it is a non-political and non-religious association, politics does play an integral part. The guest list of the 2006 FOBANA meeting included some corrupt ministers and political figures from Bangladesh. Most of them, after a political changeover, are now, at the time of drafting this chapter (September 2007), being tried on charges of corruption.

The intrusion of politics has created factionalism in various organisations as well as in the umbrella organisation itself. In 1994, in 1995 and in 1996, parallel conventions of FOBANA took place. In 1995, there were parallel meetings in Montreal where some participants moved from one to the other to enjoy the shows and the food. In these conventions they invite leading artists from Bangladesh and organise fairs to showcase saris and other items for the participants. The main reason why many attend these annual events is to meet old friends and to expose their children to Bangladeshi/Bengali culture. Seminars and discussions on issues related to national development or the overseas Bangladeshi community are also organised. Many Bangladeshi professionals also attend such events to display their high professional and class status. Others come to enjoy a sense of community and to renew their social bonding.

Class and *bhadralok* status

In the mid-1970s a huge number of Bangladeshi workers went to the Gulf to work as construction workers. It may be useful to separate contract workers who have no choice but to return to their country of origin from those who exercise some choice, thus agency, over the country and home as their destination. I use diaspora strictly to capture the latter group, i.e. the *bhadralok* migration. It is important to understand that *bhadralok* is more than a class, it is a status group. Literally, it means 'the gentlemen class', a category that some of the intellectually-oriented British civil servants-*cum*-historians coined to describe the social structure of Bengal. There are certain demarcating features of this *bhadralok* class or as they are also known as part of 'Babu' culture. Members of this social category prefer white-collar work, and are averse to manual work and even business. Their roots can be found in the absentee landlord class. Migration for many Bangladeshis was seen as an escape from the economic hardships of their native land, it was also a social ladder to become a member of the *bhadralok* class in the shortest possible time. Yet, in climbing the social ladder, many of them had to work hard and manually. Here we find a sharp difference between Bangladeshis in the USA with those in Singapore. The openness and opportunities in American society provided many opportunities for some decaying members of the *bhadralok* class to retain their status and for others to gain that status. In Singapore, on the contrary, such class mobility is almost impossible to attain.

The importance of the host society, not only its policies towards the migrant communities but the nature of social contract with its own population, plays a role in determining the life chances of the migrants. Singapore, as host society, has strict control and monitoring of incoming migrants, which apart from reducing the number of illegal Bangladeshis to the minimum, ensures that the migrant workers return home after their tenure. The middle class professionals are clearly distinguished from the working class contract workers. Their visas are different, reflecting their differential social ranks and income. In the USA, many who started with a humble manual job climbed up the social ladder, and for others it involved trading places. In the early 1970s, a number of students dropped out of Dhaka University and ended up in New York. One of them started work in a bakery; by the late 1980s he was the owner of one of the most popular up-market Indian restaurants in New York. A Bangladeshi Air Force officer I met some time back in Los Angeles, became a bank employee for a while, tried his hand at writing a fiction narrating his migrant experience, before settling down to sell Lexus to rich Asians (mainly Chinese) in Los Angeles. Another senior Air Force officer took a more down to earth job. He became a member of the California Highway Patrols or CHIPs. Such mobility or cross-over is quite common.

The main thrust of Bangladeshi migration to the United States since 1970s has been the migration of the middle class or the *bhadralok* class. The introduction of D-visa or 'Diversity visa' apparently sought to correct the so-called 'brain drain' and make it an equal opportunity affair since the applicants were chosen on the basis of a lottery. This has resulted in a great diversity amongst the Bangladeshi migrants in the USA. A number of newspaper salesmen in New York are from Bangladesh and some of them are poorly educated even by Bangladeshi standards, and there are Bangladeshis who have attained a great deal of material success as well as social standing. There are Bangladeshi university teachers as there are investment bankers. The first South Asian to serve as an ambassador of the United States government was of Bangladeshi origin. Mr Osman Siddique, a first generation Bangladeshi-American was appointed US ambassador to Fiji by President Clinton. Another young Bangladeshi, Dina Hossain, has made a name for herself by co-producing a documentary on the legendary Lucille Ball. She has also made documentaries on Leonard Bernstein, Ella Fitzgerald and other cultural luminaries of America.

A young Bangladeshi-American, Asif Siddiqi, has received accolades as a science historian with specialisation in Soviet space. As a PhD student at Carnegie Mellon University, he published *The Soviet Space Race with Apollo* for which he won the Emme Award for Astronautical Literature in 2001. Another Bangladeshi-American scientist, Abul Hussam, received the Grainger Challenge Prize in 2007 from the National Academy of Engineering and the Grainger Foundation of USA. This award is one of the most prestigious prizes in the field of engineering and is restricted to US citizens. A young Bangladeshi-American woman, Nora Ali, won the Miss USA Junior award in 2007, which apart from national fame in both USA and Bangladesh, landed her a scholarship at Harvard University. The Nobel-laureate Professor Yunus of Bangladesh was featured in several American talk shows, which included *Oprah* and Jon Stewart's *The Daily Show*, and was accorded a warm reception at various levels in the USA partly because he was a graduate of Vanderbilt University in the USA.

The norms of meritocracy and openness in American society encourage many migrants to pursue their dreams by overcoming odds. It is not surprising that about 13 per cent of the US population are immigrants. The strong sense of career mobility and strive can be seen in one woman's struggle to help her son through college. This woman, estranged from her husband and on her own for several years, runs a kiosk in a shopping mall in Ithaca, New York, to help her son through Cornell. Even as she runs her business, she makes sure that her only son gets a home-cooked meal every day. She has developed her own network comprising the friends of her son. In one instance when she had to travel to Florida, some of her son's friends ran the kiosk, selling tid-bits and cultural items from Bangladesh and elsewhere. In another case, a young woman from a provincial town of Bangladesh entered America as part of a delegation of an international youth organisation and never returned home. She found a sales job at a shop with her college education. Her employer was not interested in her visa status. In the course of time, after she had saved enough money, she consulted a lawyer who counselled her to declare herself as a political refugee and after a legal battle she got her green card. That was one of the best days of her life. A single woman from a distant land making her way to New York she has gained in confidence. She lives modestly in an apartment at Brooklyn and commutes to her workplace at Manhattan. She is saving money to buy her own place so that she can bring her mother from Bangladesh. Singapore society with its strict rules does not allow migrants to take advantage of gaining legal status as residents through the court.

Parents sacrificing their lives for their children are a common theme in Bangladesh. Bangladeshi communities in the USA are no exception. In another instance, a Bangladeshi professional took up manual work in a city so that his children got a good education. There was a case of a 12-year-old boy who had a cancer in his eye for which he was seen by a doctor in Singapore who in turn advised that treatment of this condition was available in the USA. The boy's father, a member of the cabin crew of Biman Bangladesh Airlines, jumped ship with his family, ended up as a cab driver, got his son's surgical procedure done in New York, and now lives in New York. The boy grew up in New York, works part-time and adds to the income of the family pool. His prospect of getting a job suddenly declined after 9/11. His name is Osama.

Since the focus of this essay is identity, it is worth mentioning how Bangladeshi identity was affected by the terrorist attacks of September 11, 2001. I was in the USA in the summer of 2001, just a couple of months before the attack. I returned to the States in the summer of 2002. I was mostly in New York as my sabbatical was split between Columbia at Manhattan and Cornell at upstate New York. I was a frequent visitor to Syracuse where I had the opportunity to observe the Bangladeshi community from a close distance. My cousin, who lived in Queens, the mecca of the Bangladeshi community in New York, was a recent migrant to the US. She was a researcher in a state organisation. Her husband was a fallen businessman who had no income and no job. In New York he reinvented himself as a worker in a food store. His social mobility took a reverse direction from a middle-class businessman in Bangladesh to a working-class, struggling migrant, in the USA. Their elder son was recruited in the US Army. As Bush was planning war on Iraq, my cousin became frenetic. I was a counsellor for them at a difficult time. They were part of a *bhadralok* class and all they wanted was to retain their status. They did not plan to go to a foreign land to get involved in some war in some distant places. They wanted stability and guarantee for a secure life for which they had left home in the first place. The decision to join the services had its allure in terms of benefits, especially a scholarship to pursue a college education in engineering. As the war proceeded, the parents become more religious and possibly received 'God's attention'. The young man was spared a tour of duty in Iraq, completed his services with distinction and finished with an engineering degree from Rutgers University. Now married and with a secure civilian employment, he fulfilled the dreams of his parents. He met his wife-to-be, a Canadian Bangladeshi, at his college. The prayers of his parents were handsomely rewarded.

Resurgent Islam?

Bangladeshi Muslims are, by and large, religious people. There is a popular self-image of Bangladeshis as a moderate Muslim community. This image has been made popular particularly by the diasporic Bangladeshis. Religion in moderation is a particularly problematic term. What is evident is that the religiosity of Bangladeshis in the USA is not uniform. The posh houses of the affluent Virginia doctors were never in short supply of fine wine. I attended an event of the Bangladeshis in Syracuse which was organised in a church. On the day of the programme, a diner, one of the key organisers, received a phone call. One of the participants requested that food should be served separately for males and females. Now this caller is not really someone who observes strict rules of seclusion: she works in a K-Mart. But in the gathering of the Bangladeshis she prefers to be in seclusion. She came to the United States via one of the Gulf countries (Saudi Arabia) and brought with her a reinforced culture of religiosity. In her mind, the Bangladesh community is the 'real community' where she wants to go by the rules of her cultural norms. She wants to behave and dress like a Bangladeshi Muslim woman in her own community. The larger community norms are mere survival strategies for her. So it is not a contradiction for her to work in K-Mart as a sales assistant, and sometimes at the cashier's counter, interacting with the shoppers. The larger American community is not her community. That is a community of the others that she interacts with minimally and functionally. The roles of Bangladeshi women are varied. It cannot be reduced to a distinction between 'modern' versus 'traditional'. The roles are not to be viewed as fixed but transient. What seems like a carry over from ancestral practices rooted in hoary traditions can very well be quite a recent acquisition from a distant culture, some alien place such as Kuwait, Qatar or Saudi Arabia, a point of transition on the way to the final destination, USA.

Community activities of the Bangladeshis in Pittsburgh, Pennsylvania, USA revolve around the newly built mosque. One of the doctors played an important role in the mosque and through it on the entire community. Children go to this mosque on Sundays to take Arabic and religious lessons. This was in sharp contrast from my student days in Pittsburgh in the early 1980s. In Singapore religion is a touchy subject and even devout Bangladeshis are aware of that and they keep their faith private. The only exception is when they organise *Milad*, a small gathering at home to praise the prophet. Deaths in the family, a birth or moving into a new home are occasions for such *Milad*.

Yet religion is not completely absent in Singapore. An annual prize-giving function of a community-based school in Singapore started with prayers and ended with a fashion parade displaying Bangladeshi dresses, mainly saris and kameez suites. Even the culture of recreation was not free from the political overtones of back home. The government of Bangladesh at that time was formed by the Nationalist Party (BNP) in Dhaka, which used to combine this blend of modernity with Islam in an interesting, though ambiguous, way. The school function was a true replication of such ambiguity and confusion. Community politics in USA too, is often a replica of politics back home dominated by party line – the centrist Awami League and the rightist BNP. And sometimes politics degenerates into fist-fights. Political culture is also reproduced through widely circulated political jokes especially after the Florida election where apparently Bangladeshi consultants were used as advisers on how to rig elections.

Some of the conspiracy theories over 9/11 were popularised in Bangladesh by the overseas Bangladeshis in the USA. The vast majority of Muslims including the Bangladeshi Muslims in USA voted for George Bush in the US presidential election in 2000 because Al Gore's Vice-Presidential candidate, Senator Joe Lieberman, was of Jewish faith. Soon after the attacks of 9/11, President Bush did invite the Muslim leaders and helped pre-empt any backlash against the Muslim community.

Zaglu Bhai, a former leader of the Bangladeshi community in New Jersey, once confided to me in a matter of fact statement that there are three types of Bangladeshis and only the first two categories have the qualities to be overseas. This sort of arrogance is not uncommon among the overseas Bangladeshis, especially if they have achieved even a modicum of material success, gradually assuming the name and prestige as non-resident Bangladeshis or NRB after the non-resident Indians or NRI. Not too long ago, in a reported interview, Indian children, when they were asked what do you want to be when they grow up, answered that they wanted to be NRI. For Zaglu Bhai, the Bangladeshis can be categorised as 'A', 'B' and 'C' categories. 'A' category of people – obviously the best of the lot – are in the USA and Europe; 'B' category in Japan, Southeast Asia and elsewhere; those belonging to 'C' category are left in Bangladesh.

Internet discussion groups, blogs and so on, provide another window on the Bangladeshi community. Soc.culture Bangladesh is dominated by discussion of Bangladeshi politics mostly on partisan lines. The feuds between the two leading political parties – Bangladesh Nationalist Party or BNP and Awami League –have surpassed ethnic and religious conflicts. Politics has remained a source of identity because the difference between these two parties is essentially – with few exceptions – a divide between the centre-right versus the centre and centre left. Since its birth in the late 1970s, the centre right BNP positioned itself as anti-Indian and Islam-leaning political party to effectively counteract the so-called secularist Awami League. Under the existing circumstances when Islamist groups in the USA are under a lot of scrutiny and political pressure, a large number of pro-Islamist Bangladeshis are confronted with a deep sense of ambivalence. Many of them were quick to protest international media presentation of Bangladesh as 'a cocoon of terrorism' or a 'state of disgrace'. Many of them wrote letters or sent emails to the source of these 'negative publicities'. A BBC documentary has shown that the mosques in New York known for over-flowing attendance are now receiving fewer devotees. The ambivalence of Bangladeshis is part of the general predicament of Muslims in post-9/11 USA.

Divorce as empowerment

There are clear advantages in being a member of the upper class. A rich doctor's son who is a borderline autistic was married to a very pretty woman from Bangladesh whose family was poor. Once in the US, she found out that her husband was not fully normal. She waited and later ventured out on her own. In another case, a newly wed bride in Los Angeles was subject to abuse by her in-laws until she found her way out of the relationship with help from the local community. Another family had two daughters who were married and are now divorced and working in a gas station in Los Angeles. The breakdown of traditional gender roles was made possible due to migration. The breakdown of so-called traditional gender roles is, in fact, the story of empowerment of women. Divorce for many of them is a transition to freedom. Divorce is becoming quite common. A rich dentist's ex-wife drives her former husband's Mercedes, and lives in her ex-husband's house, awarded to her by the court as part of the divorce settlement. Another doctor was having an affair with his live-in maid from India. Once the affair was discovered, his wife, also a doctor, walked out. One of the Bangladeshi doctors in Virginia area had his own private plane and as he started commuting too frequently, he became involved in an affair with a nurse which cost him his marriage. His wife, also a doctor, had reached her limit.

Lack of divorce in Singapore among the Bangladeshi community is sometimes attributed to the lack of career opportunities for women. Someone once commented: 'Life is boring and unexciting in Singapore. Nothing happens here, not even divorce.' The divorce rate is high among Bangladeshis in the USA compared with Bangladesh and other places. In some cases, divorce has resulted in a material gain on the part of women who were awarded a large share of the property by the court. In one case a rich dot.com entrepreneur was eased out of his suburban house in New Jersey with the assistance of police as his wife went to court. In another instance, a research scientist was asked to leave home and the year-long separation ended when the couple was reconciled with help from the community. Social capital was properly utilised. In the New Jersey case the couple was not embedded in community but an extended family where the relatives of the husband were on one side, and the wife was supported by her live-in mother from Bangladesh and was assisted by the court. The USA has over the years become a favoured destination of child-birth. In the last one year at least two Bangladeshi would-be mothers from Singapore went to the USA to 'visit' their relatives where they ended up giving birth to future US citizens. In Singapore birth is not a basis of citizenship. The kinship network of these women was of great help.

Consuming culture

Food is one of the items on the cultural menu that bind people together. Bangladeshi parties are usually food fests. In fact, there are certain common features that bind different groups of people. One is Hindi films for home-viewing. In New York, especially in Queens, there are streets filled with Bangladeshi restaurants and provision shops that sell Bangladeshi food including sweets. The focus on the reproduction of culture is best illustrated in the import of Bangladeshi food as well as cooked food. The popularity of halal food is phenomenal. A book shop in the Queens area also keeps books by popular Bangladeshi authors. Someone once complained that Syed Mujtaba Ali's books were not available in these shops.

Life revolves around food and the talk of food. The power of food in holding together a nation is not widely recognised. For the diasporic community, food assumes a new meaning, a symbol, a vehicle for reproducing culture. The role of Indian films and serials on Zee TV also plays a key role in re-creating the sense of community. This is as true in Singapore as in the USA. The reproduction of community and the desire to live in one's own culture unaffected by the changing location is a constant theme. In the summer of 2002, when a young Bangladeshi was taunted by some Puerto Rican kids in Bronx, he came back with some friends armed with hockey-sticks. When the fight broke out, he was beaten to death by the Puerto Rican kids. The next day, a large number of Bangladeshis picketed in front of the police station demanding justice and immediate action. This is routine in Bangladesh. The nature of the fight, picketing, demanding, and so on are so typical of Bangladesh. This was a 'Dhaka-style' fight, which sadly ended as a death 'Dhaka-style'.

The relationship between Bangladeshis and Bengalis constitutes an important aspect of their experience with some relevance to the question of identity. Bengali-speaking people often meet in Bangladeshi grocery stores which now can be found all over. Bangladeshis in USA in general show a tendency towards particularism compared with Bengalis from the Indian state of West Bengal who tend to be more cosmopolitan. I met Sati *di* and Mainak *da* after a long time. Both of them are professors in the University of Pittsburgh. Our conversation revolved around the articles of Pankaj Misra on Indian communal riots in the August 2002 issue of the *New York Review of Books*. It is hardly inconceivable to have such a conversation with a fellow Bangladeshi. Yet, Sati *di* is a professor of statistics and her husband a professor of mechanical engineering, both of them graduates of Cornell from the mid-1970s. Their children went to Harvard and Yale and one of them has joined the State Department. The only other Bangladeshi who befriended the relatively more enlightened Bengalis in Pittsburgh area was an enlightened woman from Dhaka who dropped out of graduate school to take up a job after she broke off from her husband. Sati *di* and her friends belonged to a study group where they would read the newly published books (the best sellers of the *New York Times*) and discuss them. One of her friends, Sreerupa, an engineer, is an avid traveller.

I met them at a wedding in Pittsburgh after more than a decade. It was the marriage of a Bangladeshi boy who met a girl of Irish descent in high school and after ten years of courtship got married. The wedding ceremony took place in a beautiful park overlooking Carnegie Mellon University. It was an outdoor event, with guests in suits and background music (U2, as my son told me). The leader of the Muslim Association, an MIT-trained Bangladeshi engineer, recited from the Koran and explained beautifully the meaning and relevance of those words. He was followed by a Catholic priest who elegantly read verses from the Bible. It was an inter-faith wedding ceremony where prayers were followed by uncorking of champagne. And no one seemed to mind. Yet some elements of local culture kicked in when the father of the boy was trying to impress the guests by introducing frequently one of his distant relatives from Bangladesh as a 'retired major-general' – as if people there cared for such 'eminence'. The introduction fortunately blended with the background music as the guests consumed a meal of western delicacies. No Indian food was served, to the delight of the Bangladeshi children. The wedding was a reminder of another wedding five years before between a Bengali girl and an American from Pittsburgh with an East European heritage. The rituals of the marriage ceremony took place in a temple one afternoon because the time had to be auspicious but the wedding banquet took place in the evening of a weekend, followed by a dance. We joked that the folks back home in Kolkata will be happy and talk in hyperbole about the skin colour of the groom: 'he was really fair, very fair!'

Yet, marriage presents the ultimate metaphor to understand the future of the Bangladeshi community or for that matter any other diasporic community. This is the future, the blending of cultures, a fusion, which is sometimes sad, sometimes happy, but most of the time ambivalent. A fusion of virtuality and reality. As the world is becoming more heterogeneous and compressed at the same time, the diasporic Bangladeshis can create a globalised locality with an ease unimaginable at any other time in the past. And still the globalised local cultures they create are not the same as the local-local. What they re-create is a virtual local culture, an 'imaginary homeland' in the apt phrase of Salman Rushdie (1991).

In July 2007, I attended another Bangladeshi wedding in Washington, DC. The young bride was born in the USA to professional parents – both doctorates in chemistry who, having lived a life of wealth and luxury, are now divorced. They work in two different parts of the country, the father in Minnesota, the mother in Virginia. A month before the wedding of the daughter, the father took a new bride which broke the heart of the young girl. This was widely criticised by the Bangladeshi guests. Many female guests condemned his taking a second wife and wished he had reunited with his first wife, while men only said that the choice of timing was insensitive. 'He could have waited until his daughter's wedding,' commented one of them.

The bridegroom was from New York City where his parents owned a restaurant. Both bride and the groom were raised in America and did not see themselves as Bengalis, yet the religious pull was strong enough to follow a fairly religious marriage, *sans* alcohol.

The priest was late by nearly two hours. I asked one of the guests, an American Anglo-Saxon woman, what she thought of the wedding; her only comment was that she could not accept the delay by nearly two hours. But the proceedings of that evening were a curious mixture of a Bangladeshi and an American wedding. The priest read out the relevant passages from the holy book, translated the words into English and ended by saying now 'I pronounce you husband and wife, and you can put on the ring to your bride'.

Shankar, a popular Bengali writer from Kolkata whose novels were read widely in Bangladesh, wrote a book titled *Epar Bangla Opar Bangla* ('Bengal on this and Bengal on the other side') in the early 1970s based on his travel experience in America. He wrote that as Columbus sought to discover India and ended up discovering America, he went to discover America but instead he discovered India.

The explorations of Bangladeshis in the USA and Singapore help us to understand them not only in foreign lands but also in their native land. The imaginary homelands blend into their real homelands without the subjects realising that transmutation.

Note

1 Associate Professor Aziz shared this information in an interview with the author. Professor Aziz was one of the community leaders among the Bangladeshis in Singapore. Many of his former students in Bangladesh University of Engineering and Technology joined him as colleagues at the National University of Singapore.

References

Bartelson, J. (2000) 'Three Concepts of Globalization', *International Sociology*, 15(2): 180–96.

Chaudhuri, N. (1951) *The Autobiography of an Unknown Indian*, London: Macmillan.

Chaudhuri, N. (1992) 'Ami Keno Bilate Achi' ('Why I am living in England'), *Desh* [*Sharodia* edition].

Khondker, H.H. (2000) 'Globalization: Against Reductionism and Linearity', *Development and Society*, 29(1): 17–33.

Misra, P. (2002) 'Murder in India', *New York Review of Books*, 49(13): 34–9.

National Review (1999) 'This Week', *National Review*, 51(16): 12.

Pieterse, J.N. (1995) 'Globalization as Hybridization', in M. Featherstone, S. Lash and R. Robertson (eds) *Global Modernities*, London: Sage, pp. 45–68.

Pieterse, J.N. (2004) *Globalization and Culture: Global Melange*, Lanham, MD: Rowman and Littlefield.

Robertson, R. (1995) 'Globalization: Time–Space and Homogeneity–Heterogeneity', in M. Featherstone, S. Lash and R. Robertson (eds) *Global Modernities*. London: Sage, pp. 25–44.

Rushdie, S. (1991) *The Imaginary Homelands: Essays and Criticism, 1981–1991*, New York: Viking.

Shankar (1971) *Epar Bangla Opar Bangla* (*Bengal on This, Bengal on the Other Side*), Calcutta: Calcutta Printers.

Thambiah, S.J. (2000) 'Transnational Movements, Diaspora, and Multiple Modernities', *Daedalus*, 129(11): 163–94.

United Nations Department of Economic and Social Affairs (2006). Online. Available at: www.un-org/population/publications/2006 migration.chart.htm (accessed 10 September 2007).

Part III
Culture and changing diasporic identities

9 The attrition and survival of minor South Asian languages in Singapore

Rajesh Rai

Introduction

In 2006, the Indian diaspora in Singapore comprised approximately 319,100 (8.8 per cent) out of a total resident population of just over 3.6 million (Singapore Department of Statistics 2006: 12). The use of the term 'Indian' in official and public discourse in Singapore is, however, problematic in that it is employed as a unitary 'racial' category that refers to heterogeneous linguistic, cultural and religious groups originating from various parts of the Indian subcontinent, including what is now Bangladesh, India, Nepal, Pakistan and Sri Lanka.

The outcome of various phases of movement, the majority of Indians in Singapore belong, either as migrants or descendants, to the 'old' diaspora, the result of British colonial expansion in Southeast Asia. Largely composed of Tamil labourers, this diaspora included as well pockets of commercial and professional migrants from various parts of the Indian subcontinent and Sri Lanka. A sizeable number, however, possibly as much as between 15–20 per cent of the total Indian population in Singapore, is made up of what Vijay Mishra has described as the 'diaspora of late capital',[1] which for the purposes of this chapter have been labelled as the 'new' diaspora. This group is the product of the movement of professionals from various parts of the subcontinent since the early 1990s and constitutes an important section of what is commonly known in Singapore as 'foreign talent'.

Problematising the expression 'Indian diaspora' in Singapore serves to underline the focus of the article. Every diaspora, whether 'old' or 'new', includes its own exigencies; that is, particular ideologies, movements, or concerns from the 'homeland' or in the 'hostland' that are internalised and sustained amongst descendants of a particular trajectory and which, over time, grow to become important components of their identity. The position of the members of the 'new' diaspora is also problematic. Subject to differing ideologies and concerns that inform their identity, they are, as well, most notably caught in the dilemma of 'return' or of establishing durable roots in the 'hostland'.

Given these differential identities and concerns of groups that constitute the Indian diaspora, this chapter explores the development of minor South Asian languages in Singapore in relation to language policies adopted by the state. By 'minor' I refer to South Asian languages that do not hold the status of an official language in Singapore. Since Tamil came to be designated as the only Indian official language at the time of Singapore's independence, this study looks at the factors that have impacted on the development of Bengali (or Bangla), Gujarati, Malayalam, Hindi, Punjabi, Sindhi, Telugu and Urdu. Excluded from the education curriculum, these South Asian languages in Singapore faced the possibility of 'language death' by the 1980s. From the 1990s, however, changes in state policy vis-à-vis migration and the recognition of five other South Asian languages in the curriculum have led to considerable improvement in the situation of some of these languages. Nevertheless, whilst exercising flexibility in recognising these minor South Asian languages, the state continues to be mindful of the position of Tamil as an official language which, the chapter argues, has had an influence on the parameters of which languages have gained recognition in the education curriculum and which continue to be excluded. In addition, the chapter analyses the factors that influence the second-language choices of Indians in Singapore, and argues that often their actual 'mother tongue' has been ignored in favour of a diglossic complement due to issues of prestige, pragmatic concerns or ideological reasons linked to the 'homeland'.

Language policy after independence

Since independence, Singapore has adopted a language formula that strives to meet dual goals: an economic imperative; and a representation of its complex multicultural milieu. To meet the second objective, the state has, in the words of Nirmala PuruShotam, attempted to 'discipline difference' by using 'race' as a management category to represent its heterogeneous cultural milieu (PuruShotam 2000). Accordingly, English and three other languages, Mandarin, Malay and Tamil, reflecting the main 'races' in Singapore, were granted official status immediately after Singapore's separation from the Federation of Malaya.

A bilingual policy was instituted in education that reflected the economic and social imperatives of the state. Particularly after the Goh Report (1978) that formed the basis of educational reform in Singapore, English, whilst having a *de jure* status equal to the three other official languages, became the 'major language of dominant administrative, commercial, educational, and social status' (Gopinathan 1980: 181) and was established as the first language in education. This was justified on the grounds of 'its utilitarian value, for employment, and for guaranteeing access to the science and technology of the West' (Gopinathan 1980: 181). In addition, as a non-native language, English was seen to level the playing field between all 'races'. At the same time to ensure 'the imparting of moral values and understanding of cultural traditions', and to prevent 'loss of identity – deculturalisation – and the consequent rootlessness, seen in the acceptance of some Western values and life-styles' (Gopinathan 1980: 181), students had to take a second language based on the existing 'race'–culture–language matrix in Singapore. Each of the main 'races' came to be represented by a second language: Mandarin as the second language for Chinese students; Malay for Malay students; and Tamil for Indian students. Although from a systemic point of view, Sumit Ganguly's heralding of Singapore's language policy as 'one that has held the country in good stead in both social and economic terms' (Ganguly 2003: 256) may seem justified, a closer inspection of the hetero-geneous nature of Singapore's multicultural society may yield a more sombre assessment. Certainly not all groups benefited from the language policies of the state. In the 1980s, several South Asian languages in Singapore faced the grim prospect of language 'death'. Reflecting on language 'death' Jean Aitchison states:

> When a language dies, it is not because a community has forgotten how to speak it, but because another language has gradually ousted the old one as the dominant language, for political and social reasons. Typically, a younger generation will learn the 'old' language from their parents as a mother tongue but will be exposed from a young age to another more fash-ionable and socially useful language at school.
>
> (Aitchison 1981: 209)

Position of minor South Asian languages prior to 1990

In Singapore's multilingual setting, minor South Asian languages – Bengali, Gujarati, Hindi, Punjabi, Malayalam, Sindhi, Telugu and Urdu – always had a tentative position because initially Malay and later English were used as the primary modes of inter-ethnic communication. Moreover, due to the hetero-geneous character of Indian society in Singapore, the use of Malay (and later English) was limited not only to communication with other 'races'; it was also used as the primary language of communication between Indians of different communities.[2] Consequently interaction in the minor South Asian languages was largely confined to 'the domains of the home, for interaction with relatives ... [co-ethnic] friends, and for community related uses' (Singh 1994: 2).

In addition to the limited communicative domains for these minor South Asian languages, specific government policies at the end of the colonial period and in the postcolonial era further weakened the position of these languages. The first con-cerned the implementation of stricter migration controls from the 1950s. To the extent that new arrivals from the 'homeland' had a regenerative influence on these languages, increasingly stringent migration controls from the late 1950s 'isolated' these diasporic communities from the 'homeland'. Whilst in the cases of Hindi and Punjabi there existed community-based institutions to provide language train-ing in Singapore, the same could not be said for the other language communities whose development was contingent upon new migrants facilitating the mainte-nance of these languages at the familial or community level.

Traditional 'arranged' marriages, to some extent, mitigated these migration controls. The constant influx of South Asian brides in these communities played a crucial role in providing regenerative contact with their 'mother tongue'. As Dipika Mukherjee finds in her study of the Bengali community in Malaysia:

In the Malaysian-Bengali community, the Indian brides are valued for their conventional traits, like language ability and cultural talents, which the local Bengali women do not have. Women are expected to be language bearers and language transmitters in this community too … As most of the Indian-born Bengali wives are unable to work in Malaysia…, this often leads to these young women getting involved in community functions and gaining recognition for their contributions toward the community.

(Mukherjee 2003: 105, 115)

Dipika Mukherjee's findings on Indian-Bengali brides and their regenerative influence on Bengali language in Malaysia can be extended as well to the minor South Asian language communities in Singapore. In the late 1970s and early 1980s, however, migration controls in Singapore became even more restrictive such that foreign brides of men from the lower-income brackets were increasingly denied the possibility of gaining resident status.

The tentative position of these languages was exacerbated by the bilingual policy instituted in the education curriculum. Whilst the study of a second language was a requirement to provide 'cultural ballast', the association between second language and 'mother tongue' was problematic. In the Singapore context, 'mother tongue' did not necessarily refer to the 'language first learned by the speaker as a child' (Pei and Gaynor 1968: 141); rather, as Nirmala PuruShotam notes, it embodied 'a language … socially identified with a particular "racial" group' (PuruShotam 2000: 50).

Consequently, of the three languages accepted as a second language, only the inclusion of Malay came close to meeting the linguistic definition of a 'mother tongue' since nearly 90 per cent of those categorised as Malay identified it as such in 1957 (Kuo 1980: 41).[3] Only about 64 per cent of Indians identified Tamil, and a minuscule 0.1 per cent of the total Chinese population in 1957 identified Mandarin as their 'mother tongue'. Even in 1978, Hokkien continued to be the predominant language amongst the ethnic Chinese (Kuo 1980: 41)

Although contentious, the rationale for including Mandarin was due to its symbolic status 'tied to Chinese nationalism and Chinese-ness' (PuruShotam 2000: 46), together with its position as the official language in China. The inclusion of Tamil, however, was more problematic. Although Tamil was recognised as an official language in the Republic, Malay was the more dominant language in the Indian community in 1978. Eddie Kuo finds:

What may seem surprising is that there were in 1978 more Indians who could understand Malay than those who could Tamil. This reflects the dominant status of the Malay language even among the Indians, especially among the non-Tamil Indians who constituted approximately a third of the total Indian population in Singapore.

(Kuo 1980: 51)

Nor did Tamil, as a regional language in India, have the symbolic status of

Mandarin as the national language of China. Hindi, the official language of the Indian Union from 1950, and the closest Indian language equivalent to Mandarin in China, was not recognised for this purpose.

The inclusion of Tamil and the exclusion of Hindi was the outcome of specific developments in Singapore after the Second World War. Prior to, and during the war, leadership of the Indian community was drawn from a heterogeneous group of commercial and professional migrants 'overlaid by a pan-Indian nationalism that played down regional differences' (PuruShotam 2000: 45). Following from Indian nationalism, many of these groups advocated Hindi or Hindustani as the link language for Indians in Singapore.

However, few of these Indian commercial and professional elite had gained the support of the labouring classes made up primarily of migrants from Tamil Nadu. With the growing politicisation of labour after the war, leadership of Indians passed into the hands of leaders associated with Tamil labour. Since Tamil labourers were exposed to Tamil vernacular education, '[it] effectively placed community education in the hands of Tamil school masters [who] were fascinated by the Dravidian movement' (Rai 2004: 259) in India. The popularity of the movement, with its emphasis on Tamil language, had repercussions on language policy in Singapore. Hindi was rejected as the representative language for Indians in Singapore by the numerically and politically dominant group representing Tamil labour, not only because of the small numbers who identified Hindi as their 'mother tongue', but also due to the nature of the Tamil cultural revival, which beyond emphasising Tamil language and its literature involved a 'protracted struggle against Hindi' as the official language of the Indian Union (PuruShotam 2000: 45–6).

The adoption of Tamil as the designate 'mother tongue' for Indians, however, posed problems for the linguistically diverse community. The vast majority of non-Tamils had negligible knowledge of the language. In essence, therefore, the bilingual policy placed a severe strain on non-Tamil speaking Indian children who were required to learn two foreign languages, i.e. English and Tamil. Whilst advocates of Tamil as a link language for Indians pointed out that the policy was no different from the adoption of Mandarin for those categorised as Chinese, what must be noted is that unlike the other official languages, Tamil, as a language of a small minority in Singapore, had limited functions both in terms of socio-economic mobility as well as for both intra- and inter-ethnic communication.

Criticism of policy

A potent criticism of the second-language policy employed by the state emerged from the minor South Asian language communities. These groups argued that while Tamil was granted official status and included in the curriculum as a second language for Indians, the policy effectively ignored 36 per cent of Indians who were not of Tamil ethnic origin. Furthermore, those of North Indian origin argued that their 'mother tongue' was linguistically distinct from Tamil, with either Sanskrit (Bengali, Gujarati, Hindi, Punjabi) or Arabic/Persian (Urdu) roots. In addition the adoption of Tamil as an official language, and its inclusion as a second language in the curriculum, had a detrimental impact on the study of minor South Asian languages in Singapore. For example in the case of Hindi, Glenda Singh finds that:

> Right up to 1965, Indian students were permitted to offer Hindi at 'O' and 'A' level ... After Independence in 1965 ... Hindi could not be offered as a subject in schools. Consequently, interest in studying it declined.
>
> (Singh 1994: 21)

In an attempt to alleviate the distress of Indian students who were not of Tamil ethnic origin, the state exercised flexibility, allowing them to study any of the three second languages on offer. Consequently many of these students took up either the study of Malay, which was considered to be 'easier to pick up than Tamil or Mandarin' (Ramakanthan 1989: 43), or Mandarin, which was considered economically more useful than either Tamil or Malay.

However, the state's flexibility on the issue did not address the underlying concern of these groups that the bilingual policy did not provide the alternative of studying their own 'mother tongue' as a second language within the national curriculum. The only possibility for educating the younger generation from the minor South Asian language communities in their 'mother tongue' was through community-based efforts. Examples included Hindi language classes provided by the D.A.V. Hindi School, the teaching of Punjabi at Sikh Gurdwaras, and less formal classes usually conducted in the homes of members of the Bengali, Gujarati and Urdu community.

However, there was little motivation for the younger generation from these communities to study their 'mother tongue'. Not only was this demanding, since students had to take this up in addition to studying two foreign languages in the curriculum, there were also few tangible benefits. Given the negligible value of these minor South Asian languages in the education system and the limited communicative domains in Singapore, the younger generation had to draw on other incentives to learn their 'mother tongue': emotional reasons; to develop an oral understanding for conversation with monolingual elders at home or in the wider community, particularly in religious settings; or for entertainment – such as understanding movies from the subcontinent.

Many of the younger generation were able to sustain that level of understanding without any formal language education and thus chose not to attend classes organised by these community-based language institutions. In the case of Hindi, the decline was evident as early as the 1970s when the Netaji Hindi High School closed due to a lack of interest. Whilst the D.A.V. Hindi School continued to provide free Hindi education, the number of students usually numbered less than 40, comprising children and adults from the Hindi speaking community, and adults of other communities who had an interest in the Hindi language. Moreover, due to a lack of incentive to undertake a comprehensive programme, a high student attrition rate was evident in the school. The situation was even more dire for the smaller language communities particularly Bengali, Gujarati and Urdu. For example, in the case of Bengali, the number of students who attended classes in the late 1980s fluctuated between six and 18 with a considerable number leaving after a short period of study.[4]

By the 1980s, language proficiency in minor South Asian languages had declined considerably. According to Saravanan Gopinathan, the percentage of Singapore residents 'literate in "other" [non-Tamil] Indian languages [had] declined from 5.2 per cent in 1970 to 1.7 per cent in 1980' (Gopinathan 1998: 37). Based on theories of 'language shift', the manifest position of these minor South Asian languages in the 1980s, within their respective communities, was equivalent to that of 'third generation migrants' who, while having some spoken knowledge of their 'mother tongue', were more comfortable in using the dominant language, i.e. English, even at home (Singh 1994: 41).

The 1990s, however, marked a remarkable turnaround for these languages in Singapore. Hindi and Punjabi, in particular, and to a lesser extent Bengali, Gujarati and Urdu have seen considerable progress in Singapore from the dire situation in the late 1980s. On the other hand, the situation of Malayalam and Telugu, the two main non-Tamil South Indian languages, has continued to deteriorate.

A life-line for some of these minor South Asian languages in Singapore stemmed from a relaxation of migration controls. From the late 1980s, the state embarked on a policy of recruiting professionals first from China and later from India to maintain and renew Singapore's competitive edge following the growing out-migration of talented Singaporeans, and as a possible antidote to concerns of a 'greying' population from the 1980s. Chinese and Indian professionals were preferred, not only because they were relatively inexpensive, but also due to the perception that they could easily assimilate with their existent co-ethnic counterparts in Singapore. As well, the influx of these professional migrants provided an instrument for the state's desired goal of maintaining the 'racial profile' of the Singaporean population (*Straits Times*, 23 April 1990) especially as it was perceived that because of their higher fertility rate, Malays were more able to sustain their erstwhile population ratio than the Chinese or Indians.[5]

As a result, a new group of first-generation Indian migrant professionals emerged in the late 1980s and 1990s. This group of Indian professionals make up a significant portion of the number of Indians in Singapore although, due to various levels of resident status in Singapore (for instance, 'citizens', 'permanent residents' and 'work permit holders'), their total number is unclear. Unlike the earlier generation of Indian migrants who were overwhelmingly from Tamil Nadu, these new migrants, in ethno-linguistic terms, are more heterogeneous than the earlier population of Indian immigrants in Singapore. For the minor South Asian language communities, these new migrants played a crucial role in providing 'regenerative contact' with their 'mother tongues'.

Even more than the migration of professionals, the fortunes of minor South Asian languages improved as a consequence of sustained lobbying, particularly by the Punjabi- and Hindi-speaking communities, for the inclusion of their 'mother tongue' in the curriculum. Their arguments were two fold: (a) that studying their 'mother tongue' would enable children from these communities to understand their culture better; and (b) that students from minor South Asian language communities were having difficulty in coping with Tamil, Chinese or Malay as a second language as these differed linguistically from their 'mother tongue' (Jin 1990: 24).

A high-level task force investigating Indian underachievement in education confirmed these observations:

> The second language grades obtained by non-Tamil Indian students, who are unable to take their mother tongue for the purpose, have weakened their overall performance in primary school examinations. The Indian pass rate in second language at 'O' levels, at 85 per cent in 1990, also falls short of the Chinese pass rate of 94 per cent. This is despite the Indian pass rate in Tamil (TL2) being on par with Chinese students' performance, and reflects the special weakness of non-Tamil Indian students in the second language.
>
> (Singapore Action Committee 1991: 11)

The weakness of students from minor South Asian language communities in second language (see Figure 9.1) and the detrimental impact this had on their Primary School Leaving Examinations (PSLE) scores resulted in many of these students either not being able to meet the criteria for choice schools or, which was much worse, being forced into the 'Normal' stream that required them to take an extra year of secondary education, prior to taking the 'O' level examination.[6] According to then President of the Sikh Advisory Board, Bhajan Singh:

> A 1989 survey of 133 Sikh youths aged 16–18 years showed that 33 per cent of them had trouble with Malay ... about 40 per cent of Sikh students ended up in the Normal stream in secondary school possibly because of their inability to cope with Malay.
>
> (*Straits Times*, 28 March 1994)

This discrepancy was not limited to the PSLE and the 'O' levels but also included 'AO' level examinations where a pass in the second language was a requirement for entry into tertiary institutions in Singapore. Consequently, the failure of students from the minor South Asian language communities to achieve this minimum requirement was often the cause of their inability to gain entry into tertiary institutions in Singapore. To meet the shortcomings of these students at these crucial levels, the task force in 1991 recommended that:

> The Ministry of Education should take quick steps to recognize the efforts of the non-Tamil Indian communities to provide quality education in their own languages. Recognition of examination in these subjects at PSLE,

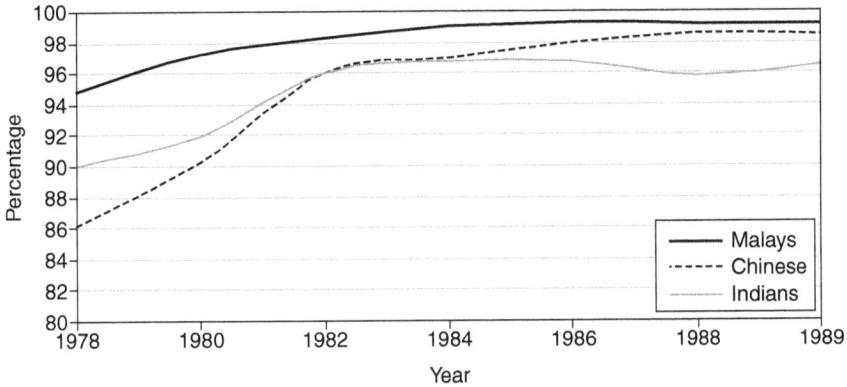

Figure 9.1 Singapore: second language passes at the Primary School Leaving Examination (PSLE) by ethnic group (1978–89) (source: Singapore Action Committee on Indian Education (1991: 12)).

besides GCE O-level and A-level, would reduce the disadvantage faced by students from those communities.

(*Straits Times*, 28 March 1993: 45)

In 1990, the Ministry of Education, as part of larger reforms in second-language study that included the possibility of studying Mandarin, Malay and Tamil as first languages in select schools, altered its policy, recognising five South Asians languages, i.e. Bengali, Gujarati, Hindi, Punjabi and Urdu at 'O' levels, and extended provision for these subjects in 1991 at 'AO' levels, in 1992 at 'N' level and in 1994 at PSLE level. However, unlike the official languages, the government adopted a policy of limited intervention vis-à-vis these languages. As the small numbers made it unfeasible to offer education in minor South Asian languages in schools, the government informed community organisations that although where possible school premises could be used for lessons (*Straits Times*, 7 October 1989: 24), provision for education in these languages would be dependent on the initiative of the respective communities. In addition, unlike the four official languages, government campaigns, official media and public functions would neither use nor promote these languages.

More crucial, however, was the fact that neither Malayalam nor Telugu was included in the list of minor South Asian languages that were recognised. As the second largest Indian ethno-linguistic community in Singapore, the demand for Malayalam to be recognised as a second language was as compelling, if not more so, than any of the other South Asian languages that had come to be recognised by the Ministry of Education. As for the Telugu community, whilst significantly smaller than the Malayali community, its numbers were similar to the smaller language groups, i.e. Bengali, Gujarati and Urdu, that had been recognised.

Various reasons have been cited for the exclusion of these languages. One is that Tamil, Malayalam and Telugu are all Dravidian languages (PuruShotam 2000: 36–7). However, if the issue of linguistic roots were relevant to that of recognition, there was no reason for five separate South Asian languages, since at least four, i.e. Hindi, Punjabi, Gujarati and Bengali, had common roots. Another interpretation for the exclusion of these languages may possibly be linked to pressures from the Tamil lobby in Singapore, some of whom even opposed the recognition of the five minor South Asian languages in the curriculum. In part the opposition stems from an insecurity amongst advocates of Tamil that the position of Tamil as an official language would be significantly weakened by the recognition of other South Asian languages. Certainly this insecurity and opposition was evident when these languages were initially recognised in the curriculum. A letter in the forum page of the *Straits Times* stated:

> Many Indians, especially non-Tamils, have 'boycotted' the Tamil language and let their children learn completely alien languages like Malay or Mandarin ... Tamil is an official language in Singapore, but this position will be threatened if the other Indian languages are taught in primary schools ... rather than introduce non-Tamil languages in primary schools, moves should be made to encourage the use of Tamil among Indians.... The introduction of other Indian languages will have an adverse effect on society. If we are not careful, soon there will be calls to accept the other Indian languages too as official languages in Singapore.
>
> (*Straits Times*, 31 May 1993)

Responding to this insecurity in the aftermath of the recognition of these five South Asian languages, Government officials were quick to reassure the Tamil community:

> The government is committed to keeping Tamil as one of the four official languages.... [Tamil] will continue to be taught in schools and used in radio and television programmes.... Tamil has a future and there was (*sic*) nothing to worry about.
>
> (*Straits Times*, 18 July 1993)

Whilst the Tamil lobby has acquiesced to the fact that it is no longer the sole representative language of all South Asians in the education system, an excess of the Dravidian movement may be the desire to maintain the position of Tamil as the link language of all South Indians in Singapore. Noting the pressure on South Indians to take Tamil, Nirmala PuruShotam states:

> a North 'Indian' does not have to be pressured into doing Tamil as the 'second language' in schools for it is not his 'mother tongue'. The South 'Indian', however, has to try harder to avoid this should he or she want to. This differential pressure in fact comes from 'Indians' themselves. The

most significant of these are proponents of Tamil language in Singapore. This group includes some with sophisticated knowledge of 'Indian' languages (particularly Tamil) as well as Tamil culture. The gist of their argument is summed up in this statement by one of my informants, 'as far as I am concerned all South "Indian" Singaporeans are Tamil'.

(PuruShotam 2000: 82)

More than ideology, however, there are real concerns. Whilst a number of Malayali students have taken Mandarin, Malay and even Hindi as a second language, nevertheless the number who take Tamil is quite significant. Consequently, recognition of Malayalam in the curriculum, unlike the other minor South Asian languages, may have a significant impact on reducing the number of students who take Tamil as a second language.

Yet, opposition by the Tamil lobby on its own is insufficient explanation for the non-recognition of Malayalam especially since the government in the 1990s has shown its willingness to disregard these sentiments. In part, the explanation rests with the Malayali community itself. An informant states that there exists 'a lack of political will' in the Malayali community to have their language recognised as a second language. Certainly the issue of language recognition was subject to considerable debate in the Malayali community in the 1990s. As Michael Fernandez, former President of the Singapore Kerala Association, stated:

Some in the Malayalee [sic] community clamour for Malayalam to be taught from kindergarten up and for it to be an examination language. On the other hand, quite a lot of people in the community, particularly the local-born Malayalees [sic] and youth, young parents, do not think it is necessary.... They don't see the economic need for mastering the language.

(*Straits Times*, 10 May 1997: 25)

Beyond 'economic need', the disjuncture in the desires of the 'old' and 'new' diaspora' for recognition may be linked to the traditional nexus of the older Malayali leadership with Tamil groups. Reflecting on this traditional connection, Nirmala PuruShotam states:

the ability [of Malayali professionals] to speak English and Tamil, at the least, meant that they could be used as intermediaries within the Indian nexus. The English-educated Malayalis were particularly desirable because it was not unusual for them to be able to communicate with Malayalam and Tamil speaking nexii.

(PuruShotam 2000: 45)

Given their position as intermediaries, it is not surprising therefore that some of the stalwarts of Tamil as a link language for Indians in Singapore came from the 'older diaspora' of Malayalis. Whilst 'local-born' Malayalis, may have acquiesced to their language not being recognised, these sentiments are not shared by many 'new migrants'. Concerned with the possibility of return to the 'homeland', Tamil, serves little real function; rather, given the nature of Indian language policy, the study of Malayalam or Hindi could be more useful if these migrants do eventually return to their land of origin.[7]

Development of minor South Asian languages since 1990

Following the government's decision to leave the provision of non-Tamil South Asian languages in the hands of the community groups, seven organisations, i.e. Bangla Language and Literary Society, Bangladesh Language and Cultural Foundation, Singapore Gujarati School, D.A.V. Hindi School, Hindi Society, Singapore Sikh Foundation, Singapore Pakistani Association and the Urdu Development Society, have shouldered the responsibility of providing for these five languages. Whilst many of these languages had less than 20 students prior to 1990, the number has grown tremendously over the last 15 years; approximately 6,000 students are now taking these languages from kindergarten upwards to 'A' levels (Figure 9.2).

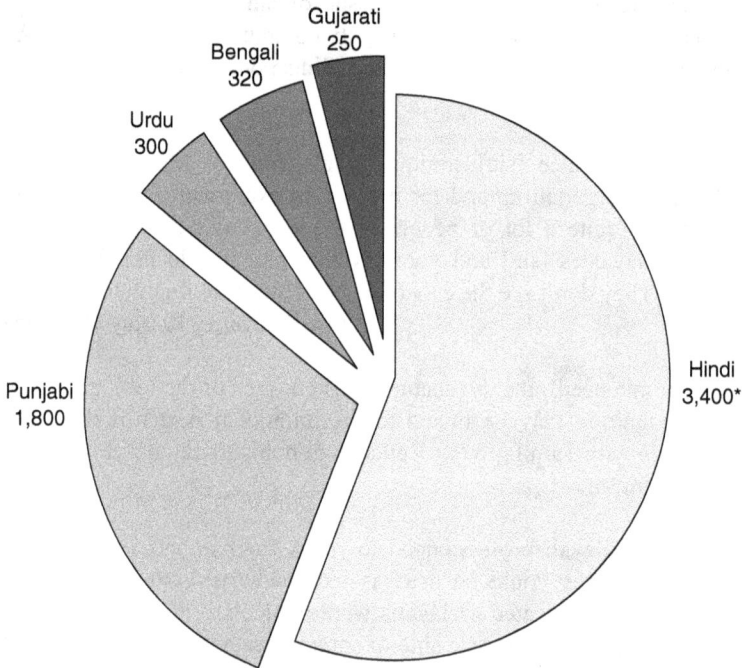

Figure 9.2 Singapore: number of students taking minor South Asian languages (2004) (source: Respondents from the Board of Teaching and Testing South Asian Languages (BTTSAL)).

Note
* Figures for Hindi do not include students studying at Indian international schools based in Singapore.

Although student numbers have increased for all groups, it is evident that Hindi has benefited most (Figure 9.3). Traditionally, Hindi in Singapore has largely found support from the eastern Uttar Pradesh (U.P.) diaspora. Whilst the eastern U.P. diaspora are themselves primarily speakers of Bhojpuri, a variety of the Hindi language, the community has long scorned its real 'mother tongue' as 'dehati bhasha' (village language) and instead emphasised the study of standard Hindi, a diglossic complement that is considered to be 'culturally superior'. Yet, even with the inclusion of the eastern U.P. diaspora, the population of those who consider Hindi as their 'mother tongue' in Singapore is less than Punjabi, although notably the number of students taking Hindi as a second language out-number those taking Punjabi.

Numerous factors explain the paradox. For one, religious politics from the subcontinent has had an impact on the 'geographical' Punjabi community that is manifest as a linguistic division. Consequently, as the Sikh community has emphasised the Punjabi language as a symbol of Sikh identity, Punjabi Hindus and Muslims have moved to support Hindi and Urdu. Consequently whilst the U.P. diaspora may have taken the lead in providing for Hindi as a 'mother

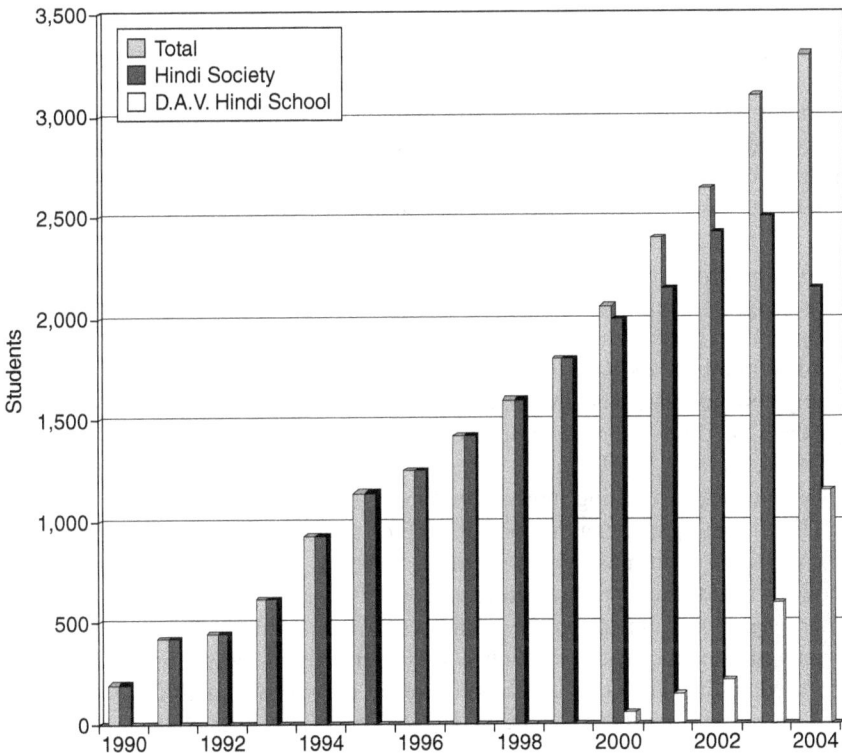

Figure 9.3 Singapore: students taking Hindi as a second language (1990–2004) (source: Respondents from Hindi Society Singapore and D.A.V. Hindi School).

tongue', it has drawn considerable support from the Punjabi Hindu community, and a large number of Hindi teachers, both in the Hindi Society and the D.A.V. Hindi School, the two Hindi language schools in Singapore, are of Punjabi origin. Similarly, religio-linguistic politics to some extent explains why the Sindhi Hindu community in Singapore has supported Hindi rather than lobbying for the Sindhi language that has traditionally been written in the Arabic/Persian script.

Even more than the religio-linguistic politics of the Punjab and Sindh, the study of Hindi in Singapore has been reinforced by the dominant position of Hindi in India, which has been attractive to the new Indian migrants. Consequently, students of Hindi as a second language are a heterogeneous group, not constrained to those who originate from Hindi-speaking regions in India. Whilst it may be that a number of new migrants from India have adopted Hindi simply because their 'mother tongue' is not be available in the curriculum (e.g. Marathi, Sindhi, Kannada, Malayalam, Telugu), their choice of Hindi is also reflective of their incipient position in Singapore. Since many new migrants perceive Singapore to be a transitory location, and harbour thoughts of return, their choice of language is influenced by language policies in India where Hindi, as the official language of the Indian Union, is compulsory in mid-primary years (Sonntag 2002: 166) in nearly all Indian states. Consequently, even when the option of learning their 'mother tongue' is available (i.e. Bengali, Gujarati, Punjabi, Tamil and Urdu), many Indians have exercised flexibility, choosing Hindi as a second language. In addition, the growth of transnational media has augmented the popularity of Hindi in Singapore. The popularity of Hindi channels on cable television and Bollywood cinema can have some influence on the choice of Hindi as the second language amongst Indian parents whose 'mother tongue' may differ.

Whilst Hindi has gained from the incipient position of the new diaspora, enlarging its numbers beyond those who consider Hindi as their 'mother tongue', its position is also vulnerable for the very same reason. Although student numbers taking Hindi show a persistent growth over the last 15 years, many new migrants have exercised their option of return to India or re-migrated to the US, UK, Australia or Canada. The development of Hindi – and also Bengali, Gujarati and Urdu – is therefore subject to the continuous migration of professionals, or existing migrants not exercising the option of return or remigration. Consequently an increase or decline in economic opportunities in India, in Singapore or in possible remigration locations; or a change in government policy towards more stringent migrant controls, are all variables that will have a more significant impact on the fortunes of Hindi, which will be more marked than with Punjabi, whose students consist primarily of those from the old diaspora. More than any other criterion, however, the survival of all these languages in Singapore is dependent on the state's policy vis-à-vis bilingualism.

Conclusion

Few issues in Singapore figure as prominently as that which concern language policies in education. Whilst the state has often been able to implement difficult decisions with relative ease, policy changes on language issues have often resulted in vigorous discontent. The vilification of the government's language policy in the *Nanyang Siang Pau* in the 1970s and criticism of the 'Speak More Mandarin, Use Less Dialect' campaign (Ganguly 2003: 257–9), following the Goh Report on the Ministry of Education in 1978 are notable cases in point. While policy decisions affecting South Asian languages are less politically salient given that Indians are a small minority of approximately 8.8 per cent, it is nevertheless a source of considerable concern for Indians in Singapore and has had a major impact on the survival of minor South Asian languages already encumbered by the lack of communicative domains.

Although the state has been the dominant player affecting the survival of these languages, with control over migration and language policy, policy decisions on language are not independent of diasporic concerns and cannot on their own fully explain the reasons for the development or underdevelopment of South Asian languages in Singapore. Since 'race' acts as an important management unit, and since representatives of racial groups may be subject to, or influenced by, 'homeland' concerns and ideologies, this can have a bearing on state policy in Singapore.

In the case of the heterogeneous Indian community in Singapore, disciplining difference through 'race' enabled larger groups, some of whom were influenced by Dravidian ideology, to advocate Tamil as the language for all Indians in the post-independence period. Not all Indians acquiesced to this, and many challenged the directive by adopting Malay or Mandarin as a second language. In any case, a consequence of the policy was that by the 1980s the future of minor South Asian languages in Singapore was clearly bleak.

Since 1990, however, numerous changes have led to considerable improvement in the situation of some of these languages whilst having a negligible impact on others. The realisation that language policy had a detrimental impact on the educational performance of students from the minor South Asian language communities resulted in a change leading to the recognition of Bengali, Gujarati, Hindi, Punjabi and Urdu in the curriculum. Seemingly though, since minor South Indian languages continue to be excluded, the parameters of this change may still be constrained by the concerns of dominant groups within the Indian community.

In addition, the migration of professionals from India since the 1990s has had an important bearing on the development of these languages. Whilst these migrants have provided important 'regenerative' contact for many minor South Asian languages, the flexibility available to Indians in choosing their 'mother tongue' has resulted in certain languages dominant in the 'homeland', particularly Hindi, benefiting beyond its immediate target community, particularly since concerns of return weigh heavily in the minds of the new diaspora.

Notes

1 Presentation by Vijay Mishra at a workshop on 'The Possibility of an Encyclopedia of Indians Overseas', Singapore, 6–8 December 2001.
2 In 1957, 88.3 per cent of Indians could speak Malay, 76.7 per cent could speak Tamil and 35.5 per cent could speak English. In 1978, 97.4 per cent of Indians could understand Malay, 79.1 per cent could understand Tamil and 67 per cent could understand English. For statistical data see Kuo (1980: 48).
3 The other Malayo-Polynesian 'mother tongues' identified in 1957 included Javanese, Boyanese, Bugis, Banjarese and Menangkabau. See Kuo (1980: 41).
4 Interview with Habibul Khondker, 10 March 2004.
5 The policy of encouraging Indian migration has resulted in a steady increase in the percentage of 'Indians' in Singapore from 7.1 per cent in 1990 to 8.8 per cent in 2006. Given that the total fertility rate for Indian women has fluctuated between 1.89 and 1.5, only slightly above the national average, the significant increase in the percentage of Indians as a proportion of the total population can largely be explained by the arrival of new migrants. See Fah and Fang (2003: 13).
6 From 1979, students entering secondary schools in Singapore were channelled into two streams. The 'Express' stream which required four years of secondary education prior to taking the 'O' levels; and the 'Normal' stream which required that these students take an 'N' level exam at the end of the fourth year. Subject to meeting the required 'N' level grades, these students would then be allowed the opportunity to take the 'O' levels at the end of the fifth year.
7 The Indian National Policy on Education (1968), reiterated in the Education Policy (1986) includes 'the study of a modern Indian language, preferably one of the Southern languages, apart from Hindi and English in the Hindi speaking states, and of Hindi along with the regional language and English in the non-Hindi speaking states'. See Mallikarjun (2002). A Malayali in Kerala would therefore be expected to study Malayalam in addition to English and Hindi.

References

Aitchison, J. (1981) *Language Change: Progress or Decay?* Glasgow: Fontana Paperbacks.
Fah, E.L.E. and Y.Y. Fang (2003) 'Singapore's Demographic Trends in 2002', *Singapore Statistics Newsletter*, (September). Online. Available at: www.singstat.gov.sg/ssn/feat/nov2003/pg10–13.pdf (accessed 24 February 2004).
Ganguly, S. (2003) 'The Politics of Language Policies in Malaysia and Singapore', in M.E. Brown and S. Ganguly (eds) *Fighting Words: Language Policy and Ethnic Relations in Asia*, Cambridge, MA: The MIT Press, pp. 239–61.
Gopinathan, S. (1980) 'Language Policy in Education: A Singapore Perspective', in E.A. Afendras and Eddie C.Y. Kuo (eds) *Language and Society in Singapore*, Singapore: Singapore University Press, pp. 175–202.
—— (1998) 'Language Policy Change 1979–1997: Politics and Pedagogy', in S. Gopinathan, A. Pakir, H.W. Kam and V. Saravanan (eds) *Language, Society and Education in Singapore: Issues and Trends*, Singapore: Times Academic Press, pp. 19–44.
Jin, C.C. (February 2 1990) 'Encouraging Number of Pupils Take Minority Indian Languages as L2'. *The Straits Times*, p. 24.
Kuo, E.C.Y. (1980) 'The Sociolinguistic Situation in Singapore: Unity in Diversity', in E.A. Afendras and Eddie C.Y. Kuo (eds) *Language and Society in Singapore*, Singapore: Singapore University Press, pp. 39–62.

Mallikarjun, B. (2002) 'Language Policy for Education in Indian States: Karnataka', *Language in India*, Vol. 2 (9 December). Online. Available HTTP: www.languageinindia. com/dec2002/karnatakaeducationpolicy.html (accessed 4 August 2004).

Mukherjee, D. (2003) 'Role of Women in Language Maintenance and Language Shift: Focus on the Bengali Community in Malaysia', *International Journal of the Sociology of Language*, 161: 105–15.

Pei, M.A. and Gaynor, F. (1968) *A Dictionary of Linguistics*, London: Peter Owen.

PuruShotam, N.S. (2000) *Negotiating Multiculturalism: Disciplining Difference in Singapore*, Berlin: Mouton de Gruyter.

Rai, R. (2004) ' "Race" and the Construction of the North–South Divide amongst Indians in Colonial Malaya and Singapore', *Journal of South Asian Studies*, 27(2): 245–64.

Ramakanthan, R. (1989) 'The Organized Management of the Tamil Language in Singapore: A Kaleidoscopic Description of the Different Aspects and the Problems Involved', MA thesis, National University of Singapore.

Singapore Action Committee on Indian Education (1991) *At The Crossroads: Report of the Action Committee on Indian Education*, Singapore: Singapore Action Committee on Indian Education.

Singapore Department of Statistics (2006) *Population Trends 2006*, Singapore: Department of Statistics, Ministry of Trade and Industry.

Singapore Statistics (2000) Key indicators of resident population. Online. Available at: www.singstat.gov.sg/keystats/c2000/indicators.pdf (accessed 27 July 2004).

Singapore Statistics (2003) Singapore Residents by Age Group and Ethnic Group. Online. Available at: www.singstat.gov.sg/keystats/mqstats/mds/mds21a.pdf (accessed 27 July 2004).

Singh, G.M. (1994) 'Sociolinguistic Influences on the Maintenance of Hindi in Singapore', MA thesis, National University of Singapore.

Sonntag, S.K. (2002) 'Minority Language Politics in North India', in J.W. Tollefson (ed.) *Language Policies in Education: Critical Issues*, London: LEA Publishers, pp. 165–78.

Straits Times (October 7 1989) 'Non-Tamils Allowed to Take Minority Indian Languages', *Straits Times*, p. 24.

Straits Times (April 23 1990) 'The Racial Balance "will be Maintained" with Move to Attract Overseas Indians', *Straits Times*, p. 47.

Straits Times (March 28 1993) 'Sikh Pupils "Should be Exempted from Malay" ', *Straits Times*, p. 20.

Straits Times (May 31 1993) 'Forget your Pride and Let Indian Kids Learn Tamil', *Straits Times*, p. 29.

Straits Times (July 18 1993) 'Tamil will Remain as an Official Language but the Community Must Uplift Itself, Say Ministers', *Straits Times*, p. 25.

Straits Times (May 10 1997) 'To Learn or Not to Learn a Minority Mother Tongue', *Straits Times*, p. 35.

10 Forging kinship with food

The experience of South Indians in Malaysia

Theresa W. Devasahayam

> Food is ... the medium through which a system of relationships within the family is expressed. Food is both a social matter and part of the provision for care of the body. Instead of isolating the food system, it is instructive to consider it frankly as one of a number of family body systems.
>
> (Douglas 1982: 86)

Mary Douglas's writings on the meal have had profound impact on the study of food and eating. Her ideas are illuminating: she highlights how food – from what is being eaten to how it is being eaten – is essentially a symbolic system of communication. Food systems, she argues, are not isolated from the rest of people's everyday lives. She goes on to show how people's lives are highly ordered (or structured) in every aspect, such as from how they care for their bodies to the clothes they adorn – each of which is connected to the other, as much as food systems.

Striking in the above quote by Douglas is the idea that food is an expression of relationships within social groups such as the family. Food is significant in another way: it is a marker that defines an in-group from an out-group. In other words, those who partake of a meal have a distinctive relationship to each other, which marks them out from those who do not share in the meal.

Food as boundary marker is an idea that exists in a multitude of communities. In India, for example, strict commensality rules provide instructions as to who may share a meal. The general rule is that a person may accept cooked food and water from a member of the same or equal or superior caste. Food received from someone of a lower caste is regarded as taboo since it is considered defiling to the person of the higher caste. As Srinivas (1984: 268) points out: 'mutual acceptability of cooked food denotes equality between the castes concerned, while the movement of food in one direction only indicates that the acceptor is inferior to the giver'. The exchange of food in the Indian context is a marker of social differentiation, separating the distinct castes. Entrance into a caste is permissible only by birth and sharing a meal signifies a shared identity.

Without a doubt, food is an important part of family life and is a symbol of community (Douglas 1984). In the context of the family, food sharing also expresses kinship. In this chapter, I shall deal with how food marks the boundaries of the family in the Indian Hindu diaspora of Malaysia. As in India, women continue to be the gatekeepers of food in the family. But the diasporic context is unique: there have been shifts in the kinds of foods distributed in the family setting. Whether the repertoire of foods purchased, prepared and presented includes new foods found in the diaspora depends largely on who is the main gatekeeper of food in the family – the older female relative represented by the mother-in-law or even mother or the younger woman or daughter-in-law or daughter.

Twenty-five women residing in Klang Valley in Peninsular Malaysia provided rich narratives on their food provisionary role in the family. These women were located through various channels: non-governmental religious and cultural organisations, women's meetings and government departments. These women have at least high-school education, with the majority holding professional jobs while seven were full-time housewives. Part of the middle class, the average household income of these women was approximately RM2,500 (US$685) per month. Since many of the women from such households also tend to be working, balancing the food provider and worker roles is critical. The two most common strategies women adopted to balance the dual roles of food provider and worker included depending on female relatives and purchasing the domestic labour of a foreign live-in maid.[1] Middle-class status meant that, in consumption habits, a greater range of convenience foods was incorporated into everyday meals.

Typically in Malaysia, Indian Hindus live in extended households (DaVanzo 1993: 148). Nine of the 25 women interviewed belonged to extended families as they lived with their husband's parent(s) in keeping with the patrilocal residence pattern of the Indians. Two women, however, lived in their natal homes. In one household, the younger woman executed the cooking and distributing of food with the assistance of her maid because her mother was too frail to undertake this task. Caste continues to play a part in the lives of Malaysian Indian Hindus. Of the 25 women, five belonged to the Brahmin caste and had arranged marriages within their caste group, while one non-Brahmin woman was married to a Brahmin man. There were three other women who married men from outside their caste although they married men of higher caste ranking. The majority of women interviewed could trace their origins to Tamil Nadu and represented various caste groups. Because of the lack of marriage partners from within the caste, and given the diverse linguistic composition of the Indian community in Malaysia, inter-caste and inter-ethnic marriages were not uncommon. Of the women interviewed, two were Malayalis, both of whom married Tamil men. Two Tamil women of Sri Lankan descent who had married within their ethnic group were also interviewed.

The female as food matriarch

Ideal notions of what it means to be a 'good' woman emphasise selfless devotion, obedience and loyalty to her husband (Wadley 1988: 43). The dominant gender ideology stems from a religious doctrine that specifically marks a woman's place in the household and in society at large. A woman's self-sacrificing qualities are also highlighted in the everyday practice of food-making and sharing – a woman's domain, highlighting her prime source of identity as nurturer to her husband and children (Appadurai 1981).

Leela Dube (as cited in Rao and Rao 1988) explains that the cooking and dis-tribution of food are important constituents of a prestigious and valued role for the Hindu woman. Tamil proverbs highlight the relationship between a woman and members of her family through her food-provisionary role. The proverb 'It is in the hands of the woman to create or destroy the family' reinforces a woman's integral role in holding the family together (Daniel 1991: 73; Egnor 1991: 26).

Malaysian Indian Hindu women are no different in conducting themselves in the family. Among nearly all the women interviewed, cooking and the sharing of food was an intrinsic part of their identities as wives and mothers. Thus, even if their husbands were keen on helping them in the daily cooking, these women were quick to turn them away. A university-educated woman in her late 20s explains:

> I actually enjoy cooking ... that's why my husband does not go into the kitchen very much ... I don't know why but in my family ... we got that complex in us ... all my brothers-in-law can cook but the women do not let them into the kitchen ... like once my mother was here, and my husband volunteered to cook ... and my mother just stared at me ... she said that if my great-grandmother was alive, she would turn in her grave ... we never let the man come into the kitchen ... my grandmother always told me this ... no matter how much you study, you must always know how to cook ... she did not directly say that a woman's place is in the kitchen ... but we still must know how to cook.

Although most women were protective of their space in the household – that is the kitchen and the activities therein – others mentioned that they would actively delimit their activities from men's, often citing their husbands' inability to prepare a decent meal.

In extended households, typically the older female relative becomes the matriarch of food provision by cooking on a daily basis (Appadurai 1981: 497). By no means does this suggest that the younger woman is freed from her obliga-tions as food provider. The younger woman whether as daughter-in-law or daughter plays a supportive role by way of food shopping and serving. The main reason why the younger woman accedes to her mother-in-law or even her own mother is because of the status held by the older woman. Whenever the older relative, usually the mother-in-law, oversees or does the cooking, in some cases, misunderstandings can and do arise (Appadurai 1981), although women reported experiencing fewer tensions should the older woman be her own mother.

But women were not taking on the food provider role solely because it formed part of their nurturing role and completed their identity as women. Indian women actively play out their food provider role because it is fairly difficult to obtain home-style cooked food from restaurants or street-vendors. By and large, the kinds of foods easily obtained in restaurants are snack foods like *dosai* (crepes made from rice and black gram), *idli* (bread made from ground rice and black gram), *idiappam* (string hoppers made from rice flour) and *sambar* (a broth made from lentils and tamarind), common to most castes in South India. Since culinary styles are caste-specific and it is not always easy to purchase certain dishes cooked within the caste group, many Indian women have little choice but to cook.

Cooking for the family is also significant for another reason. Unlike eating out, where food is a commodity to be bought and sold and is devoid of the emotions of the cook, food prepared and presented in the home is bound up with the conveying of love necessary for the forging of social relationships and kin attachments.

Cooking and sharing food: ways of incorporating 'self' and 'other'

In Indian thinking, food is regarded as a tool for forging kinship. That food cooked at home has the potential of affirming kinship bonds is predicated on the idea that when a woman cooks, a part of her emotional, mental and physical 'self' merges with the food item which then becomes transferred to the recipient whether it is her husband, children or other family members. In Indian cuisine, food preparation usually demands that the cook employs her hands when working on a food item rather than relying on kitchen tools, as is often the case in Western cooking. The use of hands is highly symbolic; substances from the hands can be transferred and intermingled with foods. Here, bodily substance and action are mutually reinforcing and inseparable (Marriot 1976; Marriot and Inden 1977). Through the process of using one's hands to cook, the woman's substance and the substance contained in the food item merges and, in turn, the gap between the self and the 'non-self' as embodied in the food item closes. Hence, the food item is an extension of the woman and when it is 'sculpted' by her and, thereafter, shared with others, kin bonds between the giver and receiver are formed or enacted.

Khare (1976: 153) makes a similar remark in his analysis of household food production in the Indian subcontinent when he describes the food item as a product of the skill of a woman in the kitchen as 'a "taste" that comes from the hands of those who are socially and emotionally near...'. This presupposes that in household cooking, food is produced by a person who, by kinship and emotion, is connected to the people who consume the food. When either the mother or someone who emotionally cares for the diners (such as the grandmother) does the home cooking, this means that the consumer becomes emotionally attached to the cook, through that which is consumed. That the food item is the supreme metaphor of the cook's love suggests that when it is received, this very act symbolises the acceptance of the cook's (and in this case the woman's) hard work and emotions that went into the handiwork.

Indeed there is a powerful link between the giving of food, giving of love and the giving of kinship, irrespective of whoever cooks – whether it is the wife/mother or husband/father. Since love is an emotion shared among those who are close, such as kindred, when food is cooked and shared over time, kin ties are enacted in the process. For this reason, women and men as well see it as imperative that a home-cooked meal is shared among family members. A lecturer in her 50s explains:

> Cooking and the sharing food is a way of building kin ties ... I have a sense of fulfilment when I serve food in my home to my family even if I may not have cooked it myself ... in fact during busy periods, my mother cooks the meals ... but when she is sick recovering from surgery or if she is away in India, I will do the cooking ... my husband has also always insisted that we eat at home.

Feeding and creating kin

Creating affinal kin

In a conjugal relationship, a woman's husband is the recipient of the food she prepares and serves. That food sharing is intrinsic to the conjugal relationship is evident in the wedding ceremonies of Indian Hindus. In ritual fashion, the bride and bridegroom literally feed each other with the meal set before them. Among couples, this public ritual signifies the beginning of an extended relationship in which they share food consumption to produce kin relations. Food sharing is significant because the couple lack kinship affinity as they are not related through blood ties which would have made them consanguines and 'their unity cannot [be] total' since they never shared food together (although they may have eaten similar foods before if they belonged to the same caste).

But the sharing of food does not end in the ritual feeding at weddings, as explained by a teacher in her late 40s:

> In Tamil culture, every couple before having their first night together are given a banana and a cup of milk to share between them ... the best part is that they have to use the same cup ... so at the beginning of the relationship as husband and wife, food becomes the first thing that they share ... but it doesn't stop there ... in India, a wife eats from the same plate after her husband has finished eating ... this idea was created so that the husband and wife can bond from the time of the marriage until their death.

Trawick (1990: 106) in her work in Tamil Nadu describes the relationship of two girls who had grown up together, Padmini and Mohana as approaching that of ' "husband and wife" [who] often ate together from the same pot or bowl'.

The concept of sharing from the same hearth and in effect even the same plate denotes strong images of a conjugal relationship. Hence, kin relations are never just created at the point of marriage; they become elaborated further when she executes the cooking for her husband. For a woman, cooking and feeding her husband expresses the existing kinship bonds because these activities encapsulate emotions and expresses statements of feelings that capture the continuity between her and her husband. Hence, the substantiality of their love and the kin relationship of the couple need to be nurtured, and it is through the preparation and sharing of food cooked by the wife on a day-to-day basis that allows for a conjugal relationship to be forged processually.

The quintessential image of the sharing of food between an Indian couple is captured when a woman waits on her husband at meals, eating any leftovers that he leaves behind on his plate. Here, not only are the leftovers considered auspicious as they are treated as *prasad*, but also the very act of consuming the leftovers. In Malaysian Indian homes, a woman may serve her husband, although he is more likely to help himself to the food. It is unlikely that women actually wait on their husbands with the intent of consuming the latters' leftovers from a meal. Nonetheless, only spouses may share food from the same plate because this implies the intermingling of bodily substances exclusive to a conjugal relationship as well as necessary for the creation of affinal ties between a man and his wife.

The sharing of food not only produces kinship but kin relationships also determine to whom food may be served. Elaborating on this point, a lecturer in her early 40s explains:

> Traditionally, we do not share the same plate or tumbler with another male ... saliva (Tamil; *ethchi*) is a definite taboo ... just like any other bodily fluid ... in traditional extended families, a young woman is also forbidden from serving food to her father-in-law ... only his wife does this.

Among Hindus, cultural norms posit that it is the wife who serves her husband regardless of whether she has cooked the food. She further explains:

> The serving of food indeed is in itself an act of intimacy ... the Indian bride is asked to serve a meal to her new husband as soon as she steps into the threshold of her new home ... the food may be pre-prepared and ready, but she is reminded that she is a host and not a guest from her very first day.

The giving and taking of food starts at the temple when food is offered to the gods as *naivedya* and it is this practice that pervades the rest of society. The marriage starts off with the woman as the gift from the bride's natal family to the groom's. In the same way a gift is never returned, the woman never returns to her own natal home. That she is host to the family she is married into serves to 'utterly sever ... the connection between the bride and her family and transforming her into an extension of the groom and his family' and in the act of offering food to her husband, this 'create[s] an indissoluble bond between husband and wife' (Trautmann 1994: 88–9).

Serving food in this case does not mean that women are enacting their subordination, as Miller (1998) would argue in the parallels he draws between women and the 'gods' they strive to please with their offerings of food. Instead they are assuming a position that embodies them with power as they are being integrated into their husbands' natal family.

Since cooking and the sharing of food are fundamental to the kinship relationship, should a woman deliberately choose not to cook or share a meal with her husband, this signals problems in the marriage. Here, the very act of not wishing to cook is indicative of a woman not wanting to produce kin bonding. Likewise, men can appropriate food as the tool for forging kinship when they choose to bond or not to bond with their wives when they accept or reject the food served to them. In an instance when a husband refuses to share in a meal cooked by his wife, this is telling of a problematic relationship. To this end, food does not just physically sustain; it goes beyond this function when it is manipulated to produce symbolically the husband–wife relationship.

Creating consanguineal kin

Unlike a woman's kin ties to her husband, the relationship with her children is created by their being related through blood. While the biological aspect of parentage does guarantee kin relations, kin bonds are enacted over time through feeding to produce a lasting kin relationship between the two. Between a mother and child, kinship is actualised at the day-to-day level through the sharing of bodily fluids at the point of birth, later to be reinforced further through the sharing of food when the child grows up. A lecturer in her late 40s explained this relationship in light of her own experience of having had two daughters:

> The relationship between a child and mother needs to be solidified after birth ... if not, the mother is nothing but a petri dish or uterus if the relationship just ends there ... we have to constantly remind the child of the relationship, like they do in Indian movies ... otherwise the child does not remember its mother.

Through feeding, the mother plays a critical role in calling to remembrance the kinship relationship between herself and her child. While the process of birthing alone is sufficient for creating kinship bonds between the biological mother and child, kin relationships, however, need to be enacted through the social activities of food sharing.

The forging of kinship with a child start at infancy when a mother breastfeeds. Here, the mother literally uses her body to build kin relationships and, as such, erasing the separation of 'self' and 'other' between them. Among the women interviewed, the older women reported going to great lengths to preserve kin relations they have with their children through breastfeeding in spite of the easy availability of commercially produced powdered milk. Among the younger working women, it was not uncommon to hear them say that ideally they would have chosen to breastfeed but the circumstances they found themselves in were not conducive to their doing so.

Given that birthing and subsequently feeding 'creates' in the woman a mother, she and her child understand who they are and where they stand in the larger kinship map within the family. The nature of this contact between a mother and child is the child's first experience with its social world. Within the family unit, the child learns who will provide it with sustenance and with whom and how food must be shared.

The sharing of milk between a mother and child, which produces kinship, is only the beginning of a kinship relationship. As a child grows older, food is appropriated instead of milk – this time to enact the kinship bonds already present between mother and child.

Change in the culinary map: from one generation to the next

South Indians in Malaysia would not contest the idea that food sharing is integral to producing kinship. The diasporic experience, however, has changed the dietary repertoire of most households in terms of the kinds of foods cooked and shared. Living with mothers-in-law or mothers invariably means that not only is the food provisionary role undertaken by the older female relative but the foods served in such families are fairly predictable in that they conform largely to what would be defined as 'Indian'.

As in India, the Brahmin community in Malaysia continues to be the bastion of culinary orthodoxy (Appadurai 1981: 497). In extended families, particularly when there is an older relative like a grandmother who is active in food matters, mostly Indian foods are served at everyday meals. Although some of these foods consist of those that may be purchased at Indian restaurants, variations to the recipes in terms of ingredients used and method account for the difference in taste. For example, Brahmins tend to routinely use *dhal* (lentils) in the preparation of the broth called *rasam*,[2] whereas the other castes tend to omit this ingredient. Some foods are not only regarded to be Indian but reputed to be quintessentially Brahmin. A typically South Indian Brahmin savoury is *thattai*. The dough, prepared from rice flour, black gram *dhal* flour, and a little Bengal gram *dhal*, black pepper, chilli powder, asafoetida, curry leaves and butter, is carved into little balls and flattened before frying.

Because it is the older female relative who is the food matriarch in these households, every festival in the Hindu calendar is an opportunity to celebrate with food offerings (*naivedya*) and rituals. *Vara Lakshmi* is one such festival, celebrated in honour of the Goddess of Wealth who brings together married women (Arunachalam 1980: 99–103). In this festival, women pray for the well-being of their husbands and families. Since the ultimate purpose is to pray for the longevity and happiness of one's husband, widows are excluded from participating, presumably because they have lost their husbands. Among Malaysian

Brahmins, this festival is celebrated at home where women carry out special rites under the supervision of older men who know the specific *mantra* (Sanskrit verses thought to have a special efficacy) for the *puja* (worship). Foods offered at the altar at this festival are *vaddai* (a deep-fried savoury snack made from black gram, onions, and dried chillies), *kolukkatai* (steamed sweet dumplings made with fillings of either grated coconut or lentil), *nai appam* (little pancakes made with rice flour and coconut milk) and *idli*. These foods are prepared from fresh ingredients by the lady of the house who participates in the ceremony. Among these foods, pre-packaged versions of the sweetmeat *vaddai* are available for purchase. Yet these sweetmeats are nearly always painstakingly prepared from scratch, especially during celebrations, mostly by the older woman, while her daughter-in-law may have helped.

For most festivals in non-Brahmin homes, food offerings tend to not to be as elaborate. Carton milk and packaged raisins are examples. Many Hindu families who were unable to buy fresh cow's milk for offering to the deities use carton milk[3] instead. One such woman in her early 50s explained:

> I usually buy carton milk ... it's a matter of what's available ... cow's milk also does not keep ... so for *Ponggal*,[4] I'll work with what I have ... it's difficult to get cow's milk in the city, quite unlike the [rubber] estates where there are usually a number of families who may keep some cows ... so in the city it is difficult to get cow's milk ... and besides, it is expensive ... so I just use the carton version even for [ritual] offering.

Brahmins are most particular about the kinds of foods used as ritual offering. While they perceive cow's milk to be mandatory, carton milk is used only in times of 'emergency' or lack of the actual food item. A Brahmin housewife in her early 30s who lived independently from her in-laws remarked:

> Every day I cook rice first thing in the morning ... so this is what I offer ... I also offer fruit and milk ... the milk is cow's milk as I get it everyday ... if the milkman does not come, I will have no choice but to offer carton milk which I will have to buy.

Brahmins tend to maintain their orthodoxy in ritual foods; but it is mostly the older female relatives or housewives who have kept alive the daily rituals of offering food, especially in extended households. The same pattern can be found in non-Brahmin families. Younger women who have careers usually leave the older woman to execute the daily ritual activities of the household while playing a more active part in food preparation particularly during festivals. As in the case in Brahmin households, everyday fare tends to be mainly Indian if the older female relative does the daily cooking. But there are extended families in which the younger woman cooks, especially when the older woman is unable to do so.

The act of cooking on the part of the younger woman becomes imperative especially if she does not share the same caste of her husband. If both husband

and wife were of the same caste, they would have ingested similar foods signifying the mingling of bodily substances to form kinship. Daniel (1984) explains how the notion of substances permeates the material and social world of the Tamils, thereby creating rank and status in society. He says that substance is also imbued in foods, which gets absorbed into the body through consumption. As such, when two people are married, they should come from the same caste since caste membership assumes similar food consumption habits, which ensures a balance of the humoral substances shared between the two. A non-Brahmin dentist who married a Brahmin man not only gave up eating meat but also learned to cook Brahmin dishes. Her decision to become vegetarian and cook Brahmin foods was prompted by her wish to be integrated into her husband's natal family, and she recognised that she could only forge kinship by sharing in the same foods. Following the 'theory [that] differs from the more conventional scholarly conception that inherited attributes, on the one hand, and interactions, on the other, are distinct sources of status in the caste system' it is evident that 'individuals continually alter their essential being through their acts' (Trautmann 1980: 520). But this woman represented the exception rather than the rule; in most cases, the older woman nearly always ends up as the food matriarch. The younger woman of a lower caste, in sharing the food from the same household hearth, becomes incorporated into the family by kinship.

By no means, however, do younger women, both Brahmin and non-Brahmin, in extended households retreat entirely from the food provisionary role. Although women who marry into the home of their husbands' natal kin have fewer opportunities to engage in food-making as compared with those who set up homes independently, these women often engaged in Western-style cooking like baking cakes and cookies or even cooking the special weekend meal. Many younger women also incorporated local dishes into the menu. In a Brahmin family I studied, the vegetarian version of *nasi lemak*[5] was a weekend treat. This local Malay coconut rice dish, originally served with fried fish or fried chicken, omelette, cucumber and a chilli paste, was presented instead with vegetarian 'mock' mutton.[6] Other common local dishes prepared by the younger women of extended households may be stir-fried vegetables in Chinese-style, flavoured with soya sauce (or oyster sauce in non-vegetarian households), and fried noodles tossed in with plenty of leafy vegetables, bean sprouts, with the addition of chicken, shrimp and egg in a non-vegetarian household.

Women living in the nuclear family set-up were the most liberated in terms of the choices they had in what they wanted to cook. Flipping through the pages of recipe books is not uncommon especially when they have more time over the weekends. But for daily meals when women are pressed for time, often convenience foods were a welcomed option. In non-vegetarian households, popular convenience foods eaten at mealtimes are frozen chicken nuggets, frozen vegetables, tinned sardines and mackerel, mushrooms, fruit, fries, burgers, sausages, frozen local breads and instant noodles. That women opt for convenience foods such as snack foods does not mean that they are never consumed at a main meal. The instant Indian bread *iddiappam* (string hoppers) is one example. A Hindu clerk in her late 40s finds these a viable alternative to making this bread herself. If made from scratch, the dough consisting of rice flour and water is forced through a press onto plates that are then placed in a steamer to be cooked. Although this bread may be bought, storing the packaged version means that she can prepare this bread whenever she wishes. When used at a main meal, there were women who said that these provided 'variety' to the kinds of foods that the family would have consumed. Families where the women worked, thus, did not see the demise of what was called 'traditional Indian foods' since convenience versions of these foods are nowadays easily purchased in select foodstores scattered across the city. For this reason, the Indians in Malaysia need not travel back to India to purchase these foods nor do they have to depend on their relatives to send them over.

Although mass-produced, the cooking and distributing of the convenience-food item does not lose its quality of being able to impart kinship since many of these foods are modified further by the cook – a creative practice of working out how it can be cooked or what foods can be prepared in combination with fresh foods. In this process, the store-bought convenience food is transformed into 'home-made' food. An example is spaghetti prepared in many Malaysian homes today. This dish has grown popular following the emergence of Western restaurants in urban areas. Often women prepare this dish at the request of their children. Rather than making the sauce from scratch, many women buy bottled spaghetti sauces, but would add first and foremost a dash of chilli powder to spice up the dish, and flavour it further by lacing it with finely diced onions and slivers of red/green chillies. Hence, when commoditised foodstuffs are introduced into the household, women are bound to personalise them.

Miller (1995: 154–6) elaborates on the link between commodified objects and kinship. It is in the context of the home, he says, that the alienating dimension of an object disappears when the woman transfers a commodity from a capitalistic context devoid of real emotional meaning into an object invested with emotional meanings as it takes on the personality and emotions of the woman. Although a convenience food is a replicated object from a mechanistic context, it ceases to be a 'simulacrum', in a Baudrillardian (1981) sense, as the distinction between the original and its copy is destroyed as it now incorporates part of herself. Home cooking, therefore, may be seen to 'particularise' (Robertson 1992: 97–114) or 'singularise' (Kopytoff 1986: 73–4) global foods such that the foreign dimension of the universal takes on a familiar meaning, especially when the woman becomes the agent of providing a personal and, hence, a familial aspect to them. The fact that cooking with convenience foods is a common feature of ordinary meals provides a context for kin bonding in everyday food consumption practice as well since in using her hands to create the food item, the food item becomes an extension of herself.

Similar to using convenience foods, a middle-class woman may also appropriate another modern-day convenience – a live-in maid who also assists in meal production (Chin 1998). While live-in maids from the Philippines and Indonesia are relatively affordable to middle-class urban families (Heyzer and Wee 1992:

38; Chin 1996: 133), in most of these homes, women almost never leave the cooking entirely to their maids. When it comes to cooking, the pattern in Indian homes is that the maid is responsible for washing, peeling, slicing, dicing and chopping up the vegetables, meats and fish – all under her female employer's supervision – while the female employer stands by the fire and executes the actual cooking. This arrangement enables the woman to make claims that she is the actual cook since she is in control of the taste of the foods through her control over the way the food is cooked, the time taken to cook the food and the actual combination of ingredients and spices added during cooking. Moreover, the female employer nearly always carries out even the marinating of meats and fish since it is she who determines the taste of each dish. Women are also conscious about distinguishing notions of purity and pollution in food preparation. Only they taste[7] the food that is prepared and never their maids, thereby suggesting that symbolically they create the 'leftovers' to be eaten by their family members and not their maids. That it is the woman who should undertake the cooking stems from the idea that food is invested with a sacred quality. Thus, food must be treated with ritual purity (Dumont 1980: 137–9), ensured only when it is cooked by those known to the consumer whether it is the wife, mother or even foreign maids; the latter, however, do not fall within the caste system and, thus, their involvement in food preparation may not be perceived as polluting by their employers (Ramanujan 1989). However, the very fact that maids only engage in the initial preparation of foods but do not transform the foods from the 'raw' to the 'cooked' suggests that they have never prepared the foods for consumption in the first place.

Hence the nuclear family is the epitome of culinary adaptation in the diasporic Indian community in Malaysia. Interestingly, younger women in such households did not experiment with the culinary culture of their own foreign live-in maids. This may be seen as a deliberate attempt on the part of the woman to differentiate her domestic worker as the 'other' in the context of the family. It is not uncommon to find women hinting at their uneasiness if their maids are applauded for their cooking abilities. As a 39-year-old Assistant Registrar notes: 'If my maid cooks better than I do, I think I would try to improve my cooking … but I wouldn't mind it if my family enjoys my mother-in-law's cooking … whether it is my husband or my children.' Her objective in outperforming her maid can only mean that she perceives her maid as a threat who has the potential of drawing her husband and children closer to herself emotionally through food sharing, thereby in turn bonding with them. Her mother-in-law, in contrast, can never be a threat since she already bears a kin relation to her husband, herself and her children.

Conclusion: changing diets, unchanging cultural practices

Food sharing in South Indian families in Malaysia, as in the Indian subcontinent, is an activity highly imbued with cultural meanings, as the discussion above has shown. On the part of the wife/mother, cooking and feeding are intrinsic to creating kin since food is objectified and tacitly accepted as the idiom for the realisation of kinship (Curtin 1991: 13). From the narratives, women more than men produce kinship through this means since the domain of cooking comes under their charge – a domain which they guard because giving food is a metaphor for giving kinship.

Food given to family need not be restricted to what is known as Indian food. The diverse ethnic fabric of Malaysia has lent to substantial cultural borrowing. But only in select families is cultural borrowing more evident. Clearly, if there is a younger woman in a household, the more likely it is that the dietary repertoire of the family extends itself to incorporate non-Indian cuisines. In this sense, women are the gatekeepers of food, although their exercise of power around food is restricted since what is cooked and consumed would have to adhere to the vegetarian/non-vegetarian[8] dichotomy in accordance to caste prescriptions (McIntosh and Zey 1989).

As much as there is strict adherence to food prescriptions laid down by religion among the Indians in Malaysia, cultural notions of food sharing as a medium for forging kinship continues to be significant. For this reason, sharing a home-cooked meal continues to be the norm among Indians while eating out as a family is less common especially since bought food is thought not to be able to assume the function of forging kinship. It is for this reason that there continues to be a marked preference for home-cooked food, accentuating the connection between the woman and her food- provisionary role.

Such cultural notions flourish but it is to the political environment that we must turn to in order to understand why food consumed in the home is granted such great importance to Indian family life. As in many countries across the world, Malaysia has shifted from a kinship-based society to one in which the State plays a central role in organising its people's lives. In the public arena, Malaysia's ethnic policy divides its citizenry along ethnic lines with the Malays comprising the largest ethnic group, followed by the Chinese and then the Indians. The separation of ethnic groups forces individuals to become more aware of the cultural differences among them. State policies have also attempted to penetrate the private sphere. National family policies, for example, have consistently emphasised women's role in the family while highlighting their contribution to the burgeoning economy of the country (Puthucheary 1991). Given the political context, it is of no surprise that familial relations in urban Malaysia mimic the 'basic Hindu association between kinship, cooking, and marriage [which] continues to hold with the modern to keep the place of the domestic hearth secure', as it has been found to be the case in South Asia. The differentiating factor is the kinds of foods cooked and shared, while the cultural ideologies of food-making and kinship making have stayed intact.

Notes

1 Live-in foreign maids cost about US$100 per month. Many women have opted for a live-in maid as they have found it cheaper than daycare, particularly if they have more

than one child. The live-in maid usually not only takes care of the children, but also assists in cooking and other household chores.

2 This is a light broth of tamarind juice boiled with ground pepper corns, garlic, cumin, turmeric, tomatoes and curry leaves.

3 In offering carton milk, it did not cross any woman's mind to offer skimmed or low-fat milk. One woman said that it seemed unthinkable to offer anything less than full-cream milk, therefore affirming the idea that only the best should be offered to the gods and, in this case, in lieu of fresh milk, carton milk may be the option. This practice is reinforced by the fact that temple authorities accept carton milk for the ritual of *abishekaram* (bathing of the deity) although when it comes to milk as a ritual food offering, it is only fresh milk that is used.

4 *Ponggal* is a four-day celebration that falls in January. It celebrates Indra the Lord of Marutam, Surya the Sun God and the cow as people's greatest helper. This festival takes its name from the Tamil word *pongu*, which means to cook, boil over and overflow, referring to the harvested rice that is cooked in a mud pot, over an open fire made in a newly formed brick oven in the yard. For more details, see Arunachalam (1980: 212–17).

5 Jaffrey (1981: 140) has noted that versions of this rice dish appear throughout coastal and Southern India, Sri Lanka, and eastward through Southeast Asia up to the Philippines. I was pleasantly surprised to see this dish on the menu card of an Indian vegetarian restaurant called Annalakshmi situated in Bangsar, an upscale, middle-class residential area in Kuala Lumpur, when I went on my rounds to the various restaurants in the city. The only components that were omitted from this dish were the meats.

6 Shaped in little cubes, textured-soy protein and soybean fibre are also called imitation or mock mutton as their taste resembles that of the actual meat. There are different varieties of imitation or mock meats ranging from beef to chicken and pork to seafood.

7 It must be noted that in most cases Indians do not taste food and return the same ladle to the pot because saliva has the effect of making the food turn rancid. The idea that when a cook tastes food rendering it symbolically to become leftovers is linked to the notion of foods offered to the gods. Here, it is never acceptable that the gods should be offered leftovers. Instead only food that is specially prepared for them should be offered so that they are in a privileged position to 'taste' these foods first.

8 Even among non-vegetarians beef is never consumed at home. In addition, during fast days, there are numerous food taboos that are observed.

References

Appadurai, A. (1981) 'Gastro-Politics in Hindu South Asia', *American Ethnologist*, 8(3): 494–511.

Arunachalam, M. (1980) *Festivals of Tamil Nadu*, Tanjavur: Gandhi Vidyalayam.

Baudrillard, J. (1981) *For a Critique of the Political Economy of the Sign*, St Louis: Telos Press.

Chin, C.B.N. (1988) *In Service and Servitude: Foreign Female Domestic Workers and the Malaysian 'Modernity' Project*, New York: Columbia University Press.

Chin, Y.F. (1996) 'Filipina Maids in Malaysia in the 20th Century', *Journal Jabatan Sejarah Universiti Malaya*, 4: 123–40.

Curtin, D.W. (1991) 'Food/Body/Person', in D.W. Curtin and L.M. Heldke (eds) *Cooking, Eating, Thinking: Transformative Philosophies of Food*, Bloomington, Indiana: Indiana University Press, pp. 3–22.

Daniel, E.V. (1984) *Fluid Signs: Being a Person the Tamil Way*, Berkeley: Berkeley University Press.

Daniel, S.B. (1991) 'Marriage in Tamil Culture: The Problem of Conflicting "Models"', in S.S. Wadley (ed.) *The Powers of Tamil Women*, Syracuse: Syracuse University Press, pp. 61–91.

DaVanzo, J. (1993) 'Living Arrangements of the Elderly', in J. Sine, T.N. Peng and J. DaVanzo (eds) *Proceedings of the Seminar in the Second Malaysian Life Survey*, Kuala Lumpur, Malaysia: National Population and Family Development Board, pp. 145–61.

Douglas, M. (1984) 'Standard Social Uses of Food', in Mary Douglas (ed.) *Food in the Social Order: Studies of Food and Festivities in Three American Communities*, New York: Russell Sage Foundation, pp. 18–39.

—— (1982) 'Food as a System of Communication', in Mary Douglas (ed.) *In the Active Voice*, London: Routledge and Kegan Paul, pp. 82–104.

Dumont, L. (1964) *Homo hierarchicus*, A. Sainsbury (trans.), Chicago: Chicago University Press.

Egnor, M. (1991) 'On the Meaning of Sakti to Women in Tamil Nadu', in S.S. Wadley (ed.) *The Powers of Tamil Women*, Syracuse: Syracuse University Press, pp. 1–34.

Heyzer, N. and Wee, V. (1992) 'Domestic Workers in Transient Overseas Employment: Who Benefits, Who Profits', in N. Heyzer, G.L. A'Nijeholt and N. Weerakoon (eds) *The Trade in Domestic Workers: Causes, Mechanisms, and Consequences of International Migration*, New Jersey: Zed Books, pp. 31–102.

Jaffrey, M. (1981) *Vegetarian Cooking: World of the East*, New York: Alfred A. Knopf.

Khare, R.S. (1976) *The Hindu Hearth and Home*, Durham, NC: Carolina Press.

Kopytoff, I. (1986) 'The Cultural Biography of Things: Commodities as Process', in A. Appadurai (ed.) *The Social Life of Things: Commodities in Cultural perspective*, Cambridge: Cambridge University Press, pp. 64–91.

Marriot, M. (1976) 'The Bifurcate Hindu Body Social', *Man* (New Series), 11(4): 594–5.

Marriot, M. and Inden R.B. (1977) 'Toward and Ethnosociology of South Asian Caste Systems', in K.A. David (ed.) *The New Wind: Changing Identities in South Asia*, The Hague: Mouton, pp. 227–38.

McIntosh, A.W. and Zey, M. (1989) 'Women as Gatekeepers of Food Consumption: A Sociological Critique', *Food and Foodways*, 3(4): 317–32.

Miller, D. (1998) *A Theory of Shopping*, Ithaca, NY: Cornell University Press.

—— (1995) 'Consumption and Commodities', *Annual Review of Anthropology*, 24: 141–61.

Milne, R.S. and Mauzy, D.K. (1986) *Malaysia: Tradition, Modernity, and Islam*, Boulder, CO: Westview Press.

Puthucheary, M. (1991) 'Government Policies and Perceptions of Policy Makers and Women Leaders of the Status and Role of Women in Society', *Status and Role of Malaysian Women in Development and Family Welfare*, Research Report No. 2. Faculty of Economics and Administration, University of Malaya, Kuala Lumpur, Malaysia.

Ramanujan, A.K. (1989) 'Is There An Indian Way of Thinking?: An Informal Essay', *Contributions to Indian Sociology*, 23(1): 41–58.

Rao, V.V.P. and Rao, V.N. (1988) 'Sex Role Attitudes of College Students in India', in Susan S. Wadley (ed.) *Women in Indian Society: A Reader*, California: Sage, pp. 109–23.

Robertson, R. (1992) *Globalization: Social Theory and Global Culture*, London: Sage Publications.

Srinivas, M.N. (1952, rpt. 1984) 'The Caste System in India', in A. Béteille (ed.) *Social Inequality: Selected Readings*, Middlesex, England: Penguin Books, pp. 265–72.

Trautmann, T.R. (1994) 'Marriage Rules and Patterns of Marriage in the Dravidian Kinship Region', in P. Uberoi (ed.) *Family, Kinship and Marriage in India*, Delhi: Oxford University Press, pp. 273–86.

—— (1980) 'Marriage and Rank in Bangali Culture', *Journal of Asian Studies*, 39(3): 519–24.

Trawick, M. (1990) *Notes on Love in a Tamil Family*, Berkeley, CA: University of California Press.

Wadley, S.S. (1988) 'Women and the Hindu Tradition', in R. Ghadially (ed.) *Women in Indian Society: A Reader*, New Delhi: Sage, pp. 23–43.

11 Bhai Maharaj Singh and the making of a 'model minority'

Sikhs in Singapore

Tan Li Jen

Introduction

In 2006, there were an estimated 15,000 Sikhs in Singapore.[1] Since the early migration of Sikhs – most notably as recruits in the security forces – to Singapore and Malaya during the colonial period, the present generation of Sikhs in Singapore have established themselves as a successful minority group characterised by a sizeable and prominent group of Sikh middle-class professionals who enjoy economic success and social mobility. In spite of their success, there exists a constant insecurity, shared in general by Sikhs in the Punjab and abroad, over the minority status of Sikhs that is reflected in the desire to maintain and assert a distinctive Singaporean Sikh identity. This insecurity has been further heightened by concerns over the marked generational, regional and caste divisions within the community, and the absence of 'neutral' figures of authority and symbols that could rally and unify the community. The proliferation of various Sikh groups and community organisations, each with their own – often conflicting – agendas, has resulted in divisive struggles for authority, legitimacy and resources within the Sikh community.

This chapter, part of a broader study on the construction of Sikh history and identity in Singapore in the postcolonial period, will explore the efforts made by the Singaporean Sikh community to assert their distinctive identity through efforts to memorialise Bhai Maharaj Singh – a prominent figure in Sikh history and religious tradition – as a community icon. There are, as yet, no historical studies on the significance of Bhai Maharaj Singh in the Singaporean Sikh community. It examines the ways in which Sikh history and identities are shaped and constructed through the multiple meanings and symbolism attached to the figure of Bhai Maharaj Singh.

Historical background

Large scale immigration from the Punjab to Southeast Asia took place in the late nineteenth and early twentieth centuries when economic and political changes brought about by the running of the British Empire led male Sikhs from the land-owning Jat caste to supplement family incomes through employment in the

British Indian Army, or through work overseas. From 1880–1920, Malaya, Singapore, Hong Kong, Thailand, Burma and China began to draw significant numbers of Sikh migrants who came in search of job opportunities (Dusenbery 1989: 5–7). By the turn of the twentieth century, Sikhs in Malaya and Singapore were already well ensconced in niche occupations as policemen, watchmen and small-time moneylenders. A large number of Sikhs came to Malaya and Singapore in search of employment with the Sikh Police Contingent, the Tanjong Pagar Dock Police Force or as militiamen in the Malay States Guides, while others found work as private watchmen, moneylenders and cattle farmers. The recruitment practices adopted by the British for the police and military service were based on their preference of Jat Sikhs from the Malwa and Mahja regions over those from the Doaba region in Punjab. This accounted for the predominance of Jat Sikhs from the Malwa and Mahja regions in Malaya and Singapore.[2]

Among the predominant Jat Sikhs, regional loyalties dominated the organisation and control of key gurdwaras and issues concerning the community. Caste and regional identities were much more pronounced in the late nineteenth and early twentieth centuries among Punjabi-Sikh immigrants. This was most clearly manifested in the factional rivalry between Sikhs from the Malwa, Mahja and Doaba regions over control and leadership of the Central Sikh Temple, one of the first gurdwaras established in Singapore (Ibrahim 1982: 36–8). The fallout between the rival groups led to the establishment in the 1920s and 1930s of region-specific gurdwaras among Jat Sikhs: Sri Guru Singh Sabha on Wilkie Road was established in 1918 by Sikhs from the Mahja region in Punjab; Khalsa Dharmak Sabha at Niven Road was formed in 1923 by Sikhs from the Malwa region; and Pardesi Khalsa Dharmak Diwan at Kirk Terrace was established in 1929 by Sikhs from the Doaba region.

Apart from region-based gurdwaras, caste-based gurdwaras also emerged: Sri Guru Nanak Sat Sangh Sabha on Wilkinson Road in Katong was established in the early 1950s by Khatris and Aroras (mercantile castes commonly referred to as the business community) who migrated to Singapore following the partition of India in 1947, and the erstwhile Khalsa Jiwan Sudhar Sabha on Buffalo Road was set up by Mazhabi Sikhs (low-caste Sikhs who were originally *Chuhras*, a sweeper caste) who felt marginalised in the Jat-dominated gurdwaras (Dusenbery 1996: 117; Singh Mehervan 1979: 47–53).

The migration of land-owning Jat Sikhs to Malaya and Singapore tapered off in the 1950s with the tightening of immigration laws. Since then, Singapore has not received any significant Sikh immigration in the postcolonial period. The social make-up of the Sikh community at present consists of second- and third-generation Singaporean Sikhs who grew up outside the Punjab. Schooled in the Western education system, these Sikhs operated in a milieu different from that to which their parents belonged. Education has given them social mobility, enabling some of them to achieve prominent social and political status. The younger generation of Sikhs who have taken up positions of community leadership are keen to steer the Singaporean Sikh community beyond what they regard as a divisive and parochial mindset among those Sikhs who still persist in maintaining caste and regional allegiances in community affairs. Their aim is to construct and assert a progressive and collective Singaporean Sikh identity defined variously by religion, nationality and ethnicity within the framework prescribed by the state.

Like other Sikhs in the diaspora, Singaporean Sikhs are experiencing a resurgence of Sikhism and Punjabi-Sikh culture, particularly in the past three decades (Barrier 2004: 220). Efforts at re-making Sikh identities in response to external circumstances and influences such as governmental policies, political developments in the Punjab, and the influence wielded by *Sants* have inevitably altered the dynamics internal to the community. Against this backdrop of external developments, Singaporean Sikhs are constantly in the process of inventing and appropriating symbols and institutions which are meant to bind the community together as well as define and represent their version of Sikh history and tradition.

Gurdwara Sahib Silat Road

An institution that has become synonymous with the Sikh community in Singapore is the Gurdwara Sahib Silat Road (henceforth Gurdwara Silat Road). Gurdwara Silat Road has emerged in the postcolonial period as a crucial site for the construction of Sikh history and identity. Along with the Central Sikh Gurdwara, the Gurdwara Silat Road is regarded as an important historic Gurdwara. Built in the early decades of the twentieth century, the two Gurdwaras played a crucial part in community-building among early Sikh immigrants as they catered to their religious and social needs. The Gurdwaras provided these migrants an access to a network of Sikh migrants based overseas. The Gurdwara Silat Road served originally to provide food and accommodation for new Sikh and non-Sikh immigrants as well as those passing in transit through Singapore to other destinations like Malaya, Hong Kong, Shanghai and Manila. It was established at Silat Road by Sikhs in the Tanjong Pagar Dock Police Contingent after they were resettled from their former barracks at Anson Road. The cost of building the Gurdwara, which was completed in 1924, was funded largely by members of the Sikh police forces, many of whom pledged a month's salary to the project. Bhai Wasawa Singh, a member of the Sikh Police Contingent in Singapore was also given leave to embark on a fund-raising campaign which took him to Malaya, Hong Kong and Shanghai.

While gurdwaras served as a focal point for the early Sikh community to conduct religious and community affairs, this function has since diminished, especially in the second half of the twentieth century. The establishment of gurdwaras along regional lines, and the reluctance of *granthis* (reciters and interpreters of holy texts and scriptures) and temple functionaries to adapt Sikh religious ceremonies and practices to the needs of Singaporean Sikhs led to the alienation, since the 1980s, of a younger generation of Sikhs from the gurdwaras, especially region-specific ones.[3] Unlike the later gurdwaras which were established along regional and caste lines, Gurdwara Silat Road is not seen to represent any particular regional interest and is regarded by many Singaporean Sikhs as a religious institution that has remained relatively unscathed by the politics of regional rivalry. An important historic gurdwara, it is a key landmark in the religious and cultural landscape of the Singaporean Sikh community.

Bhai Maharaj Singh

Another reason for the gurdwara's centrality in the Sikh community is the association between Gurdwara Silat Road and a Sikh religious and historical figure, Bhai Maharaj Singh. The link was first forged in 1966 when the *samadh* (tombstone) of a Sikh *Sant* was moved from the grounds of the Singapore General Hospital to Gurdwara Silat Road. In the period after the Second World War, Sikh devotees started worshipping at what they believed was the *samadh* of a *Sant*. The size of the Sikh congregation grew as stories of the miraculous powers of the *Sant* were circulated. The hospital grounds where the *samadh* was located became a popular religious site for Sikh devotees who held regular prayer sessions and religious functions there. The government eventually requested the Sikh community to remove the *samadh* because it felt that the hospital grounds were an inappropriate site for religious worship; there were also plans to expand the Singapore General Hospital. In October 1966, the *samadh* was relocated to Gurdwara Silat Road in compliance with the government's request and has remained there since (Singh Seva 1986: 2; Choor Singh 1991: 14). Prior to this, the Gurdwara had suffered a period of neglect as Sikhs turned increasingly to region-based gurdwaras in the 1930s. However, with the transfer of the *Sant's samadh* in 1966, the gurdwara became increasingly popular among Sikh devotees. Various written narratives on the history and origins of the *samadh* were constructed and circulated in the Sikh community: some linked the *samadh* to Bhai Maharaj Singh, while others linked it to Baba Karam Singh. Some of the oral narratives constructed by Sikh devotees refer interchangeably to the *Sant* as Baba Ji (a title of respect), Baba Karam Singh and Bhai Maharaj Singh Ji. Despite a certain degree of factual ambiguity surrounding the historical background of the *Sant*, these narratives placed him as a political prisoner exiled by the British to Malaya in the mid-nineteenth century.

The *samadh* at Gurdwara Silat Road has been a crucial site for the construction of Sikh history and identity in Singapore since the 1970s. Given the importance attached to Bhai Maharaj Singh by Sikh devotees, religious prayers and commemorations were held regularly at Gurdwara Sahib Silat Road. In July 2006, special commemorative activities were planned at Gurdwara Silat Road to celebrate the 150th *Barsi* Anniversary of Bhai Maharaj Singh and an advertisement was placed in the local newspaper, the *Straits Times*, to generate publicity for the event. A book on the life of Bhai Maharaj Singh was published by the Central Sikh Gurdwara Board under the title *Bhai Maharaj Singh Ji & Gurdwara Sahib Silat Road: A Historical Journey*. Copies of the book were printed and circulated within the community to commemorate the 150th *Barsi* (Anniversary) of

Bhai Maharaj Singh. To underscore the significance of the anniversary, a set of commemorative coins imprinted with the image of Bhai Maharaj Singh were minted to mark the event. The official opening of the Gurdwara Silat Road Sikh Centre by Singapore's President S.R. Nathan was also organised in conjunction with anniversary celebrations. The opening of a community institution can be seen as another community effort at showcasing to the government their organisation and 'self-help' initiatives.

Efforts at constructing a verifiable history of Bhai Maharaj Singh involved the reproduction of printed images and photographs related to Bhai Maharaj Singh, and the use of previously published documents, specifically British colonial records, to lend historical veracity to the narratives produced by the Singaporean Sikh community. Among the activities organised for the special anniversary celebrations in 2006 was a plan to exhibit (for the first time) some of the personal artefacts of Bhai Maharaj Singh from the *Dera* Bhai Maharaj Singh in Amritsar. Although this project did not come to fruition, photographs of the *khanga, kara, kirpan, chakras* and *gutkas* that belonged to Bhai Maharaj Singh and some of the weapons supposedly used in his struggles against the British were reproduced in print and provided as an alternative form of 'exhibition'. The commemorative practices associated with Bhai Maharaj Singh thus provided an avenue for the Sikh leadership to reinforce the relatively recent historical links established between the Singaporean Sikh community and the Sikh historical-religious figure.

Bhai Maharaj Singh as 'rebel against the British Raj'

While little is known of the history of Baba Karam Singh, Bhai Maharaj Singh occupies an important position in Sikh history and religious tradition. Bhai Maharaj Singh is situated in historical narratives as a prominent figure who led the resistance movement against British annexation of the Punjab in 1849. Details of Bhai Maharaj's role in the resistance against British expansion in the Punjab can be gleaned from a number of publications produced by authors based in India: Kirpal Singh and M.L. Ahluwalia's text on *Punjab's Pioneer Freedom Fighters* published in 1963; and a collection of archival documents on Bhai Maharaj Singh, edited and published by Nahar Singh are important sources of information (Singh Nahar 1968). Another important historical source is M.L. Ahluwalia's study on Bhai Maharaj Singh published in 1972 (Ahluwalia 1972). A publication containing documents on Bhai Maharaj Singh was again published by Nahar Singh and Kirpal Singh in 1990 as the second volume in *Rebels against the British Raj: Bhai Maharaj Singh (1810–1857)* (Singh Nahar and Singh Kirpal 1990).

These publications cast the life and history of Bhai Maharaj Singh in a nationalist vein by emphasising his role in the anti-British struggle during the period of the Anglo-Sikh Wars. Bhai Maharaj Singh's prominence in Sikh history is traced to his reputation as 'a great freedom fighter' and 'a shrewd statesman' who mobilised a powerful resistance movement against British expansion in Punjab from 1847 to 1849. The figure of Bhai Maharaj Singh resurfaced again in the nationalist discourse of Indian authors based in India with the publication of an article in the *Spokesman*, Chandigarh in August 1996. Written in a strongly nationalist tone, the article lamented the lack of knowledge Punjabis had on Bhai Maharaj Singh, which it argued was a result of 'special efforts made by the British rulers to erase the memory of his name from the minds of people and [push] his name to obscure corners of history'. The article, therefore, sought to retrieve Bhai Maharaj Singh from historical obscurity by highlighting his role as 'Punjab's unique saint-soldier, great revolutionary and topmost freedom fighter' against British rule (Singh Harcharan 1998: 21–32).

Bhai Maharaj Singh as a Sikh Sant

Bhai Maharaj Singh occupies an important position in yet another context. In his study on the development of the *Sant* movement in the Punjab, W.H. McLeod mentioned Bhai Maharaj Singh as an example of a militant religious leadership that emerged in the Punjab in the mid-nineteenth century when the Khalsa was perceived to be under serious threat from the British. Men like Bhai Maharaj Singh set a historical precedent for the emergence in the twentieth century of modern *Sants* who embraced a political and sometimes militant concept of religious duty. The significance of Bhai Maharaj Singh in the history of the Sikh *Panth* is therefore closely linked to the importance of *Sants* in Sikh history and the religious tradition of the Khalsa.

The significance of Bhai Maharaj within Sikh tradition is also discussed by Harjot Oberoi within the context of the Sanatan Sikh tradition in the nineteenth century. He argues that the potency of Bhai Maharaj as a leader the anti-British struggle stems from his stature as a *Bhai* in the Sanatan tradition (defined by Oberoi as the pluralistic and polycentric mode of Sikh tradition adopted primarily by Sikh elites in the nineteenth century). In the nineteenth century, the title Bhai, along with other titles like *Sant* and *Baba*, was given to those who were revered as holy men of the Sikh Panth. These holy men were crucial for the transmission of Sikhism among the unlettered peasant masses through their role as leaders and masters. Oberoi notes that 'to qualify for this title [Bhai] a person had to demonstrate a capacity to interpret the *Adi Granth*, communicate the wisdom of the gurus it enshrined, and be publicly recognised for his piety. If in addition he could work miracles, heal the sick and give succour to the distressed, he was sure to occupy a position of considerable reverence and influence within the community' (Oberoi 1997: 118–21).

Bhai Maharaj Singh thus came from a long established religious tradition which accorded great respect to men distinguished by their religious piety, asceticism or supernatural powers. In his childhood Bhai Maharaj Singh received instruction from Toota Singh, a Nirmala ascetic, and acquired an extensive knowledge of the *Adi Granth*. He later became a loyal follower of a famous Sikh mystic Bir Singh of Naurangabad (1768–1844) and moved to Bir Singh's *dera* at Naurangabad in Amritsar district; Bir Singh was himself the disciple of

Baba Sahib Singh of Una (1756–1834), a member of a guru lineage linked to Guru Nanak.

Bhai Maharaj Singh's prominence also stems from the myths surrounding his supernatural abilities. One popular story illustrates his ability to miraculously increase the quantity of food in the *langgar* at Bir Singh's *dera* at Naurangbad. Shortly after the capture of Bhai Maharaj Singh in 1849 for his anti-British activities, Henri Vanisttart, the deputy commissioner of Jalandhur submitted a report in which he made the following observation: 'The Gooroo [Bhai Maharaj Singh] is not an ordinary man. He is to the Natives what Jesus Christ is to the most zealous of Christians. His miracles were seen by tens of thousands and are more implicitly relied on, than on those worked by the ancient prophets' (Singh Nahar and Singh Kirpal 1990: 69–70). After his arrest by the British, Bhai Maharaj Singh was sent to Singapore as a political exile, where he is believed to have died during his internment. He is lauded in Punjab and Singapore as a *Shaheed* (martyr) who died trying to save the Sikh Kingdom from the imperialistic ambitions of the British.

Bhai Maharaj Singh as 'the first Sikh to land ashore on Singapore soil'

If Bhai Maharaj Singh features prominently in the Indian nationalist narratives highlighted above, then his exile to Singapore serves as an important point in the historical narratives of the Singaporean Sikh community. Bhai Maharaj Singh is often mentioned as one of the first Sikhs to arrive in Singapore in 1850 as a political prisoner of the British (Sandhu 1970: 347). Given the emphasis placed by the Singaporean government on the 'preservation' and promotion of cultural heritage and history among the different ethnic communities, the Singaporean Sikh community has turned to the fashioning of historical narratives and the appropriation of symbols and historical icons to define themselves.

The move to memorialise Bhai Maharaj Singh as a historical icon of the Sikh community began in the early 1990s. The process of inventing the spiritual and historical legacy left by Bhai Maharaj Singh for the Singaporean Sikh community was initiated with the proposal to construct a Bhai Maharaj Singh Memorial within the compound of Gurdwara Silat Road. Prominent members of the Sikh community were involved in a fund-raising campaign to finance the project, which cost an estimated three million dollars. In 1991, a book entitled *Bhai Maharaj Singh: Saint-Soldier* was written by Choor Singh Sidhu and published by the Central Sikh Gurdwara Board as an effort to generate greater awareness for the project.

One of the aims of the memorial project was to fashion a long and illustrious history for the community. This can be gleaned from the foreword in Choor Singh's book on Bhai Maharaj Singh:

The Sikhs in Singapore are going through an extremely interesting phase in this country. The Government has recently recognized our contribution to the development of Singapore, and to her unique flavour. Like other communities we are encouraged to preserve our cultural heritage. This requires us to delve into our past to understand who we are, and what we stand for, and how and when Sikhs came to Singapore ... Justice Choor Singh's article on Bhai Maharaj Singh is timely. It is a succinct, well-researched and highly readable account of an honourable and admirable Sikh whose heroic and saintly deeds have left an indelible impression on the hearts and minds of Singapore Sikhs. Bhai Maharaj Singh is particularly special to us because of his brief residence in this country.

(Choor Singh 1991: 2)

Choor Singh's version of the history and significance of Bhai Maharaj Singh for Singaporean Sikhs is commonly accepted as an 'official' narrative and serves as an important appendage to the history of Gurdwara Silat Road. Colonial records of Bhai Maharaj's capture by the British in Punjab and his subsequent internment in Singapore are cited in Choor Singh's narrative to provide historical verification. Even the pictorial illustration of Bhai Maharaj Singh on Choor Singh's book is replicated from that found in the collection of documents published by Nahar Singh and Kirpal Singh. A revised and updated version of Choor Singh's article was re-published by the Central Sikh Gurdwara Board after the completion of the Bhai Maharaj Singh Memorial Shrine, which was officially declared open on 23 October 1995. What is particularly interesting about this reprint is the addition made to the pictorial illustration of Bhai Maharaj Singh. The Khalsa symbol, which was not previously included in the first publication, was added to the flag staff held by the Saint. The title of the publication was also changed from *Bhai Maharaj Singh: Saint-Soldier* to *Bhai Maharaj Singh: Martyr of the Sikh Faith* (Choor Singh 1998).

As Bhai Maharaj Singh's historical trajectory spans both the Punjab and Singapore in the colonial period, his exile in Singapore offers the Singaporean Sikh community an important justification to stake a claim on him. The following is a paragraph from the preface of *Rebels against the British Raj*:

Bhaie [*sic*] Maharaj Singh was arrested in December 1849 and ordered to be sent to Singapore (China) [*sic*] ... Bhaie Maharaj Singh (1810–57) died a miserable death on 5th July 1857, almost blind on account of cataract. His strong body was reduced to a skeleton and a bundle of bones on account of sufferings. At that time there were no Hindus or Sikhs in Singapore to cremate the body. No body knows what became of it. Soon after his death his companion Khurruck Singh was transferred to Penang – Malasia [*sic*]. We earnestly request the Sikh residents of Singapore and Malaysia to collect and send us more material about Bhaie Maharaj Singh and his associate Khurruck Singh.

(Nahar Singh and Kirpal Singh 1990: xx)

The lacuna of historical detail surrounding Bhai Maharaj Singh and his companion Khurruck Singh after their exile to Malaya is particularly conducive for myth-making and the fashioning of historical narratives.[4] Official correspondence ceased after the death of Bhai Maharaj Singh and nothing is known of the fate of his companion, Khurruck Singh. Details regarding the burial of Bhai Maharaj Singh remain vague due to the absence of any written records and are, hence, open to conjecture.

Choor Singh attempts to construct a sense of historic continuity in his narrative by explaining how this lacuna dovetails with a popular belief, among Sikh devotees, that an unmarked tombstone located formerly at the grounds of the Singapore General Hospital belonged to a Sikh *Sant* imprisoned in Singapore by the British in the mid-nineteenth century. Bhai Maharaj Singh is valorised in Choor Singh's narrative as a *Shaheed* (martyr) and a 'Saint-Soldier' who effectively galvanised the resistance movement against the British. He is, therefore, portrayed as a heroic figure worthy of commemoration by the Singaporean Sikh community:

> [It] must not be forgotten that Bhai Maharaj Singh was also the Head of the Religious Order, now known as the Hoti Mardan Vali Sant Khalsa Sampardai, which had been established by Bhai Daya Singh, one of the five *Panj Payaras* of Guru Gobind Singh ... Bhai Maharaj Singh was therefore not only a revolutionary fighter who tried to save the Sikh Kingdom but also a recognized religious personage of very high standing, a true Saint of the Sikh Faith who died the death of a martyr. Some Sikhs, both in India and Singapore, even believe that he was a *Karniwala* (possessor of supernatural powers) ... Bhai Maharaj was undoubtedly one the great Saint-Soldiers of the Sikh faith, who has left behind a rich spiritual legacy and merits a memorial in Singapore, if for no other reason, then, for the simple reason that he died in Singapore. Many Singapore Sikhs unfortunately are not aware of this.
>
> (Choor Singh 1998: 27)

The emphasis on the religious and historical lineage of Bhai Maharaj Singh places him within a potent and evocative past. It is one which conjures memories of the political might of the Sikh Kingdom before the Punjab was annexed by the British in 1849; invokes the sacred/religious legacy of the tenth Sikh Guru, Guru Gobind Singh who instituted the Khalsa and the symbolism of the *Panj Pyare* (the Five Beloved); and celebrates the act of martyrdom which is highly privileged within the Sikh tradition.

Bhai Maharaj Singh, therefore, acts as a conduit linking Singaporean Sikhs to these historical and religious narratives that are central within Sikh history and iconography. The building of a memorial gurdwara to memorialise Bhai Maharaj Singh helps foster collective memory and identity for it involves the construction of a physical landmark around which Sikhs can gather for religious purposes and identify as belonging to the community. This project is also an attempt to draw the attention of the government and other communities in Singapore to the iconic status of Bhai Maharaj Singh and history behind the Gurdwara

Sahib Silat Road. The efforts of the Sikh community in promoting a national recognition of Punjabi/Sikh 'heritage' in Singapore reaped success when Gurdwara Silat Road was designated as a Historical Site by the National Heritage Board on 14 November 1999.

The choice of Bhai Maharaj Singh as an icon to represent the Singaporean Sikh community is motivated by the hope, on the part of community leaders, of finding a unifying symbol for Singaporean Sikhs. Bhai Maharaj Singh is believed to be one of the first Sikhs to arrive in Singapore. As a political prisoner of the British, Bhai Maharaj Singh was exiled to Singapore in 1850. His historical trajectory is set apart from the large-scale migration and circulation of Sikhs from Punjab to Malaya in the last quarter of the nineteenth century to the first quarter of the twentieth century. The figure of Bhai Maharaj Singh is, therefore, removed from the regional factions prevalent among the early Sikh immigrants, particularly Sikhs from the Jat caste. Though region-based identities and differences have gradually lost some of its currency among the younger generation of Singaporean Sikhs, the community is still differentiated along regional and caste lines and is also grappling with generational divisions that have emerged. Given his prominent status within Sikh history, Bhai Maharaj is thus seen as an ideal figure to be memorialised as a historical icon to represent the Singaporean Sikh community.[5]

The significance of Bhai Maharaj Singh as an anti-British Sikh martyr and a political exile is, however, downplayed by Davinder Singh in his foreword written for Choor Singh's book. Given his position then as a Member of Parliament, and a prominent member of the Sikh community, Davinder Singh was careful not to portray Bhai Maharaj Singh as a potential symbol for 'radical' political activities within Singapore. The anti-British political stance and the miraculous powers for which Bhai Maharaj is celebrated and revered, is merely hinted at in a laudatory but politically neutral acknowledgement of his 'heroic and saintly deeds' as a 'honourable and admirable Sikh' (Choor Singh 1991: 2).

Bhai Maharaj Singh and popular devotion

Besides the official narrative on Bhai Maharaj Singh written by Choor Singh in 1991, there was another book published in 1996 by a Singaporean Sikh devotee. Written originally in Punjabi, parts of the book were subsequently translated into English and published under the title *Bhai Maharaj Singh Ji, 1780–1856: Some Glimpses of His Life*. It is a hagiographic account of the significance of Bhai Maharaj Singh as a *Sant* and martyr 'who sacrificed all his life to free his country and people from foreign rule' (Singh Karam 1998: 1). The book was written for a specific readership: one that regarded Bhai Maharaj Singh as a Sikh *Sant*, and shared a religious worldview in which the belief in miracles and the worship of Sikh *Sants* co-existed with the tenets of Sikhism.

What is particularly interesting about this publication is the section documenting the miracles related to Bhai Maharaj Singh (also referred in the text as *Baba Ji*). The miracles documented (there are seven in all) are drawn from an existing oral tradition which serves as a rich repository of myths and stories related to Maharaj Singh. Clearly, the belief in miracles and the supernatural remains salient among Sikh devotees of Bhai Maharaj Singh and is, in fact, interwoven with their belief in the Sikh Gurus and the sanctity of the *Guru Granth Sahib*. This is underscored in the preface by the author who is himself a staunch devotee of Bhai Maharaj Singh:

> Just as those who receive grace by truly believing in Waheguru or Guru, Baba Ji's followers who witnessed his miracles received his help. Baba Ji fulfils the requests of those who regarding him as omnipresent, continue to serve him.... The miracles connected with Baba Ji are related in this hand-book so that there will be a record for the benefit of future generations. The miracles narrated here have been witnessed by Baba Ji's followers.... It is not a question of being Sikh or non-Sikh. It is a matter of love. Therefore those Sikhs who do not adorn long hair but make sincere requests with love have their prayers and requests answered. Then such devotees present flowers and make obeisance at his tomb as a mark of gratitude.
>
> (Singh Karam 1998: 1–2)

Among the miracles documented are accounts of non-believers (a Muslim, a North Indian Hindu and an Englishman) who became devotees after supernatural encounters with the *Sant* as well as accounts of the exorcism of evil spirits through the invocation of '*Baba Ji*' (Karam Singh 1998: 11–20). In the realm of popular devotion, the memory of Bhai Maharaj Singh is invoked in his capacity as a tutelary *Sant* or a *Karniwala* (possessor of special powers). There exists among many Sikh devotees a popular belief in the miraculous powers of Bhai Maharaj Singh. Sikhs of the older generation, especially Sikh ladies, pay homage to the *Sant* for their personal well-being, and for their supplications to be granted. This community of devotees gather frequently at the Bhai Maharaj Singh Memorial and prayer sessions are held regularly at the Memorial where devotees offer flowers and money as a token of their devotion.

Prior to efforts by the Sikh leadership to fashion a history behind the *samadh* by linking it to the figure of Bhai Maharaj Singh, Sikh devotees, who were motivated by different concerns, had already ascribed religious significance to the *samadh*. This was highlighted in Choor Singh's narrative on Bhai Maharaj Singh:

> After the Second World War, some Tamils started putting flowers at the foot of this tombstone. Some Sikhs followed suit but it was the Tamils who put up some masonry on the ground around it and made it look like a tomb-stone. Some green flags on poles were also stuck around it, probably by Muslims who believed the tombstone was a *Kramat* (memorial for a Muslim Saint). Some Sikhs started believing that it was the tombstone of Bhai Maharaj Singh while others believed it was of Baba Karam Singh. Nothing is known of this Baba Karam Singh.... The Sikhs went one step

further than the Tamils. They put up a structure over the tombstone in the grounds of the General Hospital. Very soon they installed the Granth Sahib there and the place became a full-fledged Gurdwara. Regular prayer sessions and functions were held with large crowds of devotees in attendance. Eventually the Government decided that it was no place for a regular Gurdwara and requested the Sikhs to demolish the structure.

(Choor Singh 1991: 14–15)

The above observation underscores the religious belief in saints shared by other communities of faith along with the Sikhs. Far from being exclusive to the Sikhs, the former site of the *samadh* was shared by Hindus and Muslims who grafted onto this nondescript tombstone their respective religious beliefs and symbols. Previously an open and contested site, the tombstone was eventually appropriated by Sikh devotees when they installed the *Guru Granth Sahib* at the *samadh* and held regular prayer sessions there. When the *samadh* was relocated to Gurdwara Silat Road in 1966, it effectively became a religious symbol of the Sikh community. Construction of the Bhai Maharaj Singh Memorial within Gurdwara Silat Road compound took place in the early 1990s and it was officially declared open on October 1995 by Kartar Singh Thakral, a prominent member of the Sikh business community who donated generously to the renovation of the Gurdwara Silat Road. His involvement in the memorial project is symbolically significant as it is a gesture of co-operation and unity between the Sikh business community and Sikhs from the non-business class.

The *Barsi* of Bhai Maharaj Singh is an important religious and social event held annually at the Bhai Maharaj Singh Memorial at Gurdwara Sahib Silat Road. During the *Barsi*, the *akhand path* prayer ceremony is offered in memory of the *Sant*. It is a major religious event at the Gurdwara; other programmes such as *kirtan* and prayer sessions are often organised in conjunction with the *Barsi*. The Gurdwara Sahib Silat Road is considered an important landmark in the network of Sikh religious sites that have emerged in Malaysia and Singapore. These religious sites are usually gurdwaras associated with popular Sikh *Sants*. The Gurdwara Sahib Malacca where devotees gather annually for the *Barsi* of the famous Sant Sohan Singh is another important religious site. It has become an increasingly common practice for Sikh devotees to undertake a pilgrimage of popular religious sites in Malaysia and Singapore, especially during major religious festivals for the benefits of *darsan* and *seva*. Although the *Barsi* of Bhai Maharaj Singh is a significant event for Singaporean Sikh devotees, the scale of the religious commemoration in Singapore is considerably smaller in comparison to the *Barsi* in Malacca.

The community of Bhai Maharaj Singh devotees is not made up exclusively of Punjabi-Sikhs: it also includes non-Sikhs, namely Chinese and North Indian devotees who have been known to offer prayers and offerings at the Memorial. Older Sikh ladies who form the core of Bhai Maharaj devotees serve as 'keepers' of an oral tradition built on the myths and stories of the *Sant*. It was noted that

Bhai Maharaj Singh is the favourite Saint of Sikh ladies. Some of them light candles at the back of the shrine and seek his intercession in their prayers. The belief that prayers are answered by his intercession is very strong, so much so that Ten Thousand Dollar notes and even jewellery, such as gold bangles, have on some occasions been found in the donation box of the shrine. This is ample proof that some grateful devotee's prayers have been answered by the intercession of Bhai Maharaj Singh.

(Choor Singh 1998: 28)

The belief in the miraculous powers of *Sants* and the religious merit of making pilgrimages to sacred sites associated with *Sants* is regarded with ambivalence by some of the more educated Sikhs. The worship of *Sants* is regarded by reformist elements within the Sikh community as being distinctly Hindu and hence an un-Sikh religious practice which goes against the orthodox tenets of Sikhism. This reformist impulse is articulated by Choor Singh:

It will be remembered that there are several small Gurdwaras built in the Golden Temple Complex at Amritsar in memory of Sikh martyrs, e.g. Baba Deep Singh Gurdwara. It is of fundamental importance that Sikhs who believe that prayers are granted when intercession of Bhai Maharaj Singh is invoked, should worship in his Gurdwara and not at his *samadh* (tombstone). The practice of worshipping at a *samadh* of a Saint, no matter how holy, is gross violation of the tenets of the Sikh faith. This is [why] it is imperative that there should be a Bhai Maharaj Singh Memorial Gurdwara in Singapore. It will enable and hopefully encourage those seeking his intercession, to pray in his Gurdwara instead of his *samadh*.

(Choor Singh 1991: 17)

The push for the construction of a Memorial Gurdwara to house the *samadh* of the *Sant* can be seen as an attempt by the leaders of the community to discipline and standardise religious practices according to the religious tenets of Khalsa Sikhism. What is striking about this project is the creative manner in which a rapprochement is established between the modernist approach of the Sikh leadership and the popular devotional practices of Sikh devotees. Through the imaginative use of important religious symbols like the *Guru Granth Sahib* to delineate Sikh sacred space, the worship of Bhai Maharaj Singh by devotees is justified as an accepted Sikh religious practice.

Attempts to address the contention surrounding the practice of worshipping at the *samadh* resulted in the housing of the *samadh* in a memorial where the *Guru Granth Sahib* occupies a central position. In a clever organisation of sacred space, the dais bearing the *Guru Granth Sahib* is specially constructed to hold and display the *samadh* of Bhai Maharaj Singh in an unobtrusive manner. Devotees who worship at the memorial pay homage first to the *Guru Granth Sahib* (which is placed prominently at the entrance of the memorial) before they circumambulate the dais in order to pay homage to Bhai Maharaj Singh as his *samadh* is placed at the back of the dais, facing away from the memorial's entrance.

Conclusion

In his study of the transmission of Sikh identity and cultural heritage among Sikhs in Singapore, Verne Dusenbery makes the observation that Singaporean Sikhs are 'a community of Sikhs who have come of age in the diaspora' (Dusenbery 1996: 120–1). Unlike Britain, Canada and the United States which, still receive new Sikh immigrants, the movement of Sikh immigrants into Singapore was kept in check by the tightening of immigration laws in 1953 and 1959. Subsequent additions to the local Singaporean Sikh community have consisted largely of female spouses from the Punjab and middle-class Sikh professionals from the Punjab, the United States, or Britain who stay only for the duration of their employment contracts. A number of Sikhs from the Punjab who are employed in Singapore as unskilled contract labourers are a more recent, though separate, presence within the community.

In the colonial period, Sikhism was exported along with its adherents, to new territories where Sikh communities settled and took root. The idea of Sikhs as a martial race, popularised in British colonial discourse, served as an important channel through which Sikhs were able to take advantage of the economic opportunities offered through military service. Once recruited into Sikh regiments and Sikh Police Contingents, Sikhs were required to undergo the Khalsa's *khande ki pahul* initiation rite and to maintain the external symbols of their Sikh identity which are commonly referred to as the Five Ks (McLeod 1997: 53). They also had to accept the religious authority of *granthis* installed by the colonial authorities. These measures were implemented by the British and were meant to foster and preserve a distinctly martial Khalsa Sikh identity (Ballantyne 2002: 112–13). Sikhs who served in the colonial security forces often served as the standard measure to represent the Sikh community, especially those communities based in British colonies.

The martial nature of Sikhs, which was such an important trope in British colonial discourse, has been supplemented by new discursive tropes in the national discourse on the Singaporean Sikh community: the success of Sikhs as a minority group in Singapore; their contribution to Singapore, notably through military service; their dynamism and progressive approach towards the transmission of Punjabi-Sikh heritage to the younger generation of Singaporean Sikhs. The majority of Sikhs who came to Singapore and Malaya during the colonial period were of peasant background from the Mahja, Malwa and Doaba regions of Punjab, and those who stayed on after the tightening of immigration laws in the 1950s laid the foundations of the Singaporean and Malaysian Sikh communities. Regional and caste loyalties formed a key aspect in the delineation of Sikh identities among the earlier generation of Singapore-domiciled Sikhs and this was manifested in the establishment of Gurdwaras where networks based on historically rooted regional and caste affiliations were forged and maintained.

A younger generation of Sikhs have emerged in postcolonial Singapore to assume leadership positions within the community: they are mainly middle-class, Singapore-born, male, English-educated professionals bearing a distinct *kesdhari* Sikh identity.[6] This Sikh identity has its historic antecedent in the distinctive image of the turbaned Sikh policeman represented in historical narratives on Singapore and its colonial past as a symbol of the British Empire. Even in the postcolonial period, the martial nature of Sikhs continued to hold currency in public life and Sikhs were closely associated with military service in Singapore. This has often been highlighted as a notable contribution made by Sikhs to Singapore and nation-building. The recent achievements of Sikhs in the political and legal sectors in Singapore have also cast the community in a positive light. In the course of working with the government through community initiatives to advance Sikh interests in Singapore, notable efforts were also made to construct a normative and collective Singaporean Sikh identity variously defined by nationality, religion and ethnicity.

The projects initiated by the Sikh leadership in the early 1990s such as the launching of the Singapore Sikh Education Foundation in 1990 to advance Punjabi language education among Sikh youth, and the organisation of 'The International Conference cum Exhibition on Punjabi/Sikh Heritage' in June 1992 to raise public awareness of Sikh religion and tradition are attempts by the Sikh community to construct a version of 'Punjabi-Sikh heritage' that reflected the particular needs and concerns of a generation of Singaporean Sikhs who have come of age in the diaspora.

An important concern is the construction of a collective Singaporean Sikh identity. The appropriation of Bhai Maharaj Singh as an icon for the Singaporean Sikh community serves as an illustration of the dynamics involved in the fashioning of Sikh history and identities. From his position as a political prisoner exiled to Singapore by the British in 1850, Bhai Maharaj Singh was rehabilitated as a Sikh martyr and memorialised as a heroic 'Saint of the Sikh faith' by the Singaporean Sikh community. By recounting the martyrdom of Bhai Maharaj Singh and establishing his significance in the history of Sikhs in Singapore, the Sikh leadership is attaching to their community the same qualities of heroism, fortitude, and piety associated with Bhai Maharaj Singh. The appropriation of a prominent historical and religious figure in Sikh history also allows for the construction of a long and illustrious historical narrative for the Singaporean Sikh community. The act of memorialising of Bhai Maharaj Singh is in tandem with efforts to revive the historic significance of the Gurdwara Silat Road in the Sikh community. The designation of Gurdwara Sahib Silat Road as a historical site by the National Heritage Board in 1999 was seen as an important milestone for the Singaporean Sikh community. It was highlighted by the Sikh community as an important acknowledgement on the national level of the 'strong historical contribution of Bhai Maharaj Singh Ji and the contribution of the Sikh Police Contingent to nation building' (Central Sikh Gurdwara Board 2006: 70).

This chapter, by focusing on the role of Sikh community organisations and the links forged between Bhai Maharaj Singh, Gurdwara Sahib Silat Road and the Singaporean Sikh community, seeks to illustrate the complex and creative ways in which members of the community negotiate 'the colonial past and the postcolonial present' in the construction of Sikh historical narratives and identities (Ballantyne 2004: 171). A key concern shaping the construction of Singaporean Sikh identities lies in 'transforming the image of Sikhs from just providers of security and defence of the nation to that of being successful in any career from defence to academics and from medicine to international entrepreneurs' (Central Sikh Gurdwara Board 2006: 69). Singaporean Sikhs will constantly be fashioning and rewriting historical narratives and appropriating new symbols to reflect this transformation.

Notes

1 The estimate of the Singaporean Sikh population in 2006 was provided by Mr Dilbagh Singh, a prominent figure in the Sikh community in Singapore.
2 Sikhs from Malwa region in Punjab formed the largest group followed by those from the Majha region while Sikhs from Doaba were the smallest group among the three.
3 It has been suggested that one of the causes behind this alienation was the continued use of Punjabi as a principal mode of religious instruction by *granthis*, who are usually employed from the Punjab on a contractual basis. Meanwhile, an increasing number of Singaporean Sikhs were more comfortable and fluent in English than they were in Punjabi.
4 The last written record on Bhai Maharaj was sent by G.M Blundel, Governor of the Straits Settlements, to the colonial office in British India. Dated 12 July 1856, the dispatch conveyed news of the death of Bhai Maharaj. 'I have the honour to report to you for the information of the Right Hon'ble the Governor General of India-in-Council, that the State Prisoner, "Bhaie Maharaj Singh" died on the 5th instant.' Document No. 86. See Singh, Nahar and Singh, Kirpal (2nd edn 1990).
5 British Sikhs too have appropriated the figure of Maharaja Dalip Singh, the last sovereign ruler of the Sikh Kingdom of Punjab, as a symbol to unify a community plagued by caste and generational divisions. See Ballantyne (2004: 151–75).
6 A *kesdhari* Sikh is a Sikh with uncut hair. Having uncut hair (*kes*) is one of the five markers of the Khalsa identity. A *kesdhari* Sikh is not necessarily an initiated member of the Khalsa. An *amritdhari* Sikh, on the other hand, is an initiated member of the Khalsa who adheres to the religious practices and external markers of the Khalsa.

References

Ahluwalia, M.L. (1972) *Bhai Maharaj Singh*, Patiala: Punjabi University.
Ballantyne, T. (2002) *Orientalism and Race: Aryanism in the British Empire*, Hampshire: Palgrave.
—— (2004) 'Maharaja Dalip Singh, History and Negotiation of Sikh Identity', in Pashaura Singh and N.G. Barrier (eds) *Sikhism and History*, New Delhi: Oxford University Press, pp. 151–75.
Barrier, N.G. (2004) 'Authority, Politics and Contemporary Sikhism: The Akal Takht, the SGPC, *Rahit Maryada*, and the Law', in Pashaura Singh and N.G. Barrier (eds) *Sikhism and History*, New Delhi: Oxford University Press, pp. 194–229.
Central Sikh Gurdwara Board. (2006) *Bhai Maharaj Singh Ji & Gurdwara Sahib Silat Road: A Historical Journey*, Singapore: Central Sikh Gurdwara Board.

Dusenbery, V.A. (1989) 'Introduction: A Century of Sikhs Beyond Punjab', in V.A. Dusenbery and N.G. Barrier (eds) *The Sikh Diaspora: Migration and Experience Beyond Punjab*, Delhi: Chanakya Publications, pp. 1–28.

—— (1996) 'Socialising Sikhs in Singapore: Soliciting the State's Support', in Pashaura Singh and N.G. Barrier (eds) *The Transmission of Sikh Heritage in the Diaspora*, Delhi: Chanakya Publications, pp. 113–48.

Ibrahim, B. (1982) 'A Study of the Sikh Community in Singapore', Thesis (M.Soc.Sci.), National University of Singapore.

McLeod, H. (1997) *Sikhism*, England: Penguin Books.

Oberoi, H. (1997) *The Construction of Religious Boundaries: Culture, Identity and Diversity in the Sikh Tradition*, Delhi: Oxford University Press.

Sandhu, K.S. (1970) 'Sikh Immigration into Malaya during the Period of British Rule', in J. Ch'en and N. Tarling (eds) *Studies in the Social History of China and Southeast Asia*, Great Britain: Cambridge University Press, pp. 335–54.

Singh, Choor (1991) *Bhai Maharaj Singh: Saint-Soldier*, Singapore: Central Sikh Gurdwara Board.

—— (1998) *Bhai Maharaj Singh: Martyr of the Sikh Faith*, Singapore: Central Sikh Gurdwara Board.

Singh, Harcharan (reprint 1998) 'Bhai Maharaj Singh – The First Great Warrior who endeavoured to break the shackles of slavery', *Spokesman*, Chandigarh, August 1996.

Singh, Karam (1998) *Bhai Maharaj Singh 1780–1856: Some Glimpses of his Life*, Singapore: Bhai Karam Singh.

Singh, Mehervan (1979) *Sikhism East and West*, Singapore: Mehervan Singh.

Singh, Nahar (1968) *Documents relating to Bhai Maharaj Singh*, Punjab: Sikh History Source Material Search Association.

Singh, Nahar and Kirpal Singh (2nd edn 1990) *Rebels against the British Raj: Bhai Maharaj Singh (1810–1857)*, Volume II, New Delhi: Atlantic Publishers & Distributors.

Singh, Seva (1986) *Early Pioneers in Singapore*, Singapore: Seva Singh Gandharb.

12 'The familiar temporariness'

Naipaul, diaspora and the literary imagination: a personal narrative

Vijay Mishra

> So much of this I saw with the literary eye, or with the aid of literature.
>
> (Naipaul 1987: 22)

11 October 2001: the Nobel laureate in literature (the hundredth as it turned out) was V.S. Naipaul. Many years before I sent Naipaul a copy of a book I edited for the centenary of the arrival of Indians in Fiji. The book's title, *Rama's Banishment*, had clearly impressed him as he sent me a warm letter of thanks in which he remarked, 'the topic is close to my heart, as it has to be'. I had hoped for more – for instance, his own attitude to the agony of displacement that I had captured by referring to the defining myth of the Hindi speaking Hindu. About this and other matters he remained silent. But the letter was important in as much as it acknowledged that we understood each other. A week after the Nobel announcement I wrote a deeply personal and celebratory homage for Naipaul, which was published in 2002 (Mishra 2002a, 2002b).

I have returned to that homage and to much of its substance to rethink the question of the links between a very colonial literary imagination and V.S. Naipaul's writings, especially in so far as they take us to a specifically 'old Indian diasporic' link between a colonial education and the aesthetic. At the heart of the link is a trauma about belonging (to a nation-state) and ownership of a language not one's own. The discourse I adopt here is, after a phrase used in Shakespeare criticism, 'memorial reconstructions', which I believe in this instance has a special place. Memorially constructing one's response to texts at their first moments of encounter is, after all, one way of locating oneself more immediately in an author's writing. Of course, critical judgment – the scholarly enterprise – requires something else; it requires detachment and the placing of the speaking subject under erasure; it presupposes judgment and analysis only after the corpus has been re-read in its entirety, only after the bibliography has been more or less exhausted. It requires a dispassionate engagement with the subject matter. I am, therefore, undertaking something which sits a little uncomfortably with scholarly judgment by rethinking, in an intensely personal manner, the literary intertexts of the old (plantation) Indian diaspora via V.S. Naipaul and doing so through memory, and through the genre of homage. If there is a certain urgency in my prose, a rush to connect ideas, a pressure from within to round off matters even before the analytic is complete, it is because Naipaul is like an indwelling spectre – in my style, in my attempt to break into the grand narratives of English literary history, even, shamefully, in my barely suppressed nostalgia for the Pax Britannica. I have lived with Naipaul for some 40 years and very much in his shadow. I own first editions of all his works. He has also denied me the privilege of critical originality by being everywhere before me – the Indian plantation diaspora, Oxford, India – as indeed, to have mine back for the moment, Conrad denied Naipaul that privilege by being everywhere before him.

The word *homage*, of course, carries power of an unusual kind. Not a word with 'indigenous roots', it came to Middle English from the French '(*h*)*omage*' which in turn may be traced back to medieval Latin '*homināticum*', that is '*homo, homin*' ('man') + '*aticum*' (the suffix '–age') which has the meanings of a 'journey', 'belonging to', and the like. Although of the three meanings (as a noun) of the word *homage* – in feudal law a formal and public acknowledgment of allegiance; a body of persons owning allegiance; acknowledgment of superiority in respect of rank, worth, beauty … reverence, dutiful respect, or honour shown – it is the third which is appropriate for my use, the concept of allegiance always haunts its usage and with it a sense of reverence, honour and respect. Hence Milton: 'All these are Spirits of air, and woods, and springs, Thy gentle ministers who come to pay Thee homage, and acknowledge thee their Lord' (*Paradise Regained*, II, 376–8). To Naipaul himself the etymology of a word – the kind of etymology traced above – has special meaning because etymology is an act of dispassionate labour, the work of monkish discipline, an abstract, silent, discipline with little functional value. Monkish, detached, remote, and very English – colonial education for the people of the plantation diaspora was like that. The syllabus throughout the English-speaking plantation diaspora, and probably in much of the Empire generally, was controlled by the Cambridge University Syndicate and the School Certificate (awarded in three divisions, first, second and third) was the Cambridge Overseas School Certificate. In my own final year in a Methodist Mission High School in Fiji (the Lelean Memorial School) the Literature syllabus included Francis Palgrave's *Golden Treasury*, an anthology of English verse later much derided by Naipaul (2007: 8), Joseph Conrad, Thomas Hardy, Shakespeare and Sheridan. How did that educational system affect Naipaul's imagination? What impact did that educational system have on the children of the old Indian plantation diaspora? A passage from Naipaul's recently published collection of essays is revealing:

> First in school you have English Composition, maybe a page or two in an exercise book, with perhaps an occasional piece of précis running to half a page; and then many years later, in a graver place, you have Essays, literary pieces, of many foolscap pages. The pen runs along the ruled page, with hardly a correction. This can give an illusion of maturity and power. But you may not find it easy to move from those essays, full of required reading, full of other men's ideas and language, to what you may already have begun

to think of as proper writing, writer's writing, something personal, with authority, something you might imagine printed in a book.

That was how it happened to me.

(2007: 127)

For me the long shadow of Naipaul began in the second of the two years that the colonial government granted us to undertake post-Senior Cambridge education at the 'European and part-European only' Suva Grammar School in Fiji. This was in 1963 and I have, in another essay (1990) recounted my first moment of encounter with Naipaul's works. One morning in the English class (George Eliot or one of the bard's histories, probably *Henry IV Part I*, was the set text) a Christian colleague, Oliver by name (the rest of the Indians being predominantly Hindu were far too timid, the Fijians excessively deferential or polite), improbably interjected, 'But Mrs R, I've just borrowed this book from the British Council Library and it is fantastic'. (Mrs R, wife of the Commissioner of Police, had come recently to Suva Grammar with good English Honours – which in Britain means it wasn't a third class – from the University of London.) The teacher was taken aback but was not dismissive. She asked for the book and read it that night. The next morning she said, 'This is a difficult book, I couldn't get into it try as I might, it seemed to wobble so much, lacked a sense of unity, of design, and the language was, in part, so odd. I'm sorry we can't possibly read it in class.' Oliver was downcast; the rest of the class, knowing no better, accepted the teacher's judgment, not that disagreement would have mattered even if our defence were stronger. The book in question was V.S. Naipaul's masterpiece, *A House for Mr Biswas*, among two or three of the great books written in English in the second half of the twentieth century. I read what I could of the book during morning and lunch recess. However, I was not a member of the British Council and not being a city person (I travelled by bus to Suva Grammar from the Methodist Mission sanctuary of Dilkusha, across the river from Nausori where the first sugar mill was established by the Colonial Sugar Refining Company), I had little understanding of how libraries worked. So I had to wait until a colonial government scholarship took me to Wellington the following year before I read Naipaul's novel in its entirety. It was a similar scholarship which took Naipaul to Oxford in 1950.

Monkish education, seeing things with an [English] literary eye, being sensitive to the history of a word, Naipaul had said. A peculiar Anglophone (or Francophone or Dutch) sensibility, an almost colonial outlook to things in the old plantation diaspora – these are matters not explored well enough in studies of the Indian diaspora. The old Indian diaspora, dragged into modernity through the production of one commodity, sugar, and part of a system (of indenture) which remained unchanged for almost eighty years, affected nation-states in the making in ways that the new diaspora of late capital has never been able to do. In Trinidad, in Guyana, in Fiji, in Mauritius, in Suriname especially, in South Africa perhaps only marginally, the old diaspora informed the nation and

affected its social structures. And since this was a peasant diaspora, largely illiterate and without any understanding of a pan-Indian culture, it internalised the
discourses of the master, created a surrogate motherland (England, France,
Holland) and mimicked her cultural norms as if these were its own. When
trouble began in these half-baked postcolonial societies (the phrase echoes
Naipaul's own), the diaspora migrated to either the land of their imperial
masters or to white settler nations. Except for a few members of the comprador
class, no one returned to India. For people not brought up in that diaspora, this
strange adulation, which verges on a fetish, is difficult to understand. Since
everything about India was effectively alien – its high culture languages, religion, art and so on – and since, on the other hand, the coloniser's culture was
everywhere in the educational system (culminating in the ubiquitous curriculum
of the Cambridge Overseas School Certificate) what developed was a borrowed
sensibility, a way of understanding the world, which this diaspora internalised in
a very unselfconscious fashion. The exemplary text here is Naipaul's first published novel *The Mystic Masseur* (1957).

The Mystic Masseur begins with the narrator being taken to the home of
Ganesh Ramsumair, a mystic masseur, for treatment for a swollen foot. The foot
remains untreated in spite of Ganesh's home-made medicine (which the narrator
was asked to take three times a day – but never after meals) and finally it is a
trained doctor who removes the abscess. But what the narrator remembers is
Ganesh's library in a house which was no more than a thatched hut. Ganesh
Ramsumair, who had 'surprised everybody by passing [the Cambridge School
Certificate] in the second grade' (Naipaul 1957: 18), was the proud owner of a
huge library of some 1,500 volumes. The moment of revelation, which is also a
statement about the centrality of books in the colonial and postcolonial indenture
(plantation) imaginary, needs to be cited in full.

> 'Leela,' Ganesh said, 'the boy want to know how much book it have here.'
> 'Let me see,' Leela said, and hitched up the broom to her waistband. She
> started to count off the fingers of her left hand. 'Four hundred Everyman,
> two hundred Penguin – six hundred. Six hundred, and one hundred Reader's
> Library, make seven hundred. I think with all the other book it have about
> fifteen hundred good book here.'
>
> (11)

Everyman, Penguin, Reader's Library books made their way into British
Council Libraries in the plantation Indian diaspora with Everyman collection,
the ultimate prize. Its titles covered every major work of world literature; its
ownership signifying elevated taste. Before the narrator leaves the hut, Ganesh
gives him a copy of his first published booklet, *101 Questions and Answers on
the Hindu Religion*, Ganesh's first attempt to be a writer so that his name could
be placed alongside the red, blue, green, brown and yellow Everyman dust
jackets. The achievement – which reflected rote-learning and plagiaristic
transcription of the worst kind – is rendered with gentle comic irony, an

achievement which finally leads Ganesh Ramsumair to mimic the colonial absolutely as the narrator recalls at the end of the novel:

> 'Pundit Ganesh!' I cried, running towards him. 'Pundit Ganesh Ramsumair!'
> 'G. Ramsay Muir,' he said coldly.

(215)

To read *The Mystic Masseur*, for which the 'source text' is none other than Ganesh Ramsumair's own autobiography, '*The Years of Guilt* (Ganesh Publishing Co. Ltd., Port of Spain)' (14), is to enter into the mystique of the English language and its literature, its publishing practices and its valued genres, which came to this diaspora through a very English educational system. Ganesh's aunt, The Great Belcher, speaks accusingly to him: 'you sitting down here, scratching. Scratching not like hoeing, you know. It can't grow food.' To which Ganesh replies, 'I ain't scratching, man. I reading and I writing' (110). The act of hoeing is linked to plantation labour, the hoe being a key implement for sugar cane cultivation. Against that act (which the aunt considers as real labour) Ganesh offers the act of writing as his real vocation. The power of writing, this bookish knowledge which was prized above all, in the end also contains within it an incipient anglophilia, a nostalgia for the Pax Britannica which Naipaul also carries. For Ganesh Ramsumair it finally took the form of a memorable 'defence of British colonial rule' (214). The diaspora identity is marked by an inherent contradiction: at once anti-colonial and at the same time so firmly located in colonial discourses even when, as Naipaul confesses much later, upon finding that neither Graham Greene nor Somerset Maugham's writings spoke to him 'My material was too far away from [theirs]; it was my own' (2007: 56). It is this contradiction which energises the literature that has emerged from that quarter and it is precisely the contradiction that is at the heart of Naipaul's art.

In a work published 30 years after *The Mystic Masseur*, Naipaul writes from near Salisbury, in Albion's druidic shore with its pre-Christian Stonehenge and the 'Fairies of Albion' (after William Blake), about himself, his origins in a faraway Caribbean island, his engagement with the English language and the challenge facing the colonial writer when confronted with the great discourse of imperialism, the discourse of Romanticism which captured at once an energising poetic movement as well as the high point of European expansionism. The book he produces is an autobiography styled as a novel in five parts and it carries a title which Apollinaire gave to one of Giorgio de Chirico's paintings, *The Enigma of Arrival* (1987). This is an early surrealist painting which Naipaul describes in some detail. A classical scene it is, Mediterranean or ancient-Roman. A wharf, the mast of an 'antique vessel', two figures on a deserted street, one a visitor perhaps, the other a native of the city; it is a desolate scene, mysterious and enigmatic, as the title suggests. Naipaul is struck by the 'mystery of arrival' (91–2). The painting occasions a strong desire to compose a novel around its themes. Naipaul meditates on this possibility: how, if he were to write a novel on the subject, a man would arrive at this port, do his business, get involved in the affairs of the city but then become its sacrificial victim. He escapes and manages to reach the quayside. He thinks he is saved but something is missing: 'Above the cut-out walls and buildings there is no mast, no sail. The antique ship has gone' (92). The plantation diaspora also found that the ship had gone, and we were left on the wharf to gather our goods in a gunny sack and make some sense of our lives. Bereft of an adequate language, without the social organisation of village life, we struggled to find meaning in our lives. For those with a creative imagination, hope came from the colonial masters themselves, which is why, as we read Naipaul, we are struck so much by his 'Englishness' and this Englishness is not to be confused with a perverse racism, the celebration of the white man; instead it is the condition of plantation quotidian life. This is what we are.

The novel opens with a disarmingly simple sentence, 'For the first four days it rained' (11). What follows is an account of how one masters the land, reads it as a native informant ought to have, and then internalises it as one's own, procedures which the old Indian diaspora had been engaged in for almost a century and half. To be able to distinguish 'water meadows' or 'wet meadows' from 'downs', to know that 'avon' means a river and 'hound' any dog, and 'both "Walden" and "shaw" meant wood' (13) require a peculiarly English sensibility. It confirms a bookish, monkish knowledge, the mastery of which is one thing; a 'rawness of response' to the country quite another. And it is this ambivalence – perfect mastery of the language (Naipaul's style is so very English, critics from Pritchett to Ricks have maintained) – high on the heels of a certain 'strangeness', a 'solitude' so that 'every incursion into a new part of the country' was for him 'like a tearing at an old scab' (13) which is at the crux of his writing. The metaphor – 'rawness of response' – is painful but incisive as it captures a singular distance, a distance which is also a consciousness of how the language and its significations were laboriously learnt. Naipaul looks at the golden hay in a shed which is again linked to bookish memory and to a comparison with grass always freshly cut for cattle in Trinidad, 'never browned into hay' (17).

The old and the new, words which recur in this novel, words which also capture the two Indian diasporas, the plantation and the late modern, the old built around the concept of labour where the *materièl* was the hoe and the cane knife, the new governed by the logic of late modern capitalism with its cyber-technology and global economy. The idea of 'ruin and dereliction' (19), the idea that the subject of the old diaspora comes to a putative 'motherland' (how strange the word sounds in the context of the imperial centre) to capture a romantic nostalgia only to find that it is no longer there. Not surprisingly, the artist pauses to examine Jack's father-in-law, 'a figure of literature in the ancient landscape'. 'He seemed a Wordsworthian figure', writes Naipaul, 'bent, exaggeratedly, going gravely about his peasant tasks, as if in an immense Lake District solitude (20)', 'the subject of a poem Wordsworth might have called "The Fuel-Gatherer"' (26). This knowledge could only come to someone who understood the English literary tradition albeit with the 'nerves of the stranger'. The challenge is enormous, the discourse of romanticism so hallowed, the legacy of the English language, as received in the colonies, so frighteningly complex. This diaspora, descendants of illiterate peasants with neither a high culture nor tradition, the flotsam and jetsam of history, panic-ridden and traumatised, in embracing the occupation of writing has to out perform the master, which is why the literature of the old diaspora carries in it a consciousness of the great tradition of English writing. Writing in English is in itself a homage to the coloniser's language even when, in the case of so many writers, Naipaul included, the demotic invades the dominant discourse. The point is made, without this kind of theoretical explanation, by Naipaul himself. In *The Enigma of Arrival*, 'longing for Shakespeare, longing to be put in touch with the early language', Naipaul returns to *King Lear* to make sense of Kent's speech, 'Goose, if I had you upon Sarum Plain, I'd drive ye cackling home to Camelot'. The passage strikes Naipaul because on the radio Naipaul had heard that in the 'days of the Roman Empire geese could be walked to market all the way from the province of Gaul to Rome' (22). The passage from *King Lear* (II. ii. 80–1) has Kent railing at Oswald, a duplicitous steward of Lear's daughter Goneril. Skilled editors of this play, Kenneth Muir included, have found this passage obscure. To Naipaul, Kent's words, after the story of geese making their way from Gaul to Rome, are quite clear: 'Sarum Plain, Salisbury Plain; Camelot, Winchester – just twenty miles away' (22). Naipaul had arrived at a meaning which had confounded textual critics. Would it follow that an editor of *King Lear* will now quote Naipaul to explain what 'commentators had found obscure'?

Seeing England through the conventions of literature, 'the days shortening', filling Naipaul 'with thoughts of winter pleasures' – these thoughts lead to a craving to connect with an even earlier language, to seasons captured in the Middle English poem *Sir Gawain and the Green Knight*: Bot þen hyʒes heruest, and hardenes hym sone,/Warnez hym for þe winter to wax ful rype ('But then the harvest season (autumn) hastens on and encourages it at once, warms it to ripen for fear of the winter') (II. 521–2). On the face of it, this is more than postcolonial mimicry for it verges on adulation, or a far too obvious anglophilia. But this is not how I read Naipaul's engagement with England and the English literary tradition given my understanding of the ways in which cultural capital actually worked in the plantation diaspora. Naipaul is aware of this, hence his constant return to the rawness of nerves, for it is this rawness, and with it a sense of a loss, which gives Naipaul's prose so much of the fin de siècle mood. Two key passages have to be quoted in full:

[A]lready I lived with the idea of decay. (I had always lived with this idea. It was like my curse: the idea, which I had had even as a child in Trinidad, that I had come into a world past its peak.) Already I lived with the idea of death, the idea, impossible for a young person to possess, to hold in his heart, that one's time on earth, one's life, was a short thing. These ideas, of a world in decay, a world subject to constant change, and of the shortness of human life, made many things bearable.

(26)

To see the possibility, the certainty, of ruin, even at the moment of creation: it was my temperament. Those nerves had been given me as a child in Trinidad partly by our family circumstances: the half-ruined or broken-down houses we lived in, our many moves, our general uncertainty. Possibly, too, this mode of feeling went deeper, and was an ancestral inheritance, something that came with the history that had made me: not only India, with its ideas of a world outside men's control, but also the colonial plantations or estates of Trinidad, to which my impoverished Indian ancestors had been transported in the last century – estates of which this Wiltshire estate, where I now lived, had been the apotheosis.

(52)

The idea of decay, of a world exhausted and past its prime, the 'special anguish attached to the career' of a writer (94), experience transformed into an aesthetic, came from a colonial education and the demands it made on the recipient of that education. *The Enigma of Arrival* represents another kind of homage, a homage to the English language and a homage to values of the Enlightenment which were intrinsic to plantation life. The book – and Naipaul's life itself – stands as a critique of a postcolonial world view which uncritically celebrates difference. For what Naipaul stands for, and what the old Indian diaspora has always stood for (which is so different from the difference-based, multiculturally inclined new Indian diaspora of late capital) is a willingness to intervene into the grand narratives of the Empire and declaring that they, the plantation diaspora, too are a part of that narrative; it is theirs too not through any racial connection but by right of vision. This argument stands uncomfortably with an activist postcoloniality or multiculturalism, which is why so many postcolonial critics, magisterial Edward Said among them, thought of Naipaul as no more than a 'colonial renegade', and this why too in studies of the Indian diaspora, and especially in respect of its cultural interventions, the old plantation diaspora is so willfully ignored.

To read Naipaul was to re-live an entire life, a colonial life in the Indian diaspora, separated from both the colonial masters and other races, both indigenous and slave-diasporic. It was to understand not only our diasporic selves but also our half-lives; lives to which were denied the vibrancy of other socio-racial life-worlds around us because in the end we remained 'afraid of the unknown, afraid to leave the familiar temporariness' (Naipaul 1961: 174), afraid to move out of our secure and confined constituencies. 'The familiar temporariness': so often I have returned to this phrase, so often in the many places I have lived I have experienced this sense of the temporarily familiar and the dread of the new. In moments of critical self-reflection I have so often felt that my life has been imitating art. Diaspora that we were, we became static and in this stasis relapsed into mythology, initially through epic remembrance of the Indian past and subsequently though Bombay cinema. Nor did our lives in the end find an alternative vitality through the postcolonial celebration of the hybrid; rather we remained half and half, masters of neither our own language (we spoke in dialect) nor of those of our masters. We lived, to quote from the last words of

Naipaul's late novel *Half a Life* (the title itself sums it up), lives that remained incomplete, lives that were in halves, lives that belonged nowhere, that could not be grounded in either geography or epistemology. Naipaul had opened *A Bend in the River* (1979) – a damning indictment of the failure to complete the project of the Enlightenment in postcolonial Africa – with the words 'the world is what it is; men who are nothing, who allow themselves to become nothing, have no place in it'. It seemed we were nothing, our half-lives incapable of self-redemption. In tragi-comedy, that genre of halves, a genre, which through Thomas Hardy especially, came to us via the Cambridge Overseas School Certificate curriculum, we found solace, which is why Naipaul's early tragi-comic novels about the Indian diaspora – *A House for Mr Biswas* especially – spoke to us directly and which is why, again, Subramani's magnificent novel in Fiji Hindi, *Daukā Purān* (the first in the demotic), pays silent tribute to V.S. Naipaul by naming the ethnographic researcher, 'Vidiadhar' Shrivastava.

The Prologue to the great novel *A House for Mr Biswas* ends with the words:

> But bigger than them all was the house, his house.
> How terrible it would have been, at this time, to be without it: to have died among the Tulsis, amid the squalor of that large, disintegrating and indifferent family; to have left Shama and the children among them, in one room; worse, to have lived without even attempting to lay claim to one's portion of the earth; to have lived and died as one had been born, unnecessary and unaccommodated.
>
> (12–13)

It is a moving passage; indeed, for me, among the most moving in literature. And yet it is so very peculiar to a particular sociality, a particular kind of desire for ownership of a house. Mr Biswas is oppressed by the Indian extended family where a room is where one belonged and communal living is the norm. The rebellious spirit, the right to own, to escape from the trauma of barrack life where indentured labourers lived, the latter such a recent memory for people like Mr Biswas, become the thematic centres of this novel. For Biswas's father 'fate had brought him from India to the sugar-estate, aged him quickly and left him to die' (15). Colonial education had taught his children otherwise, the Protestant work ethic was there for everyone and individualism was the answer to Indian fate. The house – the central trope of the book – and the possession of it, marks out this diaspora in ways rather different. In owning it, one lays claim to a portion of the earth. Ownership, belonging, the land being ours through act of labour, these become the cornerstones of life. It has always struck me how the new diaspora from New York to Perth owns homes differently, reflecting values of a different, late modern, 'materialist India': 'India is hard and materialist', writes Naipaul (2007: 45, 193). Differently, therefore, in the sense that owning a house is a sign of success, of having made it; a sign of material well-being, the bigger the better. In Naipaul's novel, home marks a belonging, an inalienable right, an experience which, transformed into art, signifies something more than bricks and mortar or Lysaght iron and wood; home suggests an ownership through naming and transforming the landscape. And yet how very 'English' Naipaul's prose is; the balanced phrases, the economical language; the build-up to the two key words: 'unnecessary and unaccommodated'. Yes, unnecessary and unaccommodated, for we were unwanted, the detritus of indenture history, always struggling to be meaningful. Which is why we turned to the language of the Empire, blasted it open – for indeed the language behind the overt text is either demotic Hindi or Creole – and accommodated ourselves.

Vidiadhar continues to shadow me. During two extended trips to India (1977–8 and 1990) I responded to our ancestral homeland by writing about it through Naipaul's works (1978, 1992–3), the first account through *India: A Wounded Civilization* (1977), a strident, panic-driven critique; the second through *India: A Million Mutinies Now* (1990), an over-compensatory work from a Naipaul who in the intervening period had returned to the memory of his father, to a celebration of the Indian democratic spirit, and to a relentless condemnation of Islam as a regressive religion afraid of modernity and reason. I was trapped not because I didn't know any better (unlike Naipaul I speak fluent Hindi and Urdu and read Sanskrit, and unlike him I cannot claim English as my mother tongue) but because the power of the precursor, the power of Naipaul's foundational discourses was so pervasive, so consuming even, that I could not escape from them, for, like him, I too had gone to India with 'jangling nerves' (Naipaul 2007: 124). India then had somehow failed the test in its attempt to complete the project of (post)colonial Enlightenment. Like the early Naipaul I too saw Indian lives as 'unnecessary and unaccommodated' as if the essential message of Krishna in the field of battle – there is no life without acts, inaction is also action – had been lost on this once grand civilisation. The later Naipaul, as I've said, began to see differently and silently admired democratic India's creative energies; but with the admiration came a loosening of the critique, the erstwhile perspective of the always sad, always unhappy, always panic-ridden writer from a liminal society was no longer there. Happily for me by 1990 there was another voice in Naipaul, a post *The Enigma of Arrival* voice. *The Enigma of Arrival*, as we have seen, was that postcolonial intervention into the most hallowed of all English discourses, that of the Romantic imagination – a voice tinged with ennui, a *fin de siècle* exhaustion with the world, as if the writer had arrived in this world too late, in a world past its prime, a world that could no longer lock itself into meaning, a world itself living in halves, a world in which the realist novel, always so redemptive, was dead. This later Naipaul, a Naipaul for whom the picaresque comedy of life, the comedy so essential for diasporic survival in colonial plantation cultures (like my own) is no longer the defining literary form, is a sombre figure for whom 'there was a special anguish attached to the career' of a writer (1987: 94).

And yet this figure, in spite of his later rejection of Trinidad and its Indian diaspora, became a gifted artist precisely because of the freedom that came to him from what he has scathingly referred to as half-baked societies. These societies, poor flotsam and jetsam of imperialism, without the power of settler communities to destroy native peoples, these societies had a perspective that came not from any smug sense of having triumphed through sly mimicry or hybridism, but through a need to fill the void, to see the world afresh, to make sense of their lives. These societies were bonded to a strange legacy of imperialism, the legacy which even in its most perverse forms still left behind the grammar of the possibility of a just society, the latter so obvious in the very late discovery of the politically charged letters of an unusual champion of indentured labourers in Guyana, one Bechu, who, although a 'bound coolie' himself was extraordinarily fluent in English (Seecharan 1999). This is why these diasporic societies have had such a tough time in those postcolonial nation-states where liberal values, values of the Enlightenment, have been overtaken by primal, atavistic values: Trinidad, Guyana, Suriname, Fiji, even South Africa, Malaysia, Kenya, Tanzania, Uganda and Zimbabwe. What they wanted most was simply to lay claim to 'one's portion of the earth', the hope of Mohun Biswas in *A House for Mr Biswas*.

Understandably my work on the Indian 'diasporic imaginary' (2007) owes much to Naipaul. But even elsewhere, the influence has been strong. Some years ago I began to revise my preface to my book on Bombay (Bollywood) cinema (2002). I had written the standard preface complete with thank yous and an outline of the argument. But it lacked a sense of immediacy, a sense of growing up with this cinema; it lacked a centre. I wrote many drafts but somehow these too lacked spirit. It was then that the habit of flipping though a writer whose works I knew so well produced serendipitous delight. I saw in Naipaul's *Finding the Centre* (1984) and in his essay 'Conrad's Darkness' (1980) the way forward. In the latter Naipaul recalled how Marlow chanced upon Towser or Towson's book on seamanship as he made his journey towards Kurtz. It wasn't the value of the book's content – dated and irrelevant to the largely unchartered river – that attracted Marlow but the owner's (a Russian sailor whom we meet later as the figure in motley, the harlequin) careful restitching of the book and his marginalia in what Marlow (for he did not read Russian) thought was coded cypher. The book in the heart of darkness connected Marlow, for the moment, with the idea of book as signifying meaning regardless of content, book as connecting the reader to values inherent in its very materiality, values so essential to civilisation. In a sense this chance encounter with the book is meant to persuade the reader to locate another centre in the novel, a centre that lacks the extended discourse around Kurtz but which is nevertheless a defining moment in the text. In *Finding the Centre* (1984) Naipaul seeks out an old acquaintance in Venezuela, a wanderer living only half a life whose words had given him the opening lines of the first book he wrote but the third to be published (*Miguel Street* (1959)) so that he could write a fragment of his own autobiography. These were valuable clues for me and I went and re-examined my notes, some of which went back many years and were written in many different libraries. I found in amongst these notes a brief commentary on Indian films in Fiji written by a certain S. Pratap in the *Indian Cinema Annual* of 1933. Like Marlow's discovery of the Russian sailor's lovingly restitched book or Naipaul's need to discover the person behind the voice in his earliest novel, I saw beneath Pratap's matter-of-fact style and undercontextualised analysis the voice of someone who had been there before me. And through this discovery I found a way of giving a centre, a shape to my own preface. The preface gained a design of its own and became much more than a series of acknowledgments. When I returned to the preface as I composed this homage, I was struck by how closely the style, in the first two pages at any rate, was an imitation of Naipaul. My cinema book too gained a centre, as I feverishly revised it, and I ceased to feel inadequate or defenceless. Of all the books I have written, this book on Bombay cinema became mine in another way too: it completed what Naipaul could only refer to in fragments, a song from the Bombay (Bollywood) film *Jhoola* (1941) in *The Suffrage of Elvira* (1958: 103, 120), another, a sullen dirge, quite possibly from the film *Achūt Kanya* (1936), in *A House for Mr Biswas* (1961: 160), and yet another, from *Manmohan* (1936), which wakes him up from sleep, in *An Area of Darkness*. The latter song – *tumhin ne mujhko prem sikhāyā*, 'you gave love meaning' – came to Naipaul as 'pure mood' which took him to another world, a world back home where, as he recalled much later, 'Indian culture was the Indian cinema' (2007: 122). As he walks in the bazaar he sees harmoniums, 'one of which had lain broken and unused … in my grandmother's house' (1964: 272).

I owe Vidiadhar a lot. The day after the Nobel Prize was announced I was on my way to Oxford by coach on the so-called 'London–Oxford tube'. I bought two newspapers, *The Times* and the *Guardian*, specifically to read their accounts of Naipaul. At another time Naipaul's win would have made front-page head-lines. This week, the events in Afghanistan being what they were, *The Times* devoted page 15 to him and the *Guardian* page 12. The *Guardian*, however, carried a fine essay by the West Indian British writer Caryl Phillips in its *Guardian Friday Review* section. I read these pages very quickly but paused, and slowed down, reverting to my old self as a very slow reader, when it came to Caryl Phillips's essay. Phillips goes to the heart of Naipaul's contradiction: hostility towards half-baked, hybrid societies yet at the same time a product of that very same culture, himself a 'towering contradiction to his own argument'. At this point Phillips recounts a conversation he had with Derek Walcott, that other West Indian Nobel laureate, in New York on Sunday:

> 'Caz, you think Vidia will win the Nobel?' I looked at Derek. 'I don't know. It seems likely,' I said. Derek threw out a few other names, and then he paused. 'You know, I hope he does. For no matter what he says, it's bigger than him. It will mean something for the region. It will provide some substance to the achievement'.

Phillips too, like me, must acknowledge Naipaul's scandalous failure to go beyond his closed world, the failure that brought on him the critical ire of Said, Achebe, Lamming and even Walcott, Rushdie and Phillips himself. But also like me, Phillips responds to Naipaul as someone to whom he can relate (after all he wrote the screenplay of *The Mystic Masseur* for the Ismail Merchant film) and although Naipaul unforgivingly excluded any mention of Trinidad from his thank you list when informed about the Nobel award (he mentioned Britain and his ancestral homeland India), it is the Caribbean, as Phillips says, that gave Naipaul his great theme: loss. Which is why, concludes Phillips, 'throughout the Caribbean, people are celebrating this most dyspeptic of sons. Not so much, "Well, done Sir Vidia," but "You hear about Vido? Naipaul's boy. He done good, eh?' More generally, the old Indian plantation diaspora, in its many dialects from demotic Fiji Hindi to patois French and Creole English said the same.

On my way back from Oxford, I walked into Blackwells on Broad Street to see if Naipaul was suddenly displayed in the window shelves. Yes he was with a congratulatory note from the bookseller. I lingered around to see if some of his earlier books were on display elsewhere. No such luck, but in another bookstore nearby I chanced upon a very short book of no more than 15,000 words by him titled *Reading and Writing* (2000). I read the book on my journey back to London. There are two essays here and they deal, in an autobiographical fashion, with the vocation of the writer. Much of the information in this book of two essays I had read in different form elsewhere and what I hadn't read I had got to know by virtue of simply reading his books so closely. But there was greater clarity here, a sharper narrative, a more forthright manner of speaking. I read the importance of his diasporic past in Trinidad to his critical works, how he had to 'go back to the beginning ... to those early literary experiences, some of them not shared by anybody else' before he could write. This material came to him from Trinidad and from Indian indenture experience. But the experience itself came to him 'separated ... by place' and was fixed. It could not be added to, only recalled, only reshaped into fiction. In the novel form – that great art form of modernity – he found a way of transforming that material but in the end the form itself he found wanting. And so it was to travel writing that he went, to a genre which he believed would come easily to him but which exposed him to archives that were disturbing. In this short book I read the wish to break free of the limitations of the novel form so that he could observe and write about matters that concerned him as a human being. I read in this context Naipaul's pathos about the lost worlds of aboriginal peoples:

> [The records I consulted] showed me the aboriginal peoples, masters of sea and river, busy about their own affairs, possessing all the skills they had needed in past centuries, but helpless before the newcomers, and ground down over the next two hundred years to nonentity, alcoholism, missionary reserves, and extinction. In this manmade wilderness then, in the late eighteenth century, the slave plantations were laid out, and the straight lines of the new Spanish town.

(32–3)

And finally I read his critique of the novel form, which had been fetishised, for so he argued, beyond its use value in the late twentieth century. The novel, he wrote, comes with metropolitan assumptions, predicated upon 'the availability of a wider learning, an idea of history, a concern with self-knowledge'. 'Where those assumptions are wrong', he continued, 'where the wider learning is missing or imperfect, I am not sure whether the novel can offer more than the externals of things.' The late twentieth century, Naipaul felt, needs a genre other than the novel to 'interpret it'. Which is why, I suspect, Naipaul himself experimented with autobiography and travel, combining ethnography with the novelist's eye for detail. If the (realist) novel is dead, it can only 'distort the unaccommodating new reality'. In his characteristically transparent style Naipaul concluded: 'It is the vanity of the age (and of commercial promotion) that the novel continues to be literature's final and highest expression.'

I meditated on these remarks as the bus so very slowly made its way to the Notting Hill underground tube. I had read and understood much literary theory, some very difficult, and here, in such lucid prose, I read much that had come to me after many years of sustained work. Naipaul, it seemed, had understood those essential connections between the bourgeois novel and society, he understood that genres exhaust themselves and need to be renewed. He understood, as he wrote, that every creative talent burns itself out, every literary form gets to the end of what it can do. Great literary theorists – Auerbach, Bakhtin, Benjamin, Lukács – all understood this. Naipaul too knew his literary theory very well and yet his theory came to him from a very thorough reading of the texts themselves, as if the novel was a theory about itself; to interpret the novel form, or any literary form, was to theorise it from within. I was thankful for this brief book by Naipaul; it made me understand the writer so much better; it also affirmed my belief in the value of theory.

I looked at blurbs on the dust jackets of books by Naipaul. The accolades have been considerable: 'The most important import since Conrad and Henry James' (Christopher Ricks); 'The greatest living writer of English prose' (*Observer*); 'Naipaul is without peer' (*The Times*); 'One of the greatest living writers in the English language' (Elizabeth Hardwicke). The denunciations (though not as blurbs) are equally fierce: 'a colonial renegade' (Edward Said); 'an informant for the other' (Spivak); a hater of black people (Walcott, Achebe). These have not been my departure points. Nor is the Nobel Prize everything. In fact it is perhaps nothing. It is said that Patrick White, the Nobel winner for literature in 1973, when informed about his win reacted with the preamble that two of the very best of the twentieth century – Joyce and Lawrence – never made it. For me it isn't really the winning, important for postcolonial literature and the Indian diaspora as it is, that is significant. Rather Naipaul's win gave me that much needed centre around which I could compose a homage that I have always been meaning to write. Without the Nobel, that homage, were it forthcoming, would have either become defensive because of Naipaul's politics or would have become a reprise of the kind of scholarly chapter that one had already written on Naipaul.

Monkish, archival knowledge, the search for truth in an uncompromising manner even if the truth, constrained by colonial education, is misguided and hurts – these remain features of V.S. Naipaul's world. A homage verges on uncritical adulation, it distorts the evidence, it is an act of vassalage, 'a formal and public acknowledgment of allegiance', meanings which the *OED* is conscious of. Naipaul, the writer and the lexicographer, the writer with an acute sense of the nature of words, how words work, what to do with them, their meanings and significations, Naipaul takes us to the heart of an ambivalence in the plantation diaspora's engagement with the aesthetic. The latter is a colonial aesthetic mediated by the English language which had to be embraced in the absence of one's own. It led to a kind of mimicry, but not without a consciousness of the 'rawness of nerves', of the special anguish of the writer under these conditions. It is a legacy we have inherited, and we cannot, nor should we, cleanse ourselves of it. For what the legacy gives us is a challenge: how to blast open the legacy's lasting discourses and make them our own; how to locate ourselves as equal inheritors of that tradition; how to theorise about literature through a 'writer's writing, something personal, with authority'. A homage insinuates an understanding of that legacy and Naipaul's singular role in making that legacy available to us. In this respect Naipaul is, to rework a major insight of Foucault (1980), a founder of a plantation diaspora discursivity into which we, descendants of that diaspora, insert ourselves.

References

Blake, William (1988) *William Blake* [The Oxford Authors], ed. Michael Mason, Oxford: Oxford University Press.

Davis, Norman (ed.) (1968) *Sir Gawain and the Green Knight* [originally edited by J.R.R. Tolkien and E.V. Gordon, 1925], Oxford: Clarendon Press.

Foucault, Michel (1980) 'What Is an Author?', in Josué V. Harari (ed.) *Textual Strategies*, London: Methuen: 141–60.

Kant, Immanuel (1986) *The Critique of Judgement*, trans. James Creed Meredith, Oxford: Clarendon Press.

Mishra, Vijay (1978) 'Mythic Fabulation: Naipaul's India', *New Literature Review*, 4: 59–65.

—— (1990) 'Little India', *Meanjin*, 49(4): 607–18.

—— (1992–3) 'After Naipaul: An Indian Journey', *Span*, 34–5: 211–25.

—— (2002a) 'Vidiadhar and I', *Evam* 1(1&2): 248–55.

—— (2002b) 'Lives in Halves: A Homage to Vidiadhar Naipaul', *Meanjin*, 61(1): 123–6.

—— (2002c) *Bollywood Cinema: Temples of Desire*, New York: Routledge.

—— (2007) *The Literature of the Indian Diaspora: Theorizing the Diasporic Imaginary*, London: Routledge.

Naipaul, V.S. (1957) *The Mystic Masseur*, London: André Deutsch.

—— (1958) *The Suffrage of Elvira*, London: André Deutsch.

—— (1959) *Miguel Street*, London: André Deutsch.

—— (1961) *A House for Mr Biswas*, London: André Deutsch.

—— (1964) *An Area of Darkness*, London: André Deutsch.

—— (1977) *India: A Wounded Civilization*, London: André Deutsch.

—— (1979) *A Bend in the River*, London: André Deutsch.

—— (1980) 'Conrad's Darkness', in *The Return of Eva Peron* with *The Killings in Trinidad*, London: André Deutsch.

—— (1984) *Finding the Centre*, London: André Deutsch.

—— (1987) *The Enigma of Arrival*, London: Viking.

—— (1990) *India: A Million Mutinies Now*, London: Heinemann.

—— (1999) *Letters Between a Father and a Son*, ed. Gillon Aitken, London: Little, Brown and Company.

—— (2000) *Reading and Writing*, New York: New York Review Book.

—— (2002) *Half a Life*, London: Picador.

—— (2007) *A Writer's People: Ways of Looking and Feeling*, London: Picador.

Said, Edward W. (1986) 'The Intellectual in the Post-Colonial World', *Salmagundi*, 70–1: 44–64.

Seecharan, Clem (1999) *Bechu: 'Bound Coolie' Radical in British Guiana 1894–1901*, Kingston, Jamaica: University of West Indies Press.

Shakespeare, William (1982) *King Lear*, ed. Kenneth Muir, London: Methuen.

Subramani. (2001) *Daukā Purān*, New Delhi: Star Publications.

van Buitenen, J.A.B. (1981) *The Bhagavadgītā in the Mahābhārata*, Chicago: University of Chicago Press.

Wordsworth, William (1981) 'Resolution and Independence', in John O. Hayden (ed.) *William Wordsworth, The Poems*, New Haven, CT: Yale University Press.

Index

saint-soldier 181–4
salary 109, 178; *see also* wages
Sanatan Dharma 101–2, 113, 121n6; *see also* Hindus/Hinduism
Sanskritisation 100
Sant 178, 179, 181, 184–8
sarraf 28–9
secular 125, 136
September 11 (2001) 129, 133, 135, 136, 133
sex ratio 47, 79, 81, 98, 114
Shakespeare, William 193–4, 199
Shia 33–4, 42, 101, 114; *see also* Islam; Muslims
Shikarpur 6, 19–20, 22–3, 25–6
ships carrying indentured labourers 89, 110, 116–17, 119
shop-keepers 82, 113
shravaks 30, 42n5
Sikhs/Sikhism 10, 82, 113, 148, 150, 154–5, 159, 176–91, 191n1–3, 191n5–6
silk 20, 23, 35, 82
Sind 6, 18–20, 22, 24–5, 27, 68
Sindhi 21–2, 25–6, 47, 58, 156; *see also* language/languages
Singapore 9–10, 26, 57, 60–2, 66n1, 71–2, 83–7, 87n1, 125–31, 135–7, 139, 139n1, 143–57, **151**, **154–5**, 158n5, 176–91
sirdar 51, 55, 91, 110, 117
slave/slavery 2, 47–8, 91–3, 105–6, 108–9, 120, 126
South Africa 18, 62, 105, 117, 195, 203
South India 75, 78, 91
South Indian 10, 18, 79, 83, 94, 101, 149, 152, 157, 160–1, 163, 167, 169, 171
Southeast Asia 2, 9, 15, 17–18, 21, 39, 41, 46, 58, 61, 71–2, **73–4**, 82–5, 87
Soviet Union 27, 60–1, 125; *see also* Russia
Sri Lanka 18, *86*, 119, 129, 143, 173
Straits Settlements 82, 191n4
street-vendors 163
Sudhir Gupta 57, 60–2, 65, 66n1, 67n3
sugar *see* plantation
Sultanpur 92, 105
Sunni 33–5, 42, 101, 114; *see also* Islam; Muslim
Surat 29–30, 34–5, 39–40, 42
Suriname 9, 108–114, *114*, 115–121, 121n1, 121n5, 121n6
Suva 100, 195
Sylhet 130
Syria 33

taboo 17, 90, 160, 165, 173
Tagore society (Singapore) 129
Tamil 18, 38, 52, 75, 78, 143, 147–8, 152–3, 161–2, 164, 169, 186–7; *see also* language/languages
Tamil Nadu 47, 147, 149, 161
Tanzania 203; *see also* East Africa
Tata Steel 60
Tazia 93
Telegu 49, 52–3, 55, 75, 78; *see also* language/languages
tertiary institutions 84, 150
textile 7, 28–9, 36, 39, 41, 82–3, 91, 113
Thailand 18, 61, 72, 84, *86*, 177
tin 35, 72, 74, 83, 116
Tinker, Hugh 48, 91
traders 2, 6–7, 16, 20, 29, 32–3, 35–6, 38–40, 42n13, 47, 52, 72, 82–3
transient 3, 9, 125, 134
transnational/transnationalism: 4–7, 25, 28, 57, 72, 127; community 4, 5, 7; media 10, 156; networks 4–7, 54–5; space 7, 25, 57, 59–60, 65–6
tribal 19, 37
Trinidad 8, 62, 89, 108, 110, 112, 114, *114,* 121, 195, 198–200, 202, 205; *see also* Caribbean

Uganda 203; *see also* East Africa
United Kingdom 3, 46, 73–4, 100, 109, 148, 189, 195, 205
United Provinces *see* Uttar Pradesh
United States of America (USA) 2–3, 9, 62, 74, 124–7, 129–130, 139, 189
untouchables 94; *see also* caste
Uttar Pradesh 91, 112–14, 155

varna 20; *see also* caste
vegetarian 169, 172–4
Vijayanagar 39
village 49, 78, 80, 89–90, 94–102, 124, 155, 198
Vora, Virji 29, 39, 42n7, 42n15
voyage *see* journey

wages 78, 80–1, 92, 98; *see also* salary
Washington D.C. 131, 138
watchmen 82, 177
weavers 42n11, 92
West Bengal 126, 128–9, 137
widows 114, 115, 167
women 7, 10–11, 23, 25, 47–8, 51, 53–4, 72, 81–2, 89, 91, 95, 98–9, 101, 108, 110, 114–15, 117, 127, 134,

For Product Safety Concerns and Information please contact our EU
representative GPSR@taylorandfrancis.com
Taylor & Francis Verlag GmbH, Kaufingerstraße 24, 80331 München, Germany

www.ingramcontent.com/pod-product-compliance
Lightning Source LLC
Chambersburg PA
CBHW050428280326
41932CB00013BA/2032